PROGRAMMING PLCs

USING ROCKWELL AUTOMATION CONTROLLERS

Jon Stenerson

Fox Valley Technical College

PEARSON

Prentice
Hall

Upper Saddle River, New Jersey
Columbus, Ohio

Library of Congress Cataloging-in-Publication Data

Stenerson, Jon.
    Programming PLCs using Rockwell automation controllers / Jon Stenerson.
        p. cm.
    Includes index.
    ISBN 0-13-094002-X
    1. Programmable controllers. 2. Microprocessors. I. Title.

    TJ223.P76S76 2003
    629.8'9--dc21   2003040579

Editor in Chief: Stephen Helba
Assistant Vice President and Publisher: Charles E. Stewart, Jr.
Assistant Editor: Mayda Bosco
Production Editor: Alexandrina Benedicto Wolf
Production Coordination: Carlisle Publishers Services
Design Coordinator: Diane Ernsberger
Cover Designer: Robin Chukes
Cover art: Digital Vision
Production Manager: Matthew Ottenweller
Marketing Manager: Ben Leonard

This book was set in Times Roman by Carlisle Communications, Ltd. It was printed and bound by R. R. Donnelley & Sons Company. The cover was printed by Phoenix Color Corp.

Pearson Education Ltd.
Pearson Education Singapore Pte. Ltd.
Pearson Education Canada, Ltd.
Pearson Education—Japan

Pearson Education Australia Pty. Limited
Pearson Education North Asia Ltd.
Pearson Educación de Mexico, S.A. de C.V.
Pearson Education Malaysia Pte. Ltd.
Pearson Education, *Upper Saddle River*, *New Jersey*

10 9 8 7 6 5 4 3 2 1
ISBN 0-13-094002-X

Dedicated to my mother Lillian

Contents

Preface

The programmable logic controller (PLC) is an amazing piece of technology. The PLC is simple to use, yet features complex technology. While the PLC has been increasing in capability and complexity, vast improvements in software and related hardware have actually made it much easier to program and integrate. The PLC can control anything we can envision. The study and use of PLCs is filled with those "AHA!" moments when we conquer another problem or application.

Programmable control has transformed manufacturing. There is a huge need for trained personnel who can program and integrate industrial controllers and devices.

I wrote this textbook for my students when I was unable to find a practical, affordable textbook that addressed Rockwell SLCs. I have included a CD that contains LogixPro programming and simulation software. The software is a great emulation of Rockwell Automation RSLogix 500 programming software. Each chapter includes questions, and some chapters include additional programming exercises. The programming and simulation software (LogixPro) CD should be used by the student to learn how to program and run the SLC. The student can actually see and troubleshoot programs in animated simulations. The Rockwell Automation instruction set reference manual is also included on the CD.

Each chapter begins with a generic approach to the topic. Each topic is clearly explained through the use of common, easy to understand examples. Chapters 1 through 3 provide the basic foundation for the use of PLCs. Chapter 1 focuses on the history and fundamentals of the PLC. Chapter 2 covers number systems. Chapter 3 covers contacts, coils, and the fundamentals of programming.

Chapter 4 focuses on Rockwell addressing and coils and contacts. Because addressing tends to be confusing for students, this chapter is intended to give them a firm understanding of addressing so that programming will be a much less frustrating task. Chapter 5 covers timers and counters and provides practical examples of the use of timers and counters and their addressing.

Chapter 6 covers I/O modules and wiring, and digital and analog modules. This chapter gives students a practical and logical approach to learning how to wire digital and analog modules, and explains the concept of analog control and resolution.

Chapter 7 covers math instructions including add, subtract, multiply, divide, and compare. In addition, the chapter covers logical operators, standard deviation, and number system conversion instructions.

Chapter 8 covers advanced programming with instructions such as copy, move, and messaging instructions. In addition, PID control and the PID instruction are covered. The newest instructions such as time stamping, ramp, and diagnostic and troubleshooting are discussed. The chapter has practical examples of sequential logic instructions.

Chapter 9 covers industrial sensors and their wiring and focuses on types and uses of sensors. Sensors include optical, inductive, capacitive, encoders, resolvers, ultrasonic, and thermocouples. The wiring and practical application of sensors is stressed.

Chapter 10 covers communications, ControlLogix, and DeviceNet. The chapter begins with an overview of the three levels of industrial communications. Control-Logix is Rockwell Automation's technology that can be used for control and communications. DeviceNet serves many purposes as well.

Chapter 11 covers safety and lockout/tagout. Students learn the basics of safety and lockout/tagout before they enter the industrial environment. Chapter 12 focuses on the installation and troubleshooting of PLC systems. The chapter discusses cabinets, wiring, grounding, noise, and troubleshooting. This chapter provides the fundamental groundwork for proper installation and troubleshooting of integrated systems.

Chapter 13 examines IEC 611313 programming, a topic that is certain to become more prevalent in industrial programming and control. This chapter is an introduction to the various types of programming available under the standard.

I sincerely hope that this book will ease the reader's task of learning to program and integrate PLCs.

ACKNOWLEDGMENTS

I would like to thank the following reviewers for their useful comments: Samuel Guccione, Eastern Illinois University; Fabian Lopez, Albuquerque TVI, New Mexico; and Saeed Shaikh, Miami Dade Community College, Florida.

I would also like to thank Bill Simpson from www.TheLearningPit.com for allowing me to include his wonderful software with this book.

Jon Stenerson

Overview of Programmable Logic Controllers

Within a short time, programmable logic controllers (PLCs) have become an integral and invaluable tool in industry. In this chapter we examine how and why PLCs have gained such wide application. We also take an overall look at the basics of a PLC.

OBJECTIVES

Upon completion of this chapter, you will be able to:

1. Explain some of the reasons why PLCs are replacing hardwired logic in industrial automation
2. Explain such terms as *ladder logic, CPU, programmer, input devices,* and *output devices*
3. Explain some of the features of a PLC that make it an easy tool for an electrician to use
4. Explain how the PLC is protected from electrical noise
5. Draw a block diagram of a PLC
6. Explain the types of programming devices available

PLC COMPONENTS

The programmable logic controller (PLC) is really just an industrial computer in which the hardware and software have been specifically adapted to both the industrial environment and electrical technician. Figure 1-1 shows the functional components of a typical PLC. Note the similarity to a computer.

Central Processing Unit

The central processing unit (CPU) is the brain of the PLC (Figure 1-2). It contains one or more microprocessors to control the PLC. The CPU also handles the communication and interaction with other components of the system. The CPU contains the same type of microprocessor as found in a microcomputer, except that the program used with the PLC microprocessor is written to accommodate ladder logic instead of other programming languages. The CPU executes the operating system, manages memory, monitors inputs, evaluates the user logic (ladder diagram), and turns on the appropriate outputs.

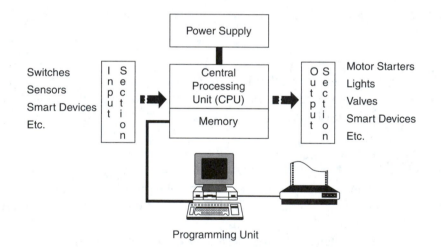

Programming Unit

Figure 1-1 Block diagram of the typical components that comprise a PLC. Note particularly the input section, the output section, and the central processing unit (CPU). The broken arrows from the input section to the CPU and from the CPU to the output section represent protection that is necessary to isolate the CPU from the real-world inputs and outputs. The programming unit is used to write the control program (ladder logic) for the CPU. It is also used for documenting the programmer's logic and troubleshooting the system.

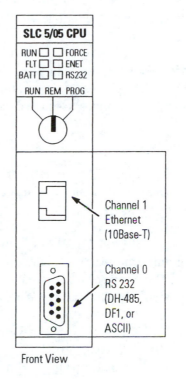

Figure 1-2 Rockwell PLC processor module (CPU). Note the many indicators for error checking and the keyswitch for switching modes between run and program mode. *(Courtesy Rockwell Automation Inc.)*

The factory floor is a noisy environment where motors, motor starters, wiring, welding machines, and even fluorescent lights create electrical noise. PLCs are hardened to be noise immune.

PLCs also have elaborate memory-checking routines to be sure that the PLC memory has not been corrupted by noise or other problems. Memory checking is undertaken for safety reasons. It helps ensure that the PLC will not execute if memory is corrupted for some reason.

CPU Modes

The keyswitch on Rockwell PLC CPUs is used to switch between program, run, and remote modes.

Program Mode In the program mode all outputs are forced to the off condition regardless of their state in the logic. The program mode can be used to:

Develop and download/upload programs

Set up input/output (I/O) forcing without them being enabled

Transfer program files to/from backup memory modules

Run Mode   In the run mode the PLC continuously scans and executes the ladder logic.

Remote Mode   In the remote mode a computer that is attached can control in which mode the processor is operating. The user can switch the SLC between the run and program modes from the computer without changing the key position.

CPU Models

5/01   The SLC 5/01 has program memory options of 1K or 4K instruction words. It can address up to 256 local I/Os. The 5/01 has DH485 peer-to-peer communications.

5/02   The SLC 5/02 has a more advanced instruction set than the 5/01. It has 4K of program memory. It can address up to 480 local I/Os that can be expanded via remote I/O or DeviceNet. Up to 4000 remote inputs and 4000 remote outputs can be addressed. The 5/02 has DH485 communications.

5/03   The SLC 5/03 has 12K words and 4K of additional data words; 960 local I/Os can be addressed. An additional 4000 inputs and 4000 outputs can be addressed remotely. The 5/03 has two communications ports: DH485 and RS232/DF1 or DH485 port. The 5/03 also has a real-time clock, online programming, indirect addressing, and additional math, block transfer, time stamping, scale instructions, and advanced diagnostics.

5/04   The 5/04 can have 12K, 28K, or 60K words of memory and an additional 4K of data words. The 5/04 has all the features and capabilities of the 5/03, as well as a Data Highway Plus (DH+) port and a RS232/DF1, DH485, or ASCII protocol. The 5/04 has a real-time clock and a math coprocessor, and can be programmed online. Networking between 5/04s is accomplished by utilizing DH+. Networking to a microcomputer network can be done through either a Rockwell KTX card or ControlLogix.

5/05   The 5/05 has the features of the 5/04 plus Ethernet communications capability. The 5/05 can be networked utilizing Ethernet communications.

Memory

PLC memory can be of various types. Some of the PLC memory is used to hold operating system memory and some is used to hold user memory.

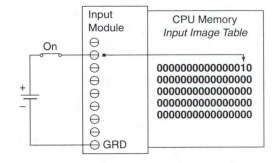

Figure 1-3 How the status of a real-world input becomes a 1 or a 0 in a word of memory. Each bit in the input image table represents the status of one real-world input.

Operating System Memory Read-only memory (ROM) is used by the PLC for the operating system. The operating system is burned into ROM by the PLC manufacturer, and controls functions such as the system software used to program the PLC. The ladder logic that the programmer creates is a high-level language. A high-level language is a computer language that makes it easy for people to program. The system software must convert the electrician's ladder diagram (high-level language program) to instructions that the microprocessor can understand. ROM is not changed by the user. ROM is nonvolatile memory, which means that even if the electricity is shut off, the memory is retained.

User Memory The memory of a PLC is broken into blocks that have specific functions. Some sections of memory are used to store the status of inputs and outputs. These are normally called I/O image tables. The states of inputs and outputs are kept in I/O image tables. The real-world state of an input is stored as either a 1 or a 0 in a particular bit of memory. Each input or output has one corresponding bit in memory (Figures 1-3 and 1-4). Other portions of the memory are used to store the contents of variables of a user program. For example, a timer or counter value would be stored in this portion of memory. Memory is also reserved for processor work areas.

Random Access Memory Random access memory (RAM) is designed so that the user can read or write to the memory. RAM is commonly used for user memory. The user's program, timer/counter values, input/output status, and so forth, are stored in RAM.

RAM is volatile, which means that if the electricity is shut off, the data in memory are lost. This problem is solved by the use of a lithium battery. The battery takes over when the PLC is shut off. Most PLCs use CMOS-RAM technology for

Figure 1-4   How a bit in memory controls one output. Using active-high logic, if the bit is a 1, the output will be on; if the bit is a 0, the output will be off.

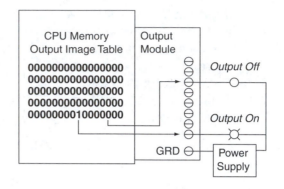

user memory. CMOS-RAM chips have very low current draw and can maintain memory with a lithium battery for a long time—2 to 5 years in many cases. A good preventative maintenance program should include a schedule to change batteries so serious losses can be avoided.

Figure 1-5 shows an example of battery replacement for a Rockwell SLC. Such processors have a capacitor that provides at least 30 minutes of battery backup while the battery is being changed. The data in RAM are not lost if the battery is replaced within 30 minutes. To replace the battery, the technician (1) removes the battery from the retaining clips, (2) inserts a new battery into the retaining clips, (3) plugs the battery connector into the socket, and (4) reinstalls the module into the rack. The battery in an SLC will last for approximately 2 years. The BATT LED on the front of the processor will light when the battery voltage falls below a threshold level.

Electrically Erasable Programmable Read-Only Memory   Electrically erasable programmable read-only memory (EEPROM) can function in almost the same manner as RAM. The EEPROM can be erased electrically. It is nonvolatile memory, and so does not require battery backup. Functionally, EEPROM is almost like a hard drive.

PLC Programming Devices

Computers are the main devices used to program PLCs. Handheld programmers also are available. Programming devices do not need to be attached to the PLC once the ladder is written, because they are simply used to write the user program for the PLC. They also may be used to troubleshoot the PLC.

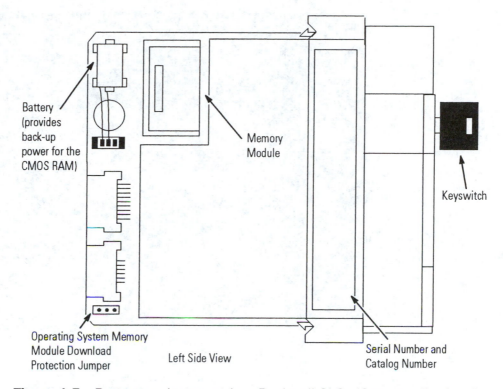

Battery (provides back-up power for the CMOS RAM)

Memory Module

Keyswitch

Operating System Memory Module Download Protection Jumper

Left Side View

Serial Number and Catalog Number

Figure 1-5 Battery replacement in a Rockwell SLC. *(Courtesy Rockwell Automation Inc.)*

Handheld Programmers Handheld programmers (terminals) (Figure 1-6) must be attached to a PLC to be used. They are handy for troubleshooting, because they can be carried easily to the manufacturing system and plugged in to the PLC. Once plugged in, they can be used to monitor the status of inputs, outputs, variables, counters, timers, and so on. This eliminates the need to carry a large programming device to the factory floor. Handheld programmers can also be used to turn inputs and outputs on or off for troubleshooting. Turning I/O off or on by overriding the logic is called forcing. Handheld programmers are designed for the factory floor. They typically have membrane keypads that are immune to the contaminants in the factory environment. One disadvantage of these programmers is they can show only a small amount of a ladder on the screen at one time.

Microcomputers The microcomputer is the most commonly used programming device. It can be used for offline programming and storage of programs. One disk

Figure 1-6 Handheld terminal.

can hold many ladder diagrams. The microcomputer also can upload and download programs to a PLC and can be used to force inputs and outputs on and off.

This upload/download capability is vital for industry. Occasionally, PLC programs are modified on the factory floor to get a system running for a short time. It is vital that once the system has been repaired, the correct program is reloaded into the PLC. It is also useful to verify from time to time that the program in the PLC has not been modified, to help avoid dangerous situations on the factory floor. Some automobile manufacturers have set up communications networks that regularly verify the programs in PLCs to ensure that they are correct.

The microcomputer also can be used to document the PLC program. Notes for technicians can be added and the ladder can be output to a printer for hardcopy so that the technicians can study the ladder diagram.

RSLogix 500 is an example of Windows-based microcomputer software for programming Rockwell Automation PLCs (Figure 1-7). RSLogix 500 is a powerful software package that allows offline and online programming. It allows ladder diagrams to be stored to a floppy disk, and then uploaded/downloaded from/to the PLC. The software allows monitoring of the ladder operation while it is executing, and the forcing of system I/Os on and off. Both features are extremely valuable for troubleshooting. RSLogix 500 also allows the programmer to document the ladder.

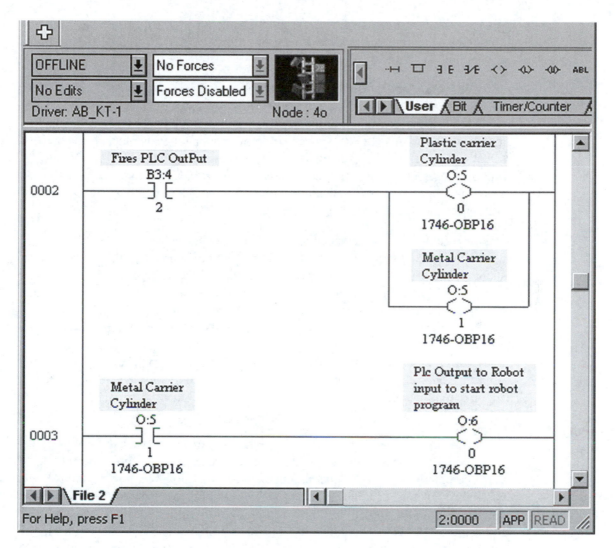

Figure 1-7 Typical PLC programming software. Note the comments and tagnames to make the ladder logic more understandable. *(Courtesy Rockwell Automation Inc.)*

This documentation is invaluable for understanding and troubleshooting ladder diagrams. The programmer can add notes, names of input or output devices, and comments that may be useful for troubleshooting and maintenance. The addition of notes and comments helps technicians to understand the ladder diagram, which allows them to troubleshoot the system, not just the person who developed it. The notes and comments could even specify replacement part numbers if so desired, to facilitate rapid repair of any problems due to faulty parts.

Previously, the person who developed the system had great job security because no one else could understand the operation. A properly documented ladder allows any technician to understand it.

IEC 1131-3 Programming   The International Electrotechnical Commission (IEC) has developed a standard for PLC programming. The latest IEC standard (IEC 1131-3) has attempted to merge PLC programming languages under one international standard. PLCs can now be programmed in function block diagrams, instruction lists, and C and structured text. The standard is accepted by an increasing number of suppliers and vendors of process control systems, safety-related systems, and industrial personal computers. An increasing number of application software vendors offer products based on IEC 1131-3.

Power Supply   The power supply is used to supply power for the central processing unit. Most PLCs operate on 115 VAC. This means that the input voltage to the power supply is 115 VAC. The power supply provides various DC voltages for the PLC components and CPU. On some PLCs, the power supply is a separate module. This is usually the case when extra racks are used. Each rack must have its own power supply.

The user must determine how much current will be drawn by the I/O modules to ensure that the power supply provides adequate current. Different types of modules draw different amounts of current. *Note:* The PLC power supply is not typically used to power external inputs or outputs. The user must provide separate power supplies to power the inputs and outputs of the PLC. Some of the smaller PLCs do supply voltage to be used to power the inputs, however.

PLC Racks   The PLC rack serves several functions. It is used to physically hold the CPU, power supply, and I/O modules. The rack also provides the electrical connections and communications between the modules, power supply, and CPU through the backplane. The modules are plugged into slots on the rack (Figure 1-8). This ability to plug modules in and out easily is one reason why PLCs are so popular. The ability to change modules quickly allows rapid maintenance and repair. Input/output numbering corresponds to a slot that holds a specific module.

Sometimes it is necessary to have more than one rack. Some midsize and large PLCs provide this feature. In certain applications, there are more I/O points than one rack can handle. There are also cases when it is desirable to locate some of the I/Os away from the PLC. For example, imagine a very large machine. Rather than run wires from every input and output to the PLC, an extra rack might be used. The I/O on one end of the machine is wired to modules in the remote rack. The I/O on the other end of the machine is wired to the main rack. The two racks communicate with one set of wiring rather than running all of the wiring from one end to the other. Many PLCs allow the use of multiple racks. When more than one rack is used it is necessary to identify the rack where the I/O is located.

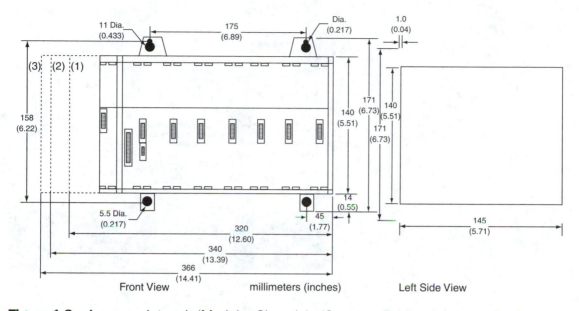

Figure 1-8 A seven-slot rack (Modular Chassis). *(Courtesy Rockwell Automation Inc.)*

Input Section The input portion of the PLC performs two vital tasks. It takes inputs from the outside world and in the process protects the CPU. Inputs can be almost any device. The input module converts the real-world logic level to the logic level required by the CPU. For example, a 250 VAC input module would convert a 250 VAC input to a low-level DC signal for the CPU.

Input Modules There are a wide variety of input modules available. Some are available for digital and analog input. Certain modules have 4, 8, 16 and 32 inputs available. Digital modules are available for AC, DC, and Transistor-Transistor Logic (TTL) (5 volt) signals. Modules are available for positive or negative input voltages. Analog modules are available to measure voltage or current. Some are user configurable to do either. There are also specialty modules available for inputs such as thermocouples, RTDs (temperature sensors), and high-speed signals such as counters or encoders. Combination I/O modules are also available.

Common input devices include switches and sensors. These are often called field devices. Field devices are gaining extensive capability, especially the ability to communicate over industrial communications networks. Other smart devices, such as robots, computers, and even PLCs, can act as inputs to the PLC.

The inputs are provided through the use of input modules. The user simply chooses input modules that will meet the needs of the application. These modules are installed in the PLC rack (Figure 1-9).

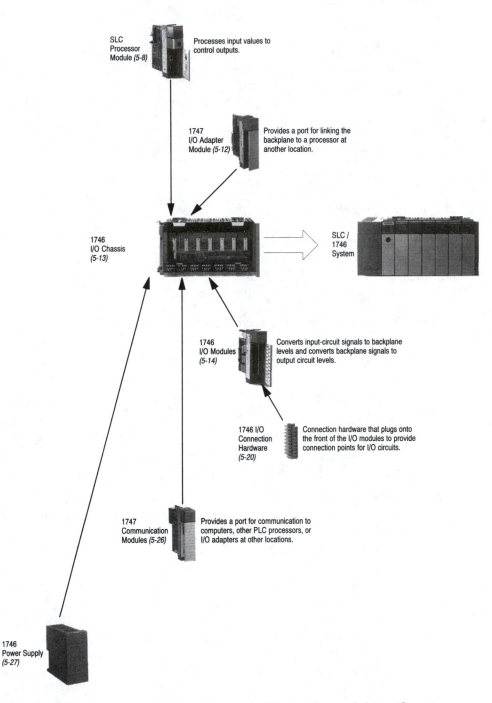

Figure 1-9 Modules, racks, and a rack filled with modules. *(Courtesy Rockwell Automation Inc.)*

Optical Isolation   The other task that the input section of a PLC performs is isolation. The PLC CPU must be protected from the outside world and at the same time be able to take input data from there. This is typically done by optical isolation, or opto-isolation (Figure 1-10). This means that there is no electrical connection between the outside world and the CPU. The two are separated optically (with light). The outside world supplies a signal which turns on a light in the input card. The light shines on a receiver and the receiver turns on. There is no electrical connection between the two.

The light separates the CPU from the outside world up to very high voltages. Even if there was a large surge of electricity, the CPU would be safe. (Of course, if the voltage is too large, the opto-isolator can fail and may cause a circuit failure.) Optical isolation is used for inputs and outputs.

Input modules provide the user with various troubleshooting aids. There are normally light emitting diodes (LEDs) for each input. If the input is on, the CPU should see the input as a high (or a 1). Input modules also provide circuits that debounce the input signal. Many input devices are mechanical and have contacts. When these devices close or open, unwanted "bounces" occur which close and open the contacts. Debounce circuits ensure that the CPU sees only debounced signals. The debounce circuit also helps eliminate the possibility of electrical noise from firing the inputs.

Inputs to Input Modules   Sensors are commonly used as inputs to PLCs, and can be purchased for a variety of purposes. They can sense part presence; count pieces; measure temperature, pressure, or size; and sense for proper packaging. There are also sensors that are able to sense any type of material. Inductive sensors can sense ferrous metal objects, capacitive sensors can sense almost any material, and optical sensors can detect any type of material. Other devices also can act as inputs to a PLC. Smart devices such as robots, computers, and vision systems, often have the ability to send signals to a PLC's input modules (Figure 1-11). This can be used for handshaking during operation. A robot, for example, can send the PLC an input when it has finished a program. Sensor types and use are covered in detail in Chapter 9.

Output Section   The output section of the PLC provides the connection to real-world output devices such as motor starters, lights, coils, and valves. These, too, are often called field devices. Field devices can be either input or output devices. Output modules can be purchased to handle DC or AC voltages. They can be used to output analog or digital signals. A digital output module acts like a switch. The output is either energized or deenergized. If the output is energized, then the output is turned on, like a switch.

Output modules can be purchased with various output configurations. Digital and analog output modules are available. Digital modules are available for DC and

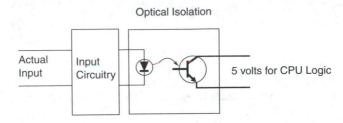

Optical Isolation

Actual Input | Input Circuitry | 5 volts for CPU Logic

Figure 1-10 Typical optical isolation circuit. The arrow represents the fact that only light travels between the input circuitry and the CPU circuitry. There is no electrical connection.

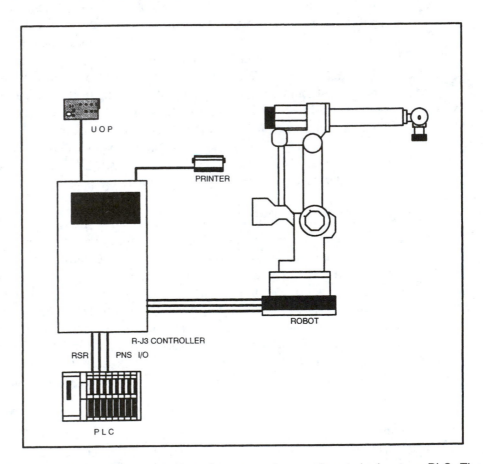

UOP

PRINTER

ROBOT

R-J3 CONTROLLER

RSR   PNS I/O

PLC

Figure 1-11 A "smart" device also can act as an input device to a PLC. The PLC also can output to the robot. Robots and some other devices typically have a few digital outputs and inputs available for this purpose. The use of these inputs and outputs allows for some basic handshaking between devices. Handshaking means that the devices give each other permission to perform tasks at some times during execution to ensure proper performance and safety. When devices communicate with a digital signal it is called primitive communication. *(Courtesy Fanuc Robotics North America, Inc.)*

AC voltages. They are available as modules with eight, sixteen, and thirty-two outputs. Modules with more than eight outputs are sometimes called high-density modules. They are generally the same size as the eight-output modules, but have many more components within the module. High-density modules therefore will not handle as much current for each output, because of the size of components and the heat generated by them.

The analog output module is used to output an analog signal. An example of this is a motor whose velocity we would like to control. An analog module puts out a voltage that corresponds to the desired speed. Analog modules are available for current or voltage. Combination modules also are available.

Current Ratings　Module specifications will list an overall current rating and an output current rating. For example, the specification may give each output a current limit of 1 ampere (A). If there are eight outputs, we would assume that the output module overall rating would be 8A; but this is poor logic. The overall rating of the module current may be less than the total of the individuals. The overall rating might be 6A. The user must take this into consideration when planning the system. Normally, each of the eight devices would not pull their 1A at the same time. Figure 1-12 shows an example of I/O wiring.

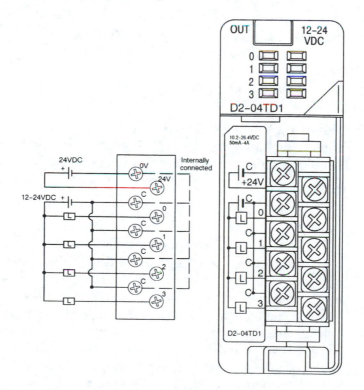

Figure 1-12　PLC I/O wiring. *(Courtesy Rockwell Automation Inc.)*

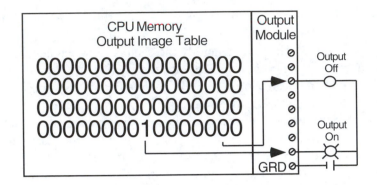

Figure 1-13 How a typical PLC handles outputs. The CPU memory contains a section called the output image table, which contains the desired states of all outputs. Using active-high logic, if there is a 1 in the bit that corresponds to the output, then the output is turned on; if there is a 0, then the output is turned off.

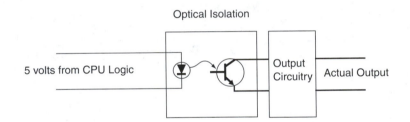

Figure 1-14 How PLC output isolation works. The CPU provides a 5-volt signal which turns on the LED. The light from the LED is used to fire the base of the output transistor. There is no electrical connection between the CPU and the outside world.

Output Image Table The output image table is a part of CPU memory (Figure 1-13). The user's logic determines whether an output should be on or off. The CPU evaluates the user's ladder logic. If it determines that an output should be on, it stores a 1 in the bit that corresponds to that output. The 1 in the output image table is used to turn on the actual output through an isolation circuit (Figure 1-14).

The outputs of small PLCs are often relays. This allows the user to mix and match output voltages or types. For example, some outputs could then be AC and some DC. Relay output modules also are available for some of the larger PLCs. The other choices are transistors for DC outputs and triacs for AC outputs. There are many types of field devices that can be connected to outputs. Figure 1-15 shows a few examples.

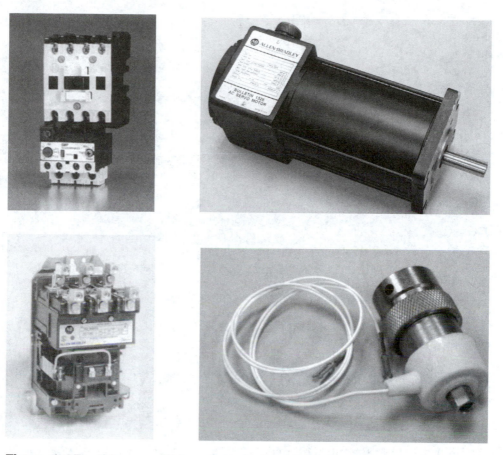

Figure 1-15   A few possible output devices including a contactor, AC motor, starter, and valve.

PLC APPLICATIONS

Programmable logic controllers are used for a variety of applications (Figures 1-16 and 1-17). They are used to replace hardwired logic in older machines, which can reduce the downtime and maintenance of older equipment. More importantly, PLCs can increase the speed and capability of older equipment. Retrofitting an older piece of equipment with a PLC for control is almost like getting a new machine. PLCs are being used to control such processes as chemical production, paper production, steel production, and food processing. In processes such as these, they are used to control temperature, pressure, mixture, and concentration. They are used to control position and velocity in many kinds of production processes. For example, they can be used to control complex automated storage and retrieval

Figure 1-16 A PLC-controlled injection molding machine. *(Courtesy Rockwell Automation Inc.)*

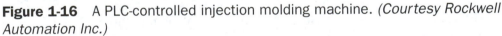

systems. They also can be used to control equipment such as robots and production machining equipment.

Many small companies have started up recently to produce special-purpose equipment, which is normally controlled by PLCs. It is quite cost effective for these companies to use PLCs. Examples are conveyors and palletizing, packaging, processing, and material handling. Without PLC technology, many small equipment design companies might not exist.

PLCs are often used for motor control applications. They can control simple stepper motor systems or complex AC and DC control of motor drives. PLCs are being used extensively in position and velocity control. A PLC can control position and velocity much more quickly and accurately than can mechanical devices such as gears and cams. An electronic system of control is not only faster, but also does not wear out and lose accuracy as do mechanical devices.

Figure 1-17 Large flexographic printing press controlled by a PLC. Flexographic presses are used to produce various packaging and printed materials.

PLCs are used for almost any process imaginable. Certain companies own PLC-equipped railroad cars that regrind and true the rail track as they travel. PLCs have been used to ring the perfect sequences of bells in church bell towers, at the exact times during the day and week. PLCs are used in lumber mills to grade, size, and cut lumber for optimal output. The uses of PLCs are limited only by the imagination of the engineers and technicians who use them.

QUESTIONS

1. The PLC is programmed by technicians using:
   a. the C programming language
   b. ladder logic
   c. the choice of language used depends on the manufacturer
   d. none of the above

2. Changing relay control type circuits involves changing:
   a. the input circuit devices
   b. the voltage levels of most I/Os

    c. the circuit wiring

    d. the input and output devices

3. The most common programming device for PLCs is the:

    a. dumb terminal

    b. dedicated programming terminal

    c. handheld programmer

    d. personal computer

4. True or false? CPU stands for central processing unit.

5. Opto-isolation is:

    a. used to protect the CPU from real-world inputs

    b. not used in PLCs, so isolation must be provided by the user

    c. used to protect the CPU from real-world outputs

    d. both a and c

6. EEPROM is:

    a. electrically erasable memory

    b. electrically programmable RAM

    c. erased by exposing it to ultraviolet light

    d. programmable

    e. a, b, and d

7. True or false? RAM typically holds the operating system.

8. Typical program storage devices for ladder diagrams include:

    a. computer disks

    b. EEPROM

    c. static RAM cards

    d. all of the above

    e. none of the above

9. The IEC 1131-3 standard specifies characteristics for:

    a. PLC communications

    b. EEPROM

    c. memory

    d. PLC programming languages

    e. none of the above

10. Input devices would include the following:

    a. switches

    b. sensors

    c. other smart devices

    d. all of the above

    e. none of the above

11. Troubleshooting a PLC system:
    a. requires special PLC diagnostic equipment
    b. is much more difficult than for relay type systems
    c. is easier because of indicators such as I/O indicators on I/O modules
    d. all of the above
    e. none of the above

12. Output modules can be purchased with which of the following output devices:
    a. transistor outputs
    b. triac outputs
    c. relay outputs
    d. all of the above
    e. both a and c

13. Field devices would include the following:
    a. switches
    b. sensors
    c. valves
    d. all of the above
    e. none of the above

14. If an output module's current rating is 1A per output and there are eight outputs, the current rating for the module is 8A. True or false? Explain your answer.

15. Describe how the status of real-world inputs are stored in PLC memory.

16. Describe how the status of real-world outputs are stored in PLC memory.

17. Define the term *debounce*. Why is it so important?

18. What is the difference between online and offline programming?

19. What does it mean to force I/O?

chapter
Overview of Number Systems 2

A knowledge of various numbering systems is essential to the use of PLCs. In addition to the decimal system, binary, octal, and hexadecimal systems are regularly used. An understanding of the systems will make the task of working with PLCs an easier one. In this chapter we examine each of these systems.

OBJECTIVES

Upon completion of this chapter, you will be able to:
1. Explain each of the numbering systems
2. Explain the benefits of typical number systems and why each is used
3. Convert from one number system to another
4. Explain how input or output modules might be numbered using the octal or hexadecimal number system
5. Use each number system properly
6. Explain such terms as *most significant, least significant, nibble, byte,* and *word*

DECIMAL SYSTEM

A short review of the basics of the decimal system will help in a thorough understanding of the other number systems. Although calculators will do the tedious work of number conversion between systems, it is vital that the technician be comfortable with the number systems. Binary, octal, and hexadecimal systems are regularly used to identify such items as inputs/outputs and memory addresses. The technician who understands and uses these systems will have an easier time with PLCs.

The decimal number system uses ten digits: 0 through 9. The highest digit is 9 in the decimal system. Zero through 9 are the only digits allowed.

The first column in decimal can be used to count up to nine items. Another column must be added if the number is larger than 9. The second column can also use the digits 0 through 9. This column is weighted, however, as shown in Figure 2-1. The second column is used to tell the number of tens. For example, the number 23 represents two 10s and three 1s. By using one column we are able to count to 9. If we use two columns we can count to 99. The first column can hold up to 9. The second column can hold up to 90 (nine 10s), exactly 10 times as much as the first column. In fact, in the decimal system, each column is worth 10 times as much as the preceding column. The third column represents the number of hundreds (10 times 10). For example, 227 would represent two 100s, two 10s, and seven 1s (Figure 2-2).

The decimal system is certainly the simplest and most familiar type of numbering system. The other systems are based on the same principles as the decimal system. It would certainly be easier if there were only one system, but the computer cannot "think" in decimal. The computer can only work with binary numbers. In fact, the other number systems are quite convenient for certain uses and actually simplify some tasks.

Decimal System					
100,000s	10,000s	1000s	100s	10s	1s

Figure 2-1   Weights of the decimal system.

Figure 2-2   Relationship between the weights of each column and the decimal number 227.

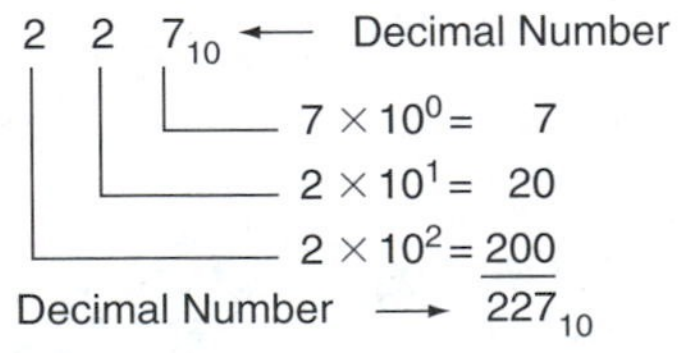

$$2 \quad 2 \quad 7_{10} \longleftarrow \text{Decimal Number}$$

$$7 \times 10^0 = 7$$
$$2 \times 10^1 = 20$$
$$2 \times 10^2 = 200$$
$$\text{Decimal Number} \longrightarrow 227_{10}$$

Binary System					
32s	16s	8s	4s	2s	1s

Figure 2-3 Weights of each column in the binary system. The first column is the number of 1s, the second is the number of 2s, and so on.

BINARY NUMBERING SYSTEM

The binary numbering system is based on only two digits: 0 and 1. A computer is a digital device. It works with voltages, on or off. Computer memory is a series of 0s and 1s.

The binary system works like the decimal system. The first column holds the number of 1s (Figure 2-3). Because the only possible digits in the first column are 0 or 1, it should be clear that the first column can hold zero 1s or one 1. Thus, we can only count up to 1 using the first column in binary. The second column holds the number of 2s. There can be zero 2s or one 2. The binary number 10 would equal one 2 plus zero 1s. The number 10 in binary is 2 in the decimal system (one 2 + zero 1s). The binary number 11 would be 3 in decimal (one 2 + one 1) (see Figure 2-4). The third column is the number of 4s. Thus, binary 100 would be equal to decimal 4. The fourth column is the number of 8s, the fifth column is the number of 16s, the sixth column is the number of 32s, the seventh is the number of 64s, and the eighth column is the number of 128s. As you can see, each column's value is twice as large as that of the previous column.

The value of the column in binary can be found by raising 2 to the power represented by that column. For example, the third column's weight could be found by raising 2 to the second power ($2 \times 2 = 4$). Remember that the first column is column 0, the second is column 1, and so on. The weight of the fourth column is 8 ($2 \times 2 \times 2$) (Figure 2-5).

Binary is used extensively because it is the only numbering system usable by a computer. It is also quite useful when considering digital logic, because a 1 can represent one state and a 0 the opposite state. For example, a light is either on or off. See Figure 2-6 for the appearance of a binary word.

BINARY CODED DECIMAL SYSTEM

Binary coded decimal (BCD) involves the blending of the binary and decimal systems. In BCD, 4 binary bits are used to represent a decimal digit. These 4 bits are used to represent the numbers 0 through 9. Thus, 0111 binary would be 7 decimal (Figure 2-7).

Figure 2-4
Comparison of the binary and decimal numbers from 0 through 15.

Binary				Decimal
8s	4s	2s	1s	
0	0	0	0	0
0	0	0	1	1
0	0	1	0	2
0	0	1	1	3
0	1	0	0	4
0	1	0	1	5
0	1	1	0	6
0	1	1	1	7
1	0	0	0	8
1	0	0	1	9
1	0	1	0	10
1	0	1	1	11
1	1	0	0	12
1	1	0	1	13
1	1	1	0	14
1	1	1	1	15

Figure 2-5 Relationship between binary and decimal. The binary number 11001101 is equal to 205 decimal.

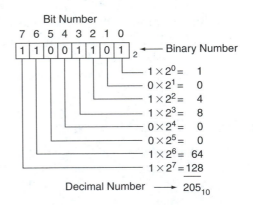

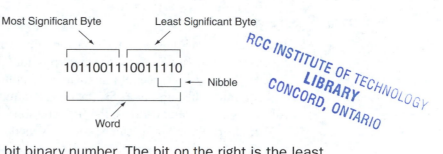

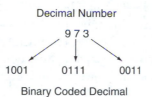

Figure 2-6 A 16 bit binary number. The bit on the right is the least significant bit. The bit on the left is the most significant bit. The next unit of grouping is the nibble. A nibble is 4 bits. The next grouping of a binary number is the byte. A byte is 8 bits. Note that the first eight digits are called the least significant byte and the last eight digits are called the most significant byte. The next grouping is called the word. The size of a word is dependent on the processor. A 16 bit processor has a 16 bit word. A 32 bit processor has a 32 bit word.

Figure 2-7 How the decimal number 973 would be represented in the binary coded decimal (BCD) system. Each decimal digit is represented by its four-digit binary number. *Caution:* BCD is not the same as binary. The decimal number 973 is 1001 0111 0011 in BCD and is 0011 1100 1101 in binary.

The difference in BCD is in the way numbers above decimal 9 are represented. For example, the decimal number 43 would be 0100 0011 in BCD. The first 4 bits (least significant bits) represent the decimal 3. The second 4 bits (most significant bits) represent the decimal 4. In BCD, the first 4 bits represent the number of 1s in a decimal number, the second 4 bits represent the number of 10s, the third 4 bits represent the number of 100s, and so on.

Use of the BCD format is popular for output from instruments. Measuring devices will typically output BCD values. Some input devices use the BCD system to output their value. Thumbwheels are one example. A person dials in a decimal digit between 0 and 9. The thumbwheel outputs 4 bits of data. The 4 bits are BCD. For example, if an operator were to dial in the number 8, then the output from the BCD thumbwheel would be 1000. PLCs can easily accept BCD input.

OCTAL SYSTEM

The octal system is based on the same principles as the binary and decimal systems except that it is base 8. There are eight possible digits in the octal system: 0, 1, 2, 3, 4, 5, 6, and 7. The first column in an octal number is the number of 1s. The second column is the number of 8s, the third column is the number of 64s, the fourth column is the number of 512s, the fifth column is the number of 4096s, and so on.

Weights of the columns can be found by using the same method as that used for binary. The number 8 is simply raised to the power represented by that column. The first column (column 0) represents 8 to the zero power (1 by definition). Remember that the first column is column 0. The weight of the second column (column 1) is found by raising 8 to the first power (8×1). The weight of the third column (column 2) is found by raising 8 to the second power (8×8) (see Figure 2-8).

The actual digits in the octal number system are 1, 2, 3, 4, 5, 6, and 7. If we must count above 7, then we must use the next column. For example, let us count to 10 in octal: 1, 2, 3, 4, 5, 6, 7, 10, 11, and 12. The 12 represents one 8 and two 1s ($8 + 2 = 10$). The number 23 decimal would be 27 in octal. Two 8s and seven 1s is equal to 23. The number 3207 octal would be 1671 in decimal. Figure 2-9 shows how an octal number can be converted to a decimal number.

Some PLC manufacturers use octal to number input and output modules, and also to number memory addresses. For example, assuming the use of input cards with eight inputs per card, the first eight inputs on the first card would be numbered 0, 1, 2, 3, 4, 5, 6, and 7. The next input card numbering would begin with octal 10, 11, 12, 13, 14, 15, 16, and 17 (Figure 2-10). This makes it easy to find the location of inputs or outputs. The least significant digit is used to specify the

Octal System					
32,768s	4,096s	512s	64s	8s	1s

Figure 2-8   Weights of the columns in the octal number system. The first column is the number of 1s, the second column is the number of 8s, and so on.

Figure 2-9   How the octal number 3207 is converted to the decimal number 1671.

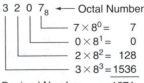

$$3 \ 2 \ 0 \ 7_8 \longleftarrow \text{Octal Number}$$
$$7 \times 8^0 = \quad 7$$
$$0 \times 8^1 = \quad 0$$
$$2 \times 8^2 = \quad 128$$
$$3 \times 8^3 = 1536$$

$$\text{Decimal Number} \longrightarrow 1671_{10}$$

Input Module 0	Input Module 1	Input Module 2	Input Module 3
I00	I10	I20	I30
I01	I11	I21	I31
I02	I12	I22	I32
I03	I13	I23	I33
I04	I14	I24	I34
I05	I15	I25	I35
I06	I16	I26	I36
I07	I17	I27	I37

Figure 2-10 I/O module addressing using the octal numbering system. The first input module is numbered 0. The first input on the module would be called input 00 (the first zero represents the first module, the second zero means that it is the first input). The eighth input on the first module would be called 07. The eighth input on the fourth module would be called input 37. (Remember that the first module is module 0; the fourth module is module 3.) The first output module would begin numbering as output module 0 and each output would be numbered just as the input modules were. For example, the fifth output on the second output module would be numbered output 14.

actual input/output number, and the most significant digit is used to specify the particular card where the input/output is located.

Octal is also used by some manufacturers for numbering memory. For example, Siemens Industrial Automation Inc. has 128 timers and counters available for the 405 series of PLCs. The timers are numbered 0 to 177 octal. This equates to 0 through 127 decimal.

HEXADECIMAL SYSTEM

The hexadecimal system normally causes the most trouble for people. Hexadecimal (or hex) is based on the same principles as the other numbering systems discussed thus far. Hex has sixteen possible digits, but with an unusual twist. It uses numbers and also the letters *A* to *F*. This can be a little confusing at first. In hexadecimal, we count 0, 1, 2, 3, 4, 5, 6, 7, 8, and 9. After the number 9, the counting changes: 10 becomes A, 11 is B, 12 is C, 13 is D, 14 is E, and 15 is F (Figure 2-11).

Figure 2-11
Comparison of the hexadecimal and decimal systems.

Hexadecimal	Decimal
0	0
1	1
2	2
3	3
4	4
5	5
6	6
7	7
8	8
9	9
A	10
B	11
C	12
D	13
E	14
F	15
10	16
11	17
12	18
13	19
14	20

The first column (column 0) in hex is the number of 1s (Figure 2-12). The second column is the number of 16s. The third column is the number of 256s, and so on.

Weights can be found in the same manner as in the binary system. In the hexadecimal system, 16 would be raised to the power of the column. For example, the weight of the third column (column 2) would be 16 to the second power ($16 \times 16 = 256$). Figure 2-13 shows how a hexadecimal number can be converted to a decimal number.

Hexadecimal numbers are easier (less cumbersome) to work with than binary numbers. It is easy to convert between the two systems (Figures 2-14 and 2-15).

Hexadecimal System					
1,048,576s	65,536s	4,096s	256s	16s	1s

Figure 2-12   Weights of the columns in the hexadecimal system. The first column is the number of 1s, the second column is the number of 16s, and so on.

Figure 2-13   Weights of the hexadecimal number system converted to the decimal weighting system.

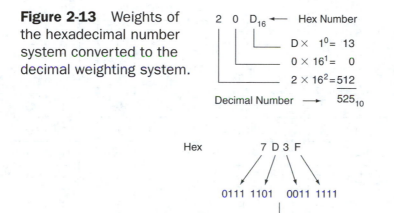

Figure 2-14   The conversion of a hexadecimal number to its binary equivalent. Each hex digit is simply converted to its four-digit binary. The result is a binary equivalent. In this case, hex 7D3F is equal to binary 0111110100111111. (Which number would you rather work with?)

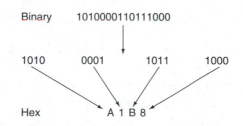

Figure 2-15   Conversion of a binary number to a hex number. The binary number is broken into four-bit pieces (4 bits are called a nibble) and each 4-bit nibble is converted to its hex equivalent. The binary number 1010000110111000 is equal to hex A1B8. (Which would you prefer to work with?)

Hexadecimal	Decimal	Octal		Binary			
		8s	1s	8s	4s	2s	1s
0	0	0	0	0	0	0	0
1	1	0	1	0	0	0	1
2	2	0	2	0	0	1	0
3	3	0	3	0	0	1	1
4	4	0	4	0	1	0	0
5	5	0	5	0	1	0	1
6	6	0	6	0	1	1	0
7	7	0	7	0	1	1	1
8	8	1	0	1	0	0	0
9	9	1	1	1	0	0	1
A	10	1	2	1	0	1	0
B	11	1	3	1	0	1	1
C	12	1	4	1	1	0	0
D	13	1	5	1	1	0	1
E	14	1	6	1	1	1	0
F	15	1	7	1	1	1	1

Figure 2-16   A comparison of the four number systems for the numbers 0 to 15.

Each hex digit is simply converted to its four-digit binary equivalent. The result is the binary equivalent of the whole hex number.

The same process works in reverse. Any binary number can be converted to its hex equivalent by breaking the binary number into four-digit pieces and converting each 4-bit piece to its hex equivalent. The resulting numbers are equal in value.

Figure 2-16 shows an overview of the four number systems.

QUESTIONS

1. Complete the following table.

	Binary	Octal	Decimal	Hexadecimal
a.	101			5
b.		11		
c.			15	
d.				D
e.		16		
f.	1001011			
g.		47		
h.			73	

2. Number the following input/output modules using the octal method.

	Input Module 0	Input Module 1	Output Module 0	Input Module 2
a.				
b.				
c.				
d.				
e.				
f.				
g.				
h.				

3. Define each of the following:
   a. bit
   b. nibble
   c. byte
   d. word

4. Why is the binary number system used in computer systems?

5. Complete the following table.

	Binary	Hexadecimal
a.	1011001011111101	
b.		1A07
c.	100100000111	
d.		C17F
e.	0010001111000010	
f.		D91C
g.	0011010111100110	
h.		ECA9
i.	0101001011000101	

6. True or false? A word is sixteen bits. Explain your answer.

7. True or false? One K of memory is exactly one thousand bytes.

8. How can the weight of the fifth column of a binary number be calculated?

9. How can the weight of the fourth column of a hex number be calculated?

10. What is the BCD system normally used for?

Fundamentals of Programming

3

In this chapter we examine the basics of ladder logic programming, including terminology and common symbols. We also learn how to write basic ladder logic programs.

OBJECTIVES

Upon completion of this chapter, you will be able to:
1. Describe the basic process of writing ladder logic
2. Define such terms as *contact, coil, rung, scan, normally open,* and *normally closed*
3. Write ladder logic for simple applications

LADDER LOGIC

Programmable controllers are primarily programmed in ladder logic, a symbolic representation of an electrical circuit. Symbols resemble those of the schematic symbols of electrical devices, to make it easy for the plant electrician to learn how to use the PLC. An electrician who has never seen a PLC can understand a ladder diagram.

The main function of the PLC program is to control outputs based on the condition of inputs. The symbols used in ladder logic programming can be divided into two broad categories: contacts (inputs) and coils (outputs).

35

Figure 3-1 A normally
open and a normally
closed contact.

Normally
Open
Contact
(XIC)

Normally
Closed
Contact
(XIO)

Contacts

Most inputs to a PLC are simple devices that are either on or off. These inputs are sensors and switches that detect part presence, empty or full, and so on. The two common symbols for contacts are shown in Figure 3-1.

Contacts can be thought of as switches. There are two basic kinds of switches, normally open and normally closed. A normally open switch will not pass current until pressed. A normally closed switch will allow current flow until it is pressed. Rockwell calls the normally open switch an examine if closed (XIC) instruction and the normally closed contact an examine if open (XIO) instruction. Think of a doorbell switch. Would you use a normally open switch or a normally closed switch for a doorbell? If you chose the normally closed switch, the bell would be on continuously until someone pushes the switch. Pushing the switch opens the contacts and stops current flow to the bell. The normally open switch is the necessary choice. If the normally open switch is used, the bell will not sound until someone pushes the button on the switch.

Sensors are used to detect the presence of physical objects or quantities. For example, one type of sensor might be used to sense when a box moves down a conveyor, and a different type might be used to measure a quantity such as heat. Most sensors are switchlike: They are on or off depending on what the sensor is sensing. Like switches, sensors can be purchased that are either normally open or normally closed.

Imagine, for example, a sensor that is designed to sense a metal part as the part passes the sensor. We could buy a normally open or a normally closed sensor for the application. If it were desired to notify the PLC every time a part passed the sensor, a normally open sensor might be chosen. The sensor would turn on only if a metal part passed in front of the sensor. The sensor would turn off again when the part was gone.

The PLC could then count the number of times the normally open switch turned on (closed) and would know how many parts had passed the sensor. Normally closed sensors and switches are often used when safety is a concern. These are examined later in the chapter.

Coils

Whereas contacts are input symbols, coils are output symbols. Outputs can take various forms, including motors, lights, pumps, counters, timers, and relays. A

Figure 3-2 Ladder logic symbol for a coil.

Coil

coil represents an output. The PLC examines the contacts (inputs) in the ladder and turns the coils (outputs) on or off depending on the condition of the inputs. The basic coil is shown in Figure 3-2. Coil symbols only appear on the right side of the rung. A specific coil number should appear only once at the right of a rung. The output that the coil represents, however, can be used many times on the left as contact(s).

LADDER DIAGRAMS

The basic ladder diagram looks similar to a step ladder. Two uprights hold the rungs that make up the PLC ladder. The left and right uprights (sometimes called power rails) represent power. If we connect the left and right uprights, power can flow through the rung from the left upright to the right upright.

Consider the doorbell example again, with one input and one output. The ladder diagram for the PLC would be only one rung (Figure 3-3). The real-world switch would be connected to input number 0 of the PLC. The bell would be connected to output number 0 of the PLC (Figure 3-4). The uprights represent a DC voltage that will be used to power the doorbell. If the real-world doorbell switch is pressed, power can flow through the switch to the doorbell.

The PLC would then run the ladder. The PLC will monitor the input continuously and control the output, a process called scanning. The amount of time it takes for the PLC to check the states of inputs, evaluate the logic, and then update the I/O table each time is called scan time. Scan time varies among PLCs. Most applications do not require extreme speed, so any PLC is fast enough; even a slow PLC scan time would be in milliseconds. The longer or more complex the ladder logic, the more time it takes to scan.

The scan cycle is illustrated in Figure 3-5. Note that this one rung of logic represents our entire ladder. Each time the PLC scans the doorbell ladder, it checks the state of the input switch *before* it enters the ladder (time period 1). While in the ladder, the PLC then decides if it needs to change the state of any outputs (evaluation during time period 2). *After* the PLC finishes evaluating the logic (time period 2), it turns on or off any outputs based on the evaluation (time period 3). The PLC then returns to the top of the ladder, checks the inputs again, and repeats the entire process. It is the total of these three stages that makes up scan time. We discuss the scan cycle more completely later in this chapter.

Figure 3-3   Simple conceptual view of a ladder diagram.

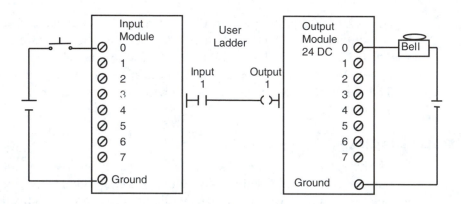

Figure 3-4   Conceptual view of a PLC system. The real-world inputs are attached to an input module (left side). Outputs are attached to an output module (right side). The center shows the logic that the CPU must evaluate. The CPU evaluates user logic by looking at the inputs and then turns on outputs based on the logic. In this case if input 0 (a normally open switch) is closed, then output 0 (the doorbell) will turn on.

Figure 3-5   An example of how a user's ladder logic is continually scanned.

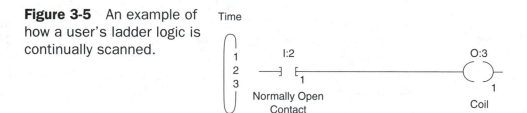

Normally Open Contacts

First we examine the normally open contact. A normally open contact does not pass power until the input associated with it is energized. A normally open contact is shown in Figure 3-5. Imagine the doorbell switch again. The actual switch is normally open. If we push the switch, it closes and passes power to sound the doorbell in the house. A normally open contact is similar to the normally open doorbell switch. In a ladder diagram this contact could be used to monitor a real-world

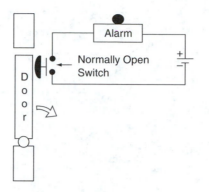

Figure 3-6 A conceptual diagram of the wrong way to construct a burglar alarm circuit. In this case, the homeowner would never know if the system failed. The correct method would be to use normally closed switches. The control system would then monitor the circuit continuously to see if the doors opened or a switch failed.

switch. If the real-world switch is closed (energized), then the normally open contact in the ladder logic would pass power.

Normally Closed Contacts

The normally closed contact will pass power until it is activated. A normally closed contact in a ladder diagram will pass power while the real-world input associated with it is off.

A home security system is an example of normally closed logic. Assume that the security system was intended to monitor the two entrance doors to a house. One way to wire the house is to wire one normally open switch from each door to the alarm, like a doorbell switch (Figure 3-6). Then if a door opened, it would close the switch and the alarm would sound. This configuration would work, but certain problems exist. Assume that the switch fails. For example, a wire may be cut accidentally, or a connection may become loose, or a switch may break. The problem is that the homeowner would never know that the system was not working. An intruder could open the door, and the switch would not work and the alarm would not sound. Obviously, this is not a good way to design a system. The system should be set up so that the alarm will sound for an intruder and will also sound if a component fails. The homeowner surely wants to know if the system fails. It is far better for the alarm to sound when the system fails with no intruder than not to sound if the system fails with an intruder.

Such considerations are even more important in an industrial setting where failure could cause an injury. The procedure of programming to ensure safety is called

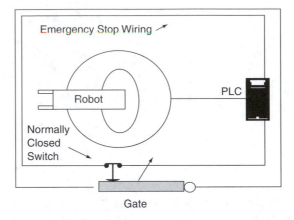

Figure 3-7 Robot cell application. Note the fence around the cell with one gate, the PLC used as a cell controller, and the safety switch to prevent anyone from entering the cell while the robot is running. If someone enters the cell, the PLC will sense that the switch opened and sound an alarm. In this case a normally closed switch is used. If the wiring or switch fails, the PLC will think someone entered the cell and sound an alarm. This system would be fail-safe.

fail-safe. The programmer must carefully design the system and ladder logic so that if a failure occurs, people and processes are safe. As shown in Figure 3-7, if the gate is opened, it opens the normally closed switch. The PLC would see that the switch had opened and would sound an alarm immediately to protect whomever had entered the work cell. (In reality, we would sound an alarm and stop the robot to protect the intruder.)

The normally closed switch as used in ladder logic can be confusing. The normally closed contact in our ladder passes electricity if the input switch is off. The switch in the gate of the cell is a normally closed switch. (The switch in the cell normally allows electricity to flow.) If the gate switch is closed, the alarm will be off, because the normally closed contact in the ladder logic will be open (Figure 3-8).

If someone opens the gate, the normally closed gate switch opens, stopping electrical flow. The PLC sees that there is no flow, the normally closed contact in the ladder allows electricity to flow, and the alarm is turned on (Figure 3-9).

What would happen if a tow motor was too close to the cell and cut the wire that connects the gate safety switch to the PLC? The alarm will sound, because the wire being cut is similar to the gate opening the switch. Is it a good thing that the alarm sounds if the wire is cut? Yes. This warns the operator that something failed in the cell. The operator could then call maintenance and have the cell repaired. This is a

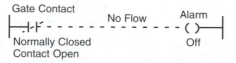

Figure 3-8 One rung of a ladder diagram. A normally closed contact is used in the ladder. If the switch associated with that contact is closed, it forces the normally closed contact open. No current flows to the output (the alarm). The alarm is off.

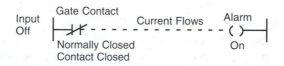

Figure 3-9 The gate switch is off. (Someone opened the gate and thus opened the switch.) The normally closed contact is true when the input is false, so the alarm sounds. The same thing would happen if a tow motor cut the wire that led to the safety sensor. The input would go low and the alarm would sound.

fail-safe system. Something in the cell failed and the system was shut down by the PLC so that no one would be hurt. The same would be true if the gate safety switch were to fail. The alarm would sound. If the switch were opened (someone opened the gate to the cell), the PLC would see that there is no power at the input (Figure 3-9). The normally closed contact in the ladder logic is then closed, allowing electricity to flow. This causes the alarm to sound. Consider the rungs shown in Figure 3-10 and determine if the output coils are on or off. (The answers follow.) Pay particular attention to the normally closed examples.

Transitional Contacts

Transitional contacts are a special type of contact. They are also called one-shot contacts. The symbol for this type of contact is shown in Figure 3-11. The one-shot rising (OSR) instruction is an input instruction that can trigger an event to occur one time, which explains why they are called one-shot contacts. When the rung conditions preceding the OSR instruction go from false to true, the OSR will be true for one scan.

There are many reasons to use the transitional contacts. They are often used to provide a pulse for timing, counting, or sequencing. They are also used when it is desired to perform an instruction only once (not every scan). For example, if an add instruction was used to add two numbers once, it would not be necessary to add

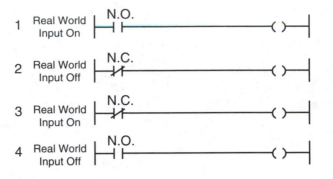

Figure 3-10 Ladder diagram exercise.

Answers to ladder logic in Figure 3-10.

1. The output in example 1 is on. The real-world input is on, so the normally open contact (or examine if closed—XIC) in the ladder would be energized and pass power to the output. In other words, the examine-on instruction is used to check if the real-world input is closed (has power). If so, the examine-on instruction passes power to the output coil in the ladder.

2. The output in example 2 is on. The real-world input is off. The normally closed contact (or examine if open—XIO) in the ladder is energized because the input is off. In other words, the examine-off instruction is used to check if the real-world input is open. If so, the XIO is energized and passes power to the output.

3. The output in example 3 is off. The real-world input is on, which forces the normally closed contact in the ladder open. In other words, the real-world input is on, so the XIO is deenergized and does not pass power. The output is off.

4. The output in example 4 is off. The real-world input is off, so the normally open contact remains open and the output off. In other words, the real-world input is off, so the XIC is deenergized and does not pass power. The output is off.

Figure 3–11 A one-shot rising instruction.   ──┤ OSR ├──

them every scan. A transitional contact would ensure that the instruction executes only on the desired transition.

MULTIPLE CONTACTS

More than one contact can be put on the same rung. For example, think of a drill machine. The engineer wants the drill press to turn on only if there is a part present and the operator has one hand on each of the start switches (see Figures 3-12 and 3-13). This would ensure that the operator's hands could not be in the press while it is running.

Note that the switches were programmed as normally open contacts. They are all on the same rung (series). All will have to be on for the output to turn on. If there

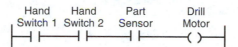

Figure 3-12   Series circuit. Hand switches 1 and 2 and the part sensor must be closed before the drill motor will be turned on, to ensure that there is a part in the machine and that the operator's hands are in a safe location.

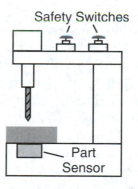

Figure 3-13   Simple drilling machine. There are two hand safety switches and one part sensor on the machine. Both hand switches and the part sensor must be true for the drill press to operate, to ensure that the operator's hands are not in the way of the drill. This is an AND condition. switch 1 and switch 2 and the part sensor must be activated to make the machine operate. The ladder for the PLC is shown in Figure 3-14.

is a part present and the operator puts both hands on the start switches, the drill press will run.

If the operator removes one hand for some reason, the press will stop. Contacts in a series such as this can be thought of as logical AND conditions. In this case, the part presence switch *and* the left-hand switch *and* the right-hand switch would have to be closed to run the drill press. Study the examples in Figure 3-14 and determine the status of the outputs.

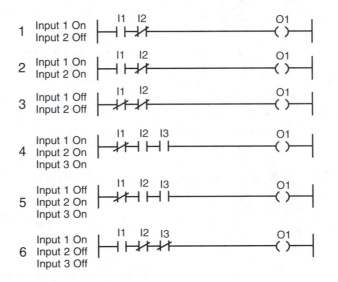

Figure 3-14   Ladder diagram exercise.

Answers to ladder logic in Figure 3-14.

1. The output for rung 1 will be on. Input 1 is on, which energizes contact 1. Input 2 is off, so normally closed contact 2 is still energized. Both contacts are energized, so the output is on.

2. The output in rung 2 is off. Input 1 is on, which energizes normally open contact 1. Input 2 is on, which deenergizes normally closed contact 2. The output cannot be on, because normally closed contact 2 is deenergized.

3. The input in rung 3 is on. Inputs 1 and 2 are off, so normally closed contacts 1 and 2 are energized.

4. The output in rung 4 is off. Input 1 is on, which deenergizes normally closed contact 1.

5. The output in rung 5 is on. Input 1 is off, so normally closed contact 1 is energized. Inputs 2 and 3 are on, which energizes normally open contacts 2 and 3.

6. The output in rung 6 is on. Input 1 is on, energizing normally open contact 1. Inputs 2 and 3 are off, which energizes normally closed contacts 2 and 3.

BRANCHING

There are often occasions when it is desired to turn on an output for more than one condition. For example, in a house, the doorbell should sound if either the front or rear door button is pushed (the two conditions under which the bell should sound). The ladder is called a branch (Figure 3-15). As shown, two paths (or conditions) can turn on the doorbell. (This can also be called a logical OR condition.)

If the front door switch is closed, electricity can flow to the bell; or, if the rear door switch is closed, electricity can flow through the bottom branch to the bell. Branching can be thought of as an OR situation. One branch *or* another can control the output. ORs allow multiple conditions to control an output. This is very important in industrial control of systems. Think of a motor that is used to move the table of a machine. There are usually two switches to control table movement: a jog switch and a feed switch (Figure 3-16). Both switches are used to turn on the same motor—an OR condition. The jog switch *or* the feed switch can turn on the table feed motor. Evaluate the ladder logic shown in Figure 3-17 to determine the output states.

Start/Stop Circuit

Start/stop circuits are extremely common in industry. Machines will have a start button to begin a process and a stop button to shut off the system. Several important

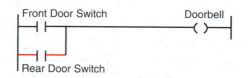

Figure 3-15 Parallel condition. If the front door switch is closed, the doorbell will sound; *or* if the rear door switch is closed, the doorbell will sound. These parallel conditions are also called OR conditions.

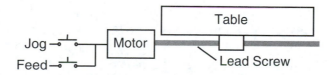

Figure 3-16 Conceptual drawing of a mill table. Note the two switches connected to the motor. These represent OR conditions. The jog switch *or* the feed switch can move the table.

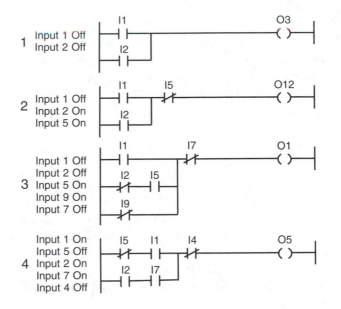

Figure 3-17 Ladder logic examples.

Answers to ladder logic in Figure 3-17.

1. The output in example 1 would be on. Input 2 is off, so that normally closed contact 2 is energized, energizing the output.

2. The output in example 2 is off. Input 5 is on, which deenergizes normally closed contact 5, so the output cannot be on whether input 1 *or* input 2 is on. Note also that in these branching examples we have combinations of ANDs and ORs. In English, this example would be input 1 *and* input 5 *or* input 2 *and* input 5 will turn on output 12.

3. The output in example 3 will be energized. Input 2 is off, which leaves normally closed contact input 2 energized *and* input 5 is on, which energizes normally open input 5 *and* normally closed input 7 is off, which energizes normally closed contact 7, which energizes output 1. In this ladder there are three OR conditions and combinations of ANDs.

4. In example 4, the output will be on. Input 5 is off, which energizes normally closed contact 5 *and* input 1 is on, which energizes normally open contact 1 *and* input 4 is off, which energizes normally closed contact 4 *and* input 4 is off, which energizes normally closed contact 4, energizing the output. Inputs 2 and 7 are also both on, energizing normally open contacts 2 *and* 7.

Figure 3-18 Start/stop circuit.

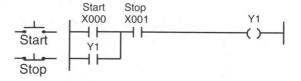

Figure 3-19 Start/stop circuit.

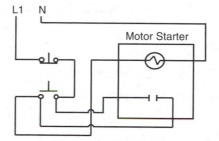

concepts can be learned from the simple logic of a start/stop circuit (Figure 3-18). Notice that the actual start switch is a normally open push button. When pressed, it closes the switch. When the button is released, the switch opens. The stop switch is a normally closed switch. When pressed, it opens.

Now examine the ladder. When the start switch is momentarily pressed, power passes through X000. Power also passes through X001, because the real-world stop switch is a normally closed switch. The output (Y1) is turned on. Note that Y1 is then also used as an input on the second line of logic. Output Y1 is on, so contact Y1 also closes. This process is called latching. The output latches itself on even if the start switch opens. Output Y1 will shut off only if the normally closed stop switch (X001) is pressed. If X001 opens, then Y1 is turned off. The system will require the start button to be pushed to restart the system. Note that the real-world stop switch is a normally closed switch, but that in the ladder, it is programmed normally open for safety reasons.

There are as many ways to program start/stop circuits (or ladder diagrams in general) as there are programmers. Figures 3-19 and 3-20 show examples of the wiring of start/stop circuits, where safety is always the main consideration.

PLC Scanning and Scan Time

Now that you are familiar with some basic PLC instructions and programming, it is important to understand the way a PLC executes a ladder diagram. Most people would like to believe that a ladder is a very sequential thing. We like to think of a ladder as first things first. We would like to believe that the first rung is evaluated and acted on before the next, and so on. We would like to believe that the CPU

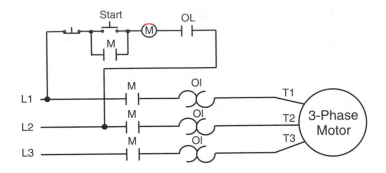

Figure 3-20 Start/stop circuit.

looks at the first rung, goes out and checks the actual inputs for their present state, comes back, immediately turns on or off the actual output for that rung, and then evaluates the next rung. Unfortunately, this is not exactly true, and misunderstanding the way the PLC scans a ladder can cause programming bugs.

Scan time can be divided into two components: I/O scan and program scan. When the PLC enters run mode it first takes care of the I/O scan (Figure 3-21). The I/O scan can be divided into the output step and the input step. During these two steps, the CPU transfers data from the output image table to the output modules (output step) and then from the input modules to the input image table (input step).

The third step is logic evaluation. The CPU uses the conditions from the image table to evaluate the ladder logic. If a rung is true, then the CPU writes a 1 into the corresponding bit in the output image table. If the rung is false, then the CPU writes a 0 into the corresponding bit in the output image table. Note that nothing concerning real-world I/O is occurring during the evaluation phase, which can be a point of confusion. The CPU is basing its decisions on the states of the inputs as they existed before the evaluation phase. We would like to believe that if an input condition changes while the CPU is in the evaluation phase, it would use the new state, but it cannot. (*Note:* It actually can use the new state if special instructions called immediate update contacts and coils are used. Most ladders will not utilize immediate instructions, however. The states of all inputs are frozen before the evaluation phase. The CPU does not turn outputs on and off during this phase either. This phase is only for evaluation and updating the output image table status.

Once the CPU has evaluated the entire ladder, it performs the I/O scan again. During the I/O scan, the output states of real-world outputs are changed depending on the output image table. The real-world input states are then transferred again to the input image table.

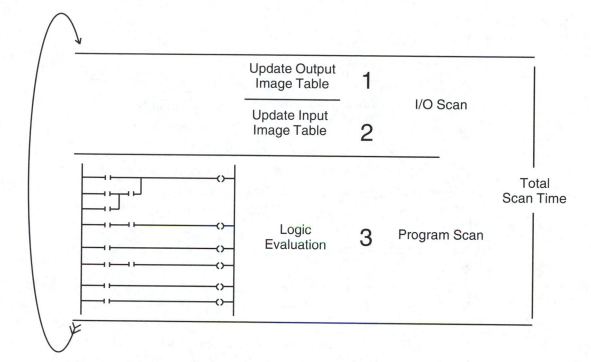

Figure 3-21   A generic example of PLC scanning.

Rockwell Automation Scan Order

Rockwell scanning occurs in the following order.

1. Input scan
2. Program scan
3. Output scan
4. Service communications
5. Overhead (timers, bits, integers, etc.)

The previous steps take only a few milliseconds (or less) to accomplish. This speed of PLCs creates problems when troubleshooting. Scan time is the sum of the times it takes to execute all of the individual instructions in the ladder. Simple contacts and coils take very little time. Complex math statements and other types of instructions take much more time. Even a long ladder diagram will normally execute in less than 50 milliseconds. There are considerable differences in the speeds of different brands and models of PLCs. Manufacturers normally will give scan time in terms of fractions of milliseconds per K of memory, to provide a rough idea of the scan times of various brands.

QUESTIONS

1. What is a contact? A coil?
2. What is a transitional contact?
3. Describe the uses of transitional contacts.
4. Explain the term *normally open* (XIC—examine if closed).
5. Explain the term *normally closed* (XIO—examine if open).
6. What are some uses of normally open contacts?
7. Explain the terms *true* and *false* as they apply to contacts in ladder logic.
8. Design a ladder that shows series input (AND logic). Use X5, X6, AND NOT (normally closed contact) X9 for the inputs and use Y10 for the output.
9. Design a ladder that has parallel input (OR logic). Use X2 and X7 for the contacts.
10. Design a ladder that has three inputs and one output. The input logic should be: X1 AND NOT X2, OR X3. Use X1, X2, and X3 for the input numbers and Y1 for the output.
11. Design a three-input ladder that uses AND logic and OR logic. The input logic should be X1 OR X3, AND NOT X2. Use contacts X1, X2, and X3. Use Y12 for the output coil.
12. Design a ladder into which coil Y5 will latch itself. The input contact should be X1. The unlatch contact should be X2.
13. Draw a diagram and thoroughly explain what occurs during a PLC scan.
14. Examine the following rungs and determine whether the output for each is on or off. The input conditions shown represent the states of real-world inputs.

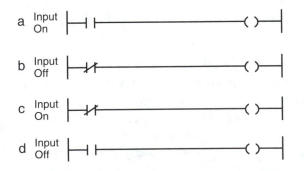

15. Examine the following rungs and determine whether the output for each is on or off. The input conditions shown represent the states of real-world inputs.

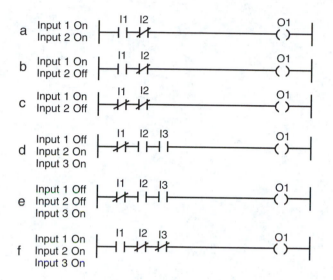

16. Examine the following rungs and determine whether the output for each is on or off. The input conditions shown represent the states of real-world inputs.

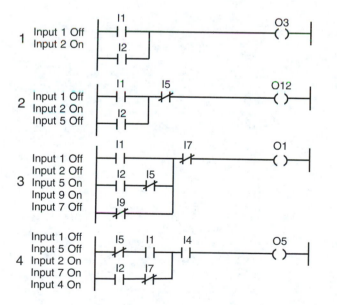

Rockwell Automation Memory Organization and Instructions 4

In this chapter we examine Rockwell Automation memory addressing and instructions. We also learn how to write basic ladder logic programs.

OBJECTIVES

Upon completion of this chapter, you will be able to:

1. Explain Rockwell Automation memory organization
2. Explain Rockwell Automation addressing
3. Define addresses for various file types
4. Explain the use of various Rockwell Automation instructions
5. Write programs that utilize Rockwell Automation instructions

UNDERSTANDING ROCKWELL FILE ORGANIZATION AND ADDRESSING

Understanding file organization and addressing can be one of the more confusing topics when learning how to program a PLC, so it is vital that you study this material carefully. This will dramatically reduce the frustration you experience as you begin to write programs. First, Rockwell Automation divides its memory system into two types: program and data (Figure 4-1). These two types of memory

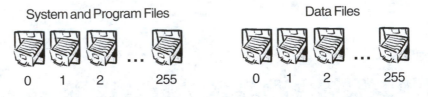

Figure 4-1 The two types of memory in a Rockwell Automation PLC.

are important to remember. Creating a mental image of the two separate memory areas may help. The program area of memory has 256 files; the data area also has 256 files.

To review, thus far you know there are two types of memory in a Rockwell Automation PLC: program and data. The program area of memory has 256 files (file 0 through file 255). The data area of memory has 256 files (file 0 through file 255). Let us now look at program memory.

Program File Memory

The 256 files in program memory (file 0 through file 255) contain controller information, the main ladder program, and any subroutine programs (Figure 4-2). The program files are as follows:

File 0 contains various system-related information and user-programmed information such as processor type, I/O configuration, processor file name, and password.

File 1 is reserved.

File 2 contains the main ladder diagram.

Files 3 through 255 are user created and accessed according to subroutine instructions residing in the main ladder program file. In other words, the user can

Program Files

Figure 4-2 System and program files in a Rockwell Automation PLC.

break the ladder diagram into logical portions of the total application program. Each portion of the ladder diagram can then be accessed, as needed from the main program in file 2. For example, the main ladder diagram in file 2 could contain the logic for the user to choose manual or automatic operation. If the user chooses automatic operation, then the logic in file 3 (or whatever file number the programmer desired) is executed. If the user chooses manual operation, then the logic in file 4 (or whatever file number the programmer desired) is executed.

Data Memory

The second type of memory that Rockwell PLCs have is data memory. As mentioned, data memory also has 256 files available. Data files are the files we need to write ladder logic. It may be helpful to imagine an office where information is stored in files. Imagine 256 files (Figure 4-1). Imagine that each file has a specific use.

Data files contain the status information associated with external I/O and all other instructions used in the main and subroutine ladder program files. In addition, these files store information concerning processor operation. You can also use the files to store "recipes" and look up tables if needed.

Data files are organized by the type of data they contain. The data file types are as follows:

File 0 is used to store the status of the outputs of the PLC. If you needed to change the status of an output you could put a 1 or 0 in the correct bit in file 0.

File 1 is used to store the status of inputs (Figure 4-3). If you needed to check the status of inputs you would look in file 1.

File 2 is reserved for PLC status information, which could be helpful for troubleshooting and program operation.

File 3 will be used to store bit information. Bits can be helpful in logic programming. They can be used to store information about conditions or as contacts or coils for non-real-world I/O.

File 4 is used for timer information.

File 5 is reserved for counter information.

File 6 is reserved for control. It is used when working with shift registers and sequencers.

File 7 is used to store integers (whole numbers).

File 8 is used to store floating point numbers (decimal numbers). This covers the files reserved for special uses. There are still many files available.

Files 9 through 255 are user configurable, meaning they are for any purpose a user would like. For example, if the user needs more room to store integers, the

File Number	Type	Use
0	Output	Stores the states of output terminals for the controller.
1	Input	Stores the states of input terminals for the controller.
2	Status	Stores the controller's operation information. This file can be useful for troubleshooting the controller and the program operation.
3	Bit	Can be used for internal relay bit storage.
4	Timer	Stores the accumulated value, preset value, and status bits for timers.
5	Counter	Stores the accumulated value, preset value, and status bits for counters.
6	Control	Stores the length, pointer position, and status bits for specific instructions such as sequencers and shift registers.
7	Integer	Can be used to store integer numbers or bit information.
8	Floating point	Can be used to store single precision nonextended 32 bit float numbers.
9–255	User defined	Can be used for any of the previously defined types by the user. Note that the whole file number must be used for the same type.

Figure 4-3   Data files and uses.

user could reserve any of the remaining files for more integers. Types may not be mixed files, however. The whole file must be reserved for integer use.

Figure 4-3 illustrates the files and their uses. Take some time to study them. It will help you to understand addressing.

Memory Addressing

I/O addressing is relatively straightforward. The first letter of the input address is called an identifier. Figure 4-4 shows the identifiers. In Figure 4-5 it is an input, so

Figure 4-4 Default file identifiers and numbers.

File Type	Identifier	File Number
Output	O	0
Input	I	1
Status	S	2
Bit	B	3
Timer	T	4
Counter	C	5
Control	R	6
Integer	N	7
Float	F	8

Figure 4-5 How address input 3 on the input module in slot 2 would be named.

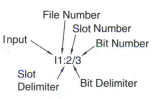

Figure 4-6 Note the input modules in slots 1, 2, and 3. The output modules are in slots 4, 5, and 6.

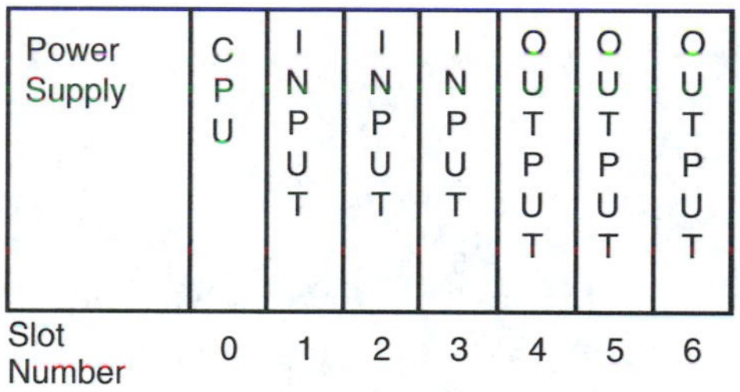

Power Supply	C P U	I N P U T	I N P U T	I N P U T	O U T P U T	O U T P U T	O U T P U T
		0	1	2	3	4	5	6

Slot Number   0 1 2 3 4 5 6

the identifier is I, indicating it will be an input. The second item in the address is a 1, which is the file number. The default number for input files is 1. The next item is a colon. This is a delimiter. A delimiter defines what will come next. If the delimiter is a colon, then the next item to follow the colon will always be the slot number of the module if we are naming inputs or outputs. Figure 4-6 shows an example of a PLC rack of modules. In our example in Figure 4-5, this input address is in slot 2. The next item is a slash. The slash is also a delimiter. The slash delimiter always means the next item will be a bit number. In this case it means that this will be input number 3. So, to review, this would be input 3 on the input module that is in slot 2.

Figure 4-7   Output
addressing example

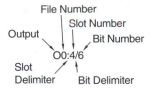

O0:5/12—Output 12 in slot 5, output file 0

O:6/7—Output 7 in slot 6, output file 0 (default file number 0)

I1:2/8—Input 8 in slot 2, input file 1

I:3/5—Input 5 in slot 3, input file 1 (default file number 1)

O0:4/12—Output 12 in slot 4, output file 0

O:5/1—Output 1 in slot 5, output file 0 (default file number 0)

I:1/9—Input 9 in slot 1, input file 1 (default file number 1)

Figure 4-8   Examples of I/O addressing.

Figure 4-9   Bit element
addressing example.

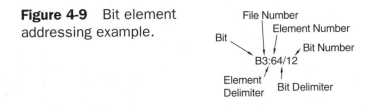

Figure 4-7 shows an example of output addressing. The first item in the address is O, for output. The next item is the file number. It is the default file number for outputs (file 0). The next item is a delimiter. It is a colon. The colon delimiter means that the next item to follow will be the slot number. In this case it is the output module in slot 4. The next item is the delimiter. The slash means that the number that follows will be the bit number (output number). In this case it is output 6 on the output module in slot 4.

Figure 4-8 has several important examples of I/O addressing. Study them carefully.

Figure 4-9 shows an example of bit element addressing. In this example the type identifier (B) specifies a bit type. The file number is 3. The element within the file is 64. The bit number is 12.

Elements for timers, counters, control, and ASCII files consist of three words. Figure 4-10 shows an example of counter addressing. In this case, the C stands for

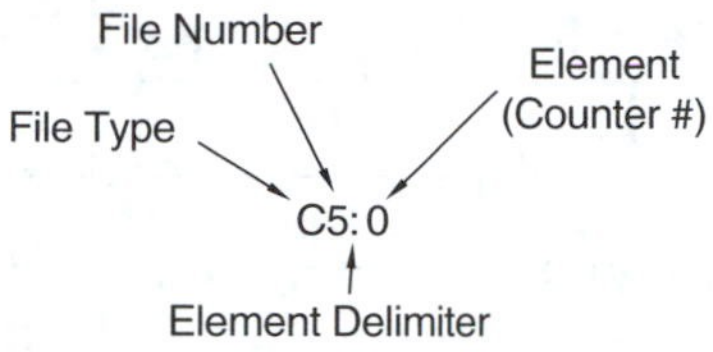

Figure 4-10 Example of a counter address.

15	14	13	12	11	10	9	8	7	6	5	4	3	2	1	0	Element
																0 C5:0
PRE/LEN																1 C5:0.PRE
ACC/POS																2 C5:0.ACC

Figure 4-11 Example of counter addressing.

Figure 4-12 Timer element addressing example.

15	14	13	12	11	10	9	8	7	6	5	4	3	2	1	0	Element
EN	TT	DN						Internal Use								0 T4:7
Preset Value PRE																1 T4:7.PRE
Accumulated Value ACC																2 T4:7.ACC

Figure 4-13 Timer memory.

counter, 5 is the file number, and the counter is 0. Figure 4-11 shows that counters occupy three words of memory. C5:0.PRE would hold the preset value and C5:0.ACC would hold the accumulated value. Timers and counters will be covered in more detail in Chapter 6.

Figure 4-12 shows an element address of T4:7.ACC. The T identifier stands for a timer. The file number is 4. The colon is the delimiter. The timer number is 7 and the ACC specifies the accumulated value word. Note that timers, like counters, utilize three words of memory (Figure 4-13). Timers will be covered in depth in Chapter 6.

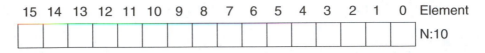

Figure 4-14   Example of the addressing of integer elements.

Figure 4-15   Integer element addressing example.

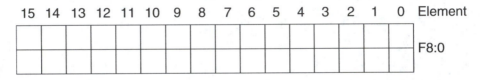

Figure 4-16   Example of the addressing of floating-point elements.

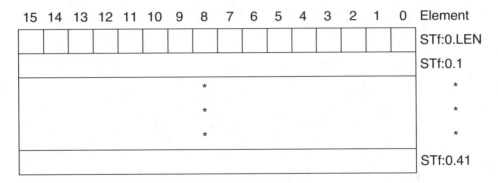

Figure 4-17   Example of the addressing of string file elements.

Figures 4-14 and 4-15 show examples of integer element addressing. In Figure 4-15 the N stands for integer, 7 is the file number, and 12 identifies the element.

Floating-point files have two-word elements. Figure 4-16 shows an example of floating-point element addressing. Note that there are two words to hold the floating-point number. In this example, the F stands for floating point, 8 is the file number, and 0 means the first two words in file 8. Remember that each floating-point number requires two words of storage.

String files have 42-word elements. Figure 4-17 shows an example. Note the use of the decimal point delimiter to specify the particular word in the string file.

User-Defined Files		
File Type	**Identifier**	**File Number**
Bit	B	
Timer	T	
Counter	C	
Control	R	9–255
Integer	N	
Float	F	
String	St	
ASCII	A	

Figure 4-18   User-defined file numbers.

USER-DEFINED FILES

Figure 4-18 shows the files that users can define. File numbers 9 through 255 are available for the user for any purpose. A whole file, however, must have the same use. For example, if the user desires to use file 10 for additional integers, file 10 can only be used for integers.

ROCKWELL AUTOMATION CONTACTS

Examine If Closed

The examine if closed instruction (XIC) is that which is normally open. If a real-world input device is on, this type of instruction is true and passes power (Figure 4-19). If the input bit from the input image table associated with this instruction is a 1, then the instruction is true. If the bit in the input image table is a 0, then the instruction associated with this particular input bit is false.

I1:2

3

Figure 4-19   Examine if closed instruction (XIC). If the CPU sees an on condition at bit I1:2/3, this instruction is true. The numbering of the input instruction is as follows: This is an input in file 1. It is located on an input module in slot 2 and it is real-world input 3 of the input module. The numbering of inputs and outputs will be covered later.

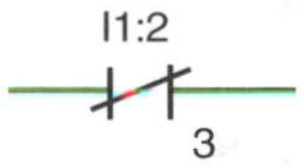

I1:2

3

Figure 4-20 Examine-off instruction (normally closed).

Examine If Open

Rockwell Automation calls its normally closed contacts examine if open contacts. The examine if open instruction (XIO) can also be called a normally closed instruction. This instruction responds in the opposite fashion to the normally open instruction. If the bit associated with this instruction is a 0 (off), then the instruction is true and passes power. If the bit associated with the instruction is a 1 (true), then the instruction is false and does not allow power flow.

Figure 4-20 shows an examine if open instruction (XIO). The input is 3 on an input module in slot 2. If the bit associated with I1:2/3 is true (1), then the instruction is false (open) and does not allow power flow. If bit I0:2/3 is false (0), then the instruction is true (closed) and allows flow.

SPECIAL CONTACTS

There are many special-purpose contacts available to the programmer. The original PLCs had few available. Sharp programmers used normally open and normally closed contacts in ingenious ways to turn outputs on for one scan, to latch outputs on, and so on. PLC manufacturers added special contacts to their ladder programming languages to meet these needs. The programmer can now accomplish these special tasks with one contact instead of a few lines of logic.

Immediate Instructions

Immediate instructions are used when the input or output being controlled is highly time dependent. For example, for safety reasons we may have to update the status of a particular input every few milliseconds. If our ladder diagram is 10 milliseconds long, the scan time would be too slow, which could be dangerous. The use of immediate instructions allows inputs to be updated immediately as they are encountered in the ladder. The same is true of output coils.

Rockwell Automation SLC 500 Immediate Input with Mask The immediate input with mask (IIM) instruction is used to acquire the present state of one word of inputs (Figure 4-21). Normally, the CPU would have to finish all evaluation of the ladder logic and then update the output and input image tables. In this case, when the CPU encounters this instruction during ladder evaluation, it interrupts the scan. Data from a specified I/O slot are transferred through a mask to the input data file. This makes

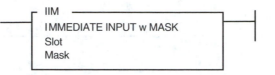

Figure 4-21 Instruction numbering. This is an immediate input with mask (IIM) instruction.

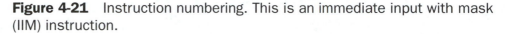

I:2	Inputs of slot 2, word 0
I:2.1	Inputs of slot 2, word 1
I:1	Inputs of slot 1, word 0

Figure 4-22 Immediate input instruction (IIM).

Figure 4-23 Rockwell Automation OSR instruction.

the data available to instructions following the IIM instruction. Thus, it gets the real-time states of the actual inputs at that time and puts them in that word of the input image table. The CPU then returns to evaluating the logic using the new states it acquired.

The IIM process is used only when time is a crucial factor. Normally, the few milliseconds a scan takes is fast enough for any job. There are cases, however, when scan time takes too long for some I/O updates. Motion control is one example. Updates on speed and position may be required every few milliseconds or less. We cannot safely wait for the scan to finish to update the I/O. In these cases immediate instructions are used.

Figure 4-22 shows an IIM addressing format. When the CPU encounters the instruction during evaluation, it will immediately suspend what it is doing (evaluating) and will update the input image word associated with I/O slot 2, word 0.

Rockwell Automation One-Shot Rising Instruction The one-shot rising (OSR) instruction is a retentive input instruction that can trigger an event to happen one time (Figure 4-23). When the rung conditions that precede the OSR go from false to true, the OSR instruction will be true for one scan. After the one scan, the OSR instruction becomes false, even if the preceding rung conditions that precede it remain true. The OSR will only become true again if the rung conditions preceding it make a transition from false to true. Only one OSR can be used per rung.

Figure 4-24   An example of latching an output on. If input 1:1/01 is true, coil O:2/09 will be energized. (Remember that contact I:1/02 is normally closed.) When coil O:2/09 energizes, it latches itself on by providing a parallel path around I:1/01. The only way to turn the latched coil off would be to energize normally closed contact I:1/02. This would open the rung and deenergize coil O:2/09.

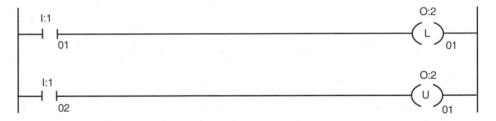

Figure 4-25   Use of a latching output. If input I:1/01 is true, output O:2/01 energizes. It will stay energized even if input I:1/01 becomes false. O:2/01 will remain energized until input I:1/02 becomes true and energizes the unlatch instruction (coil O:2/01). Note that the coil number of the latch is the same as that of the unlatch. This is an example of a Rockwell Automation latch and unlatch instruction.

Latching Instructions

Latches are used to lock in a condition. For example, if an input contact is on for only a short time, the output coil would be on for the same short time. If the programmer desired to keep the output on even if the input goes low, a latch could be used. This can be done by using either the output coil to latch itself on (Figure 4-24) or a special latching coil (Figure 4-25). When a latching output is used, it will stay on until it is unlatched. Unlatching is done with a special unlatching coil. When activated, the latched coil of the same number is unlatched.

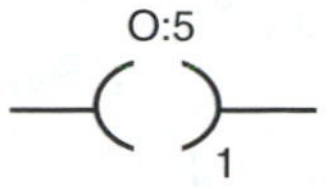

Figure 4-26 Output energize (OTE) instruction.

O:5
—( )—
1

ROCKWELL AUTOMATION COILS

Output Energize

The output energize (OTE) instruction is the normal output instruction. The OTE instruction sets a bit in memory. If the logic in its rung is true, then the output bit will be set to a 1. If the logic of its rung is false, then the output bit is reset to a 0. Figure 4-26 shows an OTE instruction. This particular example is real-world output 1 of the output module in slot 5. If the logic of the rung leading to this output instruction is true, then output bit O:5/1 will be set to a 1 (true). If the rung is false, then the output bit would be set to a 0 (false).

Rockwell Automation Immediate Outputs

The immediate output with mask (IOM) instruction is used to update output states immediately. In some applications the ladder scan time is longer than the needed update time for certain outputs. For example, it might cause a safety problem if an output were not turned on or off before an entire scan was complete. In these cases, or when performance requires immediate response, IOMs are used. When the CPU encounters an immediate instruction, it exits the scan and immediately transfers data to a specified I/O slot through a mask. The CPU will then resume evaluating the ladder logic. Figures 4-27 and 4-28 show examples of the addressing format for an IOM.

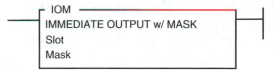

Figure 4-27 Format for an immediate output with mask (IOM) instruction.

O:2	Outputs of slot 2, word 0
O:2.1	Outputs of slot 2, word 1
O:1	Outputs of slot 1, word 0

Figure 4-28 Immediate output instruction I/O numbering.

Figure 4-29 Output latch (OTL) instruction. —(L)—

Figure 4-30 Output unlatch (OTU) instruction. —(U)—

Rockwell Automation Output Latch Instruction

The output latch (OTL) instruction is a retentive instruction. If this input is turned on, it will stay on even if its input conditions become false. A retentive output can only be turned off by an unlatch instruction. Figure 4-29 shows an OTL. In this case if the rung conditions for this output coil are true, then the output bit will be set to a 1. It will remain a 1 even if the rung becomes false. The output will be latched on. Note that if the OTL is retentive and if the processor loses power, the actual output turns off; but when power is restored, the output is retentive and will turn on. This is also true in the case of switching from run to program mode. The actual output turns off, but the bit state of 1 is retained in memory. When the processor is switched to run again, retentive outputs will turn on again regardless of the rung conditions. Retentive instructions can help or hurt the programmer. Be careful from a safety standpoint when using retentive instructions. Use an unlatch instruction to turn a retentive output off.

Rockwell Automation Output Unlatch Instruction

The output unlatch (OTU) instruction is used to unlatch (change the state of) retentive output instructions. It is the only way to turn an OTL off. Figure 4-30 shows an OTU. If this instruction is true, it unlatches the retentive output coil of the same number.

PROGRAM FLOW INSTRUCTIONS

There are many types of flow control instructions available on PLCs. Flow control instructions can be used to control the sequence in which your program is executed. Flow instructions allow the programmer to change the order in which the CPU scans the ladder diagram. These instructions are typically used to minimize scan time and create a more efficient program. They can be used to help troubleshoot ladder logic as well. They should be used with great care by the programmer. Serious consequences can occur if they are improperly used, because their use causes portions of the ladder logic to be skipped.

Figure 4-31   Rockwell Automation jump (JMP) and label (LBL) instructions.

Rockwell Automation Jump Instructions

Rockwell Automation has jump (JMP) and label (LBL) instructions available (Figure 4-31). These can be used to reduce program scan time by omitting a section of program until it is needed. It is possible to jump forward and backward in the ladder. The programmer must be careful not to jump backward an excessive amount of times. A counter, timer, logic, or the program scan register should be used to limit the amount of time spent looping inside a JMP/LBL instruction. If the rung containing the JMP instruction is true, the CPU skips to the rung containing the specified LBL and continues execution. You can jump to the same label from one or more JMP instructions.

Rockwell Automation Jump to Subroutine Instructions

Rockwell Automation also has subroutine instructions available. The jump to subroutine (JSR), subroutine (SBR), and return (RET) are used for this purpose (Figures 4-32 and 4-33). Subroutines can be used to store recurring sections of logic that must be executed in several points in the program. A subroutine saves effort and memory because you only program it once. Subroutines can also be used for time-critical logic by using immediate I/O in them.

Figure 4-32   Rockwell Automation jump-to-subroutine (JSR) instruction.

Figure 4-33   Rockwell Automation subroutine (SBR) and return (RET) instructions.

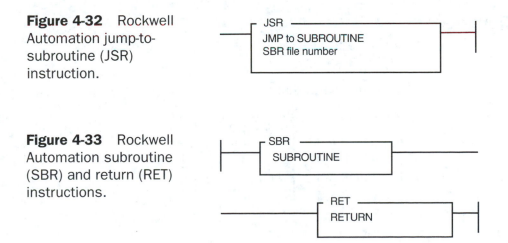

The SBR instruction must be the first instruction on the first rung in the program file that contains the subroutine. Subroutines can be nested up to eight deep. This allows the programmer to direct program flow from the main program to a subroutine and then on to another subroutine, and so on.

The desired subroutine is identified by the file number entered in the JSR instruction. This instruction serves as the label or identifier for a program file as a regular subroutine file. The SBR instruction is always evaluated as true. The RET instruction is used to show the end of the subroutine file. It causes the CPU to return to the instruction following the previous JSR instruction.

Subroutines can be very useful in breaking a control program into smaller logical sections. For example, the main file we use for our ladder logic is file 2. Many times all of the ladder logic is programmed in file 2. It makes more sense and is more understandable if the program is divided into logical modes of operation. For example, the programmer could make file 2 contain the logic needed for overall system operation; the main file (file 2) could contain logic to determine if the user wants to go into the automatic or manual mode of operation; it could also call another subroutine that monitors the system for safety. Let us use file 3 for the manual mode of operation, file 4 for the automatic mode of operation, and file 5 for the monitoring logic. We would use conditional logic to determine whether to call the manual subroutine or the automatic routine. If the user hit the manual key, the main would call the subroutine in file 3. If the user hits the auto key, the main would call the automatic subroutine in file 4. We would want the monitor subroutine to run continuously. The logic in the main can call the monitor logic or the other subroutines can call the monitor mode, as subroutines can be nested and call other subroutines. It is much simpler to program the system when it can be divided into smaller logical sections, and much easier to understand and troubleshoot.

QUESTIONS

1. What is XIO? XIC?

2. What is IOM?

3. Write the address for the first input or output for each I/O module below.

Power Supply	CPU	INPUT	INPUT	IN / OUT	OUTPUT	OUTPUT	OUTPUT
Slot Number	0	1	2	3	4	5	6

4. Design a latching circuit using a Rockwell Automation latch and unlatch instruction. Use contact I:2/7 for the latch input, I:2/8 for the unlatch input, and O:5/3 for the coil.

5. Describe the purpose and use of subroutines.

Following are sample Rockwell Automation SLC addresses. Thoroughly explain each of them.

6. B3:16/12

7. O0:1/6

8. I1:1/3

9. O0:2/5

10. I1:1/2

11. T4:7.PRE

12. C5:0.ACC

13. F8:0

14. I1:1/2

15. T4:5.EN

16. T4:3.DN

17. O0:4/9

18. I1:2/4

19. N10:3

20. I:3.0/4

21. I:2/17

22. O:7/12

23. B3:3/5

24. S:42

25. N7:12

PROGRAMMING PRACTICE

RSLogix Relay Logic Instructions

These exercises utilize the LogixPro software included with this book. To install the software, simply insert the CD into your CD-ROM drive; it should self-install. Note that the software will operate only for a limited trial period. After that (or anytime before) you may register by paying a small fee to have the full version of the software.

Description of the Software

This is a complete working version of LogixPro. In the trial or evaluation mode, only the Silo, Door, and Traffic simulations are fully available for user programming. In addition, until LogixPro has been registered, File Save and Printing functionality is disabled. For those unfamilar with RSLogix, a program file for the Silo Simulation is included to get you started. When you have LogixPro running, select the Silo Simulation, then click Load in the File Menu, and select the file "silo.rsl". Once it is loaded and you can see it, you can then "Download" it to the PLC. At this point you can place the PLC into the "RUN" mode. If all goes well, just clicking on the simulations START push button should start the whole process. We do not support online editing, so remember to place the PLC in the "PGM" mode to edit and then "Download" to the PLC before attempting to "RUN" again.

If you need help with the RSLogix addressing or instructions, you can go to two places. With your mouse, select Start, then Programs, then TheLearningPit, then LogixPro, and then you may choose the Instruction Set Reference, LogixPro, the readme file, or the student exercises. You can also log onto the Internet and go to the "LogixPro . . . Student Exercises and Documentation" page entry, which is listed on TheLearningPit.com home page. Also remember to try clicking on rungs, instructions, and so on with the right mouse button to locate popup editing menus and so forth.

First Exercise

This exercise is designed to familiarize you with the operation of LogixPro and to walk you through the process of creating, editing, and testing simple PLC programs utilizing the relay logic instructions supported by RSLogix. This is a very important exercise because it will prepare you for programming the more complex applications in later chapters. It will also enable you to achieve basic competancy in the use of Rockwell Automation RSLogix software. Go to the Student Exercises as described and complete the Relay Logic—Introductory Exercise.

Additional Exercise

1. Enter the circuit that you designed in question 4 and test it in the I/O simulator. Make sure you use appropriate addresses.
2. Go to the student exercises on the CD. Follow the instructions and program and test door simulation exercise 1. Document your program.
3. Complete student programming exercise 2 for the door simulation. Document your program.
4. Complete student programming exercise 3 for the door simulation. Document your program.

Extra Credit

Complete student programming exercise 4 for the door simulation. Document your program.

chapter

Timers and Counters

Timers and counters are invaluable in PLC programming. Industry has a need to count product and time sequences. In this chapter we examine the types and programming of timers and counters.

OBJECTIVES

Upon completion of this chapter, you will be able to:
1. Describe the use of timers and counters in ladder logic
2. Define such terms as *retentive, cascade, delay on,* and *delay off*
3. Explain the operation of TON, TOF, and RTO timers
4. Explain the use of CTU and CTD timers
5. Utilize timers and counters in ladder logic

TIMERS

Timing functions are vital in PLC applications. Cycle times are critical in many processes. Timers are used to delay actions. They may be used to keep an output on for a specified time after an input turns off, or to keep an output off for a specified time before it turns on.

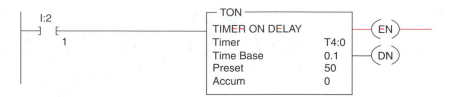

Figure 5-1   A typical block-type timer.

Many PLCs use block-style timers and counters (Figure 5-1). Regardless of the brand of PLC, timers have many similarities in the way they are programmed. Each timer will have an identifying number. The timer in Figure 5-1 is called T4:0.

Every timer will have a time base. Timers can typically be programmed with several different time bases: 1 second, 0.1 second, 0.01 second, and 0.001 second are typical time bases. If a programmer entered 0.1 for the time base and 50 for the number of delay increments, the timer would have a 5 second delay (50 × 0.1 second = 5 seconds).

Timers also must have a preset value. The preset value is the number of time increments the timer must count before changing the state of the output. The actual time delay would equal the preset value multiplied by the time base. Presets can be a constant value or a variable. If a variable is used, the timer would use the real-time value of the variable to calculate the delay. This allows delays to be changed depending on conditions during operation. An example is a system that produces two different products, each requiring a different time in the actual process. Product A requires a 10-second process time, so the ladder logic would assign 10 to the variable. When product B comes along, the ladder logic can change the value to that required by B. When a variable time is required, a variable number is entered into the timer block. Ladder logic can then be used to assign values to the variable.

Rockwell timers have one input. When this input makes a transition from low to high, the timer will begin timing.

Timers can be retentive or nonretentive. *Retentive timers* do not lose the accumulated time when the enable input line goes low. They retain the accumulated time until the line goes high again. They then add to the count when the input goes high once again. *Nonretentive timers* lose the accumulated time whenever the enable input goes low. If the enable input to the timer goes low, the timer count goes to zero. Retentive timers are sometimes called accumulating timers. They function like a stopwatch. Stopwatches can be started and stopped and retain their timed value. The stopwatch has a zero reset button; the accumulated time in a retentive timer is reset to zero with a separate reset instruction.

Figure 5-2 Format for a timer.

Bit	Set When	Remains Set Till
Timer done bit (bit 13 or DN)	Accumulated value is equal to or greater than the preset value	Rung conditions go false
Timer timing bit (bit 14 or TT)	Rung conditions are true and the accumulated value is less than the preset value	Rung conditions go false or when the done bit is set
Timer enable bit (bit 15 or EN)	Rung conditions are true	Rung conditions go false

Figure 5-3 Timer status bits.

Timer On Delay

The timer on-delay (TON) instruction turns an output on after a timer has been on for a preset time interval. The TON begins accumulating time when the rung becomes true and continues until one of the following conditions is met: The accumulated value is equal to the preset value or the rung conditions become false. Figure 5-2 shows the numbering system for timers. The T stands for timer, 4 is the file number of the timer, and 7 is the actual timer number. Note that this is what you enter in the timer block for the timer number.

Status Bit Use Timer status bits can be used in ladder logic (Figure 5-3). There are several bits available for use. Consider timer T4:0. The timer enable (EN) bit is set immediately when the rung goes true. It stays set until the rung goes false. The EN bit indicates that the timer is enabled. The EN bit from any timer can be used for logic; for example, T4:0/EN could be used as a contact in a ladder.

The timer timing (TT) bit can also be used. The TT bit is set when the rung goes true. It remains true until the rung goes false or the timer done (DN) bit is set (accumulated value equals preset value). For example, T4:0/TT could be used as a contact in a ladder.

The DN bit is not set until the accumulated value is equal to the preset value and the DN remains set until the rung goes false. When the DN bit is set, it is an indication that the timing operation is complete. For example, T4:0/DN could be used as a contact in the ladder. The preset (PRE) is also available to the ladder. For example, T4:0.PRE would access the preset value of T4:0. Note that the PRE value would be an integer.

Accumulated Value Use   The accumulated (ACC) value can also be used by the programmer. The ACC value is acquired in the same manner as the status bits and preset. For example, T4:0.ACC would access the accumulated value of timer T4:0.

Time Bases   Time bases are available in 1 second intervals, 0.01 second intervals, and 0.001 second intervals (Figure 5-4). The potential time ranges are also shown. If a longer time is needed, timers can be cascaded (see later in this chapter). Figure 5-5 shows how timers are handled in memory. Three bits are used in the first

Time Base	Potential Time Range
1 Second	To 32,767 time base intervals (up to 9.1 hours)
0.01 Second (10 MS)	To 32,767 time base intervals (up to 5.5 minutes)
0.001 Second (1 MS)	To 32,767 time base intervals (up to 0.546 minute)

Figure 5-4   Time bases available.

15	14	13	12	11	10	9	8	7	6	5	4	3	2	1	0	Element
EN	TT	DN							Internal Use							0 T4:0
Preset Value PRE																1 T4:0.PRE
Accumulated Value ACC																2 T4:0.ACC

Figure 5-5   Use of control words for timers.

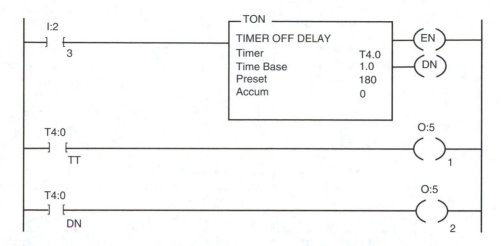

Figure 5-6 Use of a TON timer in a ladder logic program.

storage location word for this timer to store the present status of the timer bits (EN, TT, and DN). The PRE value is stored in the second 16 bits of this timer storage. The third 16 bits hold the accumulated value of the timer.

Figure 5-6 shows the use of a TON timer in a ladder. When input I:2/3 is true, the timer begins to increment the accumulated value of TON timer 4:0 in 1-second intervals. The TT bit for timer 4:0 is used in rung 2 to turn on output O:5/1, while the timer is timing (ACC < PRE). The DN bit of timer 4:0 is used in rung 3 to turn on output O:5/2 when the timer is done timing (ACC = PRE). The preset for this timer is 180, which means that the timer will have to accumulate 180 1-second intervals to time out. Note that this is not a retentive timer. If input I:2/3 goes low before 180 is reached, the accumulated value is reset to zero.

Timer Off Delay

The timer off-delay (TOF) instruction is used to turn an output on or off after the rung has been off for a desired time. The TOF instruction starts to accumulate time when the rung becomes false. It will continue to accumulate time until the accumulated value equals the preset value or the rung becomes true. The timer enable bit (EN bit 15) is set when the rung becomes true (Figure 5-7). It is reset when the rung become false. The timer timing bit (TT bit 14) is set when the rung becomes false and ACC < PRE. The TT bit is reset when the rung becomes false, or the DN bit is reset (ACC = PRE), or a reset instruction resets the timer.

The done bit (DN bit 13) is reset when the ACC value is equal to the PRE value. The DN bit is set when the rung becomes true.

Bit	Set When	Remains Set Till
Timer done bit (bit 13 or DN)	Rung conditions are true	Rung conditions go false and the accumulated value is greater than or equal to the preset value
Timer timing bit (bit 14 or TT)	Rung conditions are false and the accumulated value is less than the preset value	Rung conditions go true or when the done bit is reset
Timer enable bit (bit 15 or EN)	Rung conditions are true	Rung conditions go false

Figure 5-7   Use of TOF bits.

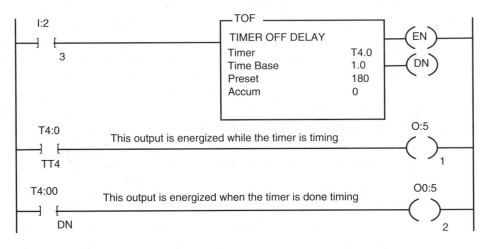

Figure 5-8   Use of a TOF timer in a ladder logic diagram.

Figure 5-8 shows the use of a TOF timer in a ladder diagram. Input I:2/3 is used to enable the timer. When input I:2/3 makes a transition from true to false, the ACC value is incremented as long as the input stays false and ACC ≤ PRE. The TT bit for timer T4:0 (T4:0/TT) is used to turn output O:05/1 on while the timer is timing. The DN bit for timer 4:0 (T4:0/DN) is used to turn on output O:5/2 when the timer has completed the timing (ACC = PRE).

To better understand the timer off delay, consider the following nonindustrial example. Think of a garage light. It would be a nice feature if a person could touch and

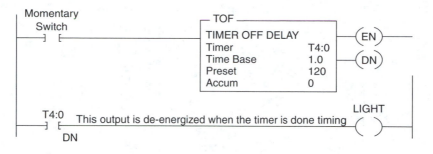

Figure 5-9 Delay-off timing circuit. If the momentary switch closes, delay-off timer T4:0 immediately begins timing when the momentary switch makes the transition from high to low. The done bit (T4:0/DN) is immediately energized, which turns on the light. When the timer reaches 2 minutes (120 seconds) it will de-energize the DN bit, which turns the light off also.

release a momentary on switch and the light would immediately turn on, and then stay on for a given time (maybe 2 minutes). At the end of the time, the light would turn off. This would allow a person time to get into the house with the light on. In this example, the output (light) turned on instantly when the input (switch) was momentarily turned on and off. The timer counted down the time (timed out) and turned the output (light) off.

In Figure 5-9, when the momentary switch is pushed and then released, the timer starts counting time intervals. The timer done bit (T4:0/DN) is used in the second rung as a contact. As soon as the momentary switch has made the high-to-low transition, the time begins timing and turns the DN bit on. If the timer DN bit is energized, the light is energized. When the timer times out (in this case 2 minutes), the contact (T4:0/DN) in rung 2 opens and the light turns off.

Retentive Timer On

The retentive timer on (RTO) instruction is used to turn an output on after a set time period (Figure 5-10). The RTO timer is an accumulating timer. It retains the ACC value even if the rung goes false. The only way to zero the ACC value is to use a reset (RES) instruction in another rung with the same address as the RTO that is to be reset. The RTO retains the accumulated count even if power is lost, or you switch modes, or the rung becomes false. Remember, the only way to zero the ACC value is to use a RES instruction, which must have the same address as the timer to be reset. Note that the RES instruction can also be used for other types of timers and counters.

The status bits can be used as contacts in a ladder diagram (Figure 5-11). The EN bit is set when the rung becomes true. When the EN bit is a 1, it indicates that

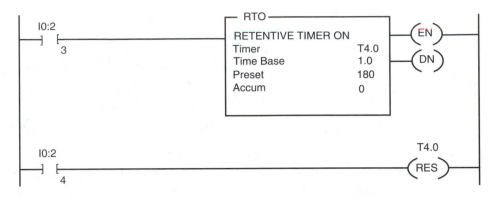

Figure 5-10 Use of an RTO timer.

Bit	Set When	Remains Set Till
Timer done bit (bit 13 or DN)	Accumulated value is equal to or greater than the preset value	The appropriate RES Instruction is enabled
Timer timing bit (bit 14 or TT)	Rung conditions are true and the accumulated value is less than the preset value	Rung conditions go false or when the done bit is set
Timer enable bit (bit 15 or EN)	Rung conditions are true	Rung conditions go false

Figure 5-11 Use of RTO bits.

the timer is timing. It remains set until the rung becomes false or a RES instruction zeros the accumulated value.

The TT bit is set when the rung becomes true and remains set until the ACC value equals the preset value or a RES instruction resets the timer. When the TT bit is a 1, it indicates that the timer is timing.

The TT bit is reset when the rung becomes false or when the DN bit is set. The DN bit is set when the timer's accumulated value is equal to the preset value. When the DN bit is set, it indicates that the timing is complete. The DN is reset with the RES instruction.

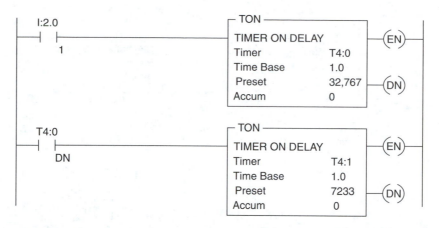

Figure 5-12 Two timers are used to extend the time delay. The first timer output, T4:0/DN, acts as the input to start the second timer. When input I:2.0/1 becomes true, timer 1 begins to count to 32,767 seconds (the limit for these timers). When it reaches 32,767, output T4:0/DN turns on. This energizes timer T4:1. Timer T4:1 then times to 7233 seconds and then turns T4:1/DN. The delay was 40,000 seconds.

CASCADING TIMERS

Applications sometimes require longer time delays than a single timer can accomplish. Multiple timers can then be used to achieve a longer delay than would otherwise be possible. One timer acts as the input to another. When the first timer times out, it becomes the input to start the second timer timing. This process is called *cascading*. Figure 5-12 shows an example of cascading timers.

COUNTERS

Counting is an important aspect in industrial applications, because the product is often counted so that another action will take place. For example, if twenty-four cans go into a case, the twenty-fourth can should be sensed by the PLC and the case should be sealed.

Counters are required in almost all applications. Several types of counters are available, including up counters, down counters, and up/down counters. The choice of which to use depends on the task to be done. For example, if we are counting the finished product leaving a machine, we might use an up counter. If we are tracking how many parts are left, we might use a down counter. If we are using a PLC to monitor an automated storage system, we might use an up/down counter to track how many are coming and how many are leaving to establish an actual, total number in stock.

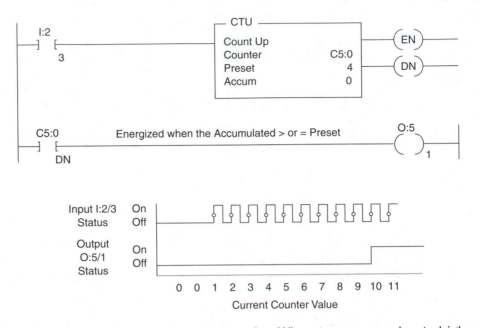

Figure 5-13 How a typical counter works. When ten or more low-to-high transitions of input I:2/3 have been made, counter C5:0/DN is energized, which energizes output O:5/1.

Counters normally use a low-to-high transition from an input to trigger the counting action. Figure 5-13 shows a generic counter. Counters have a reset input or a separate reset instruction to clear the accumulated count. Counters are similar to timers: Timers count the number of time increments and counters count the number of low-to-high transitions on the input line.

Note that the counter in Figure 5-13 is edge-sensitive triggered. The rising, or leading edge, triggers the counter. I:2/3 is used to count the pulses. Every time there is an off-to-on transition on I:2/3, the counter adds one to its count. When the accumulated count equals the preset value, the counter turns on, which turns on output O:5/1. The example just described is a count-up (CTU) counter.

A count-down (CTD) counter causes a count to decrease by one every time there is a pulse. The Micrologix PLC also has up/down counters available. An up/down counter has one input that causes it to increment the count and another that causes it to decrement the count.

Certain ladder diagram statements can utilize these counts for comparing and/or decision making. Counts can also be compared with constants or variables to control outputs.

ROCKWELL AUTOMATION COUNTERS

A Rockwell Automation counter has a counter number, a preset, and an accumulated value. The counter is numbered like the timer except that it begins with a C. The next number is a file number. The default file number for counters is 5. The third value is the counter number, which in this case is 4 (see Figure 5-14).

Your ladder diagram can access counter status bits, presets, and accumulated values (Figure 5-15). You may use the CU, CD, DN, OV, or UN bit for logic. These will each be covered a little later. You can also use the preset (PRE) and the accumulated (ACC) count.

Counter values are stored in three 16 bit words of memory. The first 8 bits of the first word are only for internal use of the CPU. The most significant bits of the first word are used to store the status of certain bits associated with the counter (Figure 5-16). The count-up enable bit (CU bit 15) is used to indicate that the counter is enabled. The CU bit is reset when the rung becomes false or when it is reset by a RES instruction. The count-up done bit (DN bit 13) when high indicates that the accumulated count has reached the preset value. It remains set

Figure 5-14 How counters are addressed.

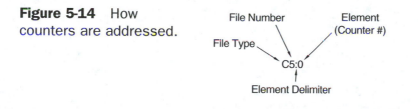

C5:4.DN	USE OF THE DONE BIT
C5:4.PRE	USE OF THE PRESET VALUE
C5:4.ACC	USE OF THE ACCUMULATED VALUE

Figure 5-15 Examples of the use of counter values.

15	14	13	12	11	10	9	8	7	6	5	4	3	2	1	0	Element
CU		DN	V	CV					Internal Use							0 C5:0
Preset Value PREE																1 C5:0.PR
Accumulated Value ACC																2 C5:0.ACC

Figure 5-16 How counter values and status bits are stored in memory.

Bit	Set When	Remains Set Till
Count-up overflow bit (bit 12 or OV)	Accumulated value wraps around to −32,768 (from +32,767) and continues counting up from there	A RES instruction that has the same address as the CTU instruction is executed or the count is decremented less than or equal to +32,767 with a CTD instruction
Done bit (bit 13 or DN)	The accumulated value is equal to or greater than the preset value	The accumulated value becomes less than the preset
Count-up enable bit (bit 15 or CU)	Rung conditions are true	Rung conditions go false or a RES instruction that has the same address as the CTU instruction is enabled

Figure 5-17   CTU counter bits.

even when the ACC value exceeds the PRE value. The DN bit is reset by a RES instruction.

The count-up overflow bit (OV bit 12) is set by the CPU to show that the count has exceeded the upper limit of +32,767. When this happens, the counter ACC value "wraps around" to −32,768 and begins to count up from there, back toward zero. (This method has to do with the way computers store negative numbers. The preset value and accumulated value are stored as a 2's complement number.) The OV bit can be reset with a RES instruction (Figure 5-17).

Count-Up Timer

Figure 5-18 shows the use of a count-up counter in a ladder diagram. Each time input I:2/3 makes a low-to-high transition, the counter ACC value is incremented by

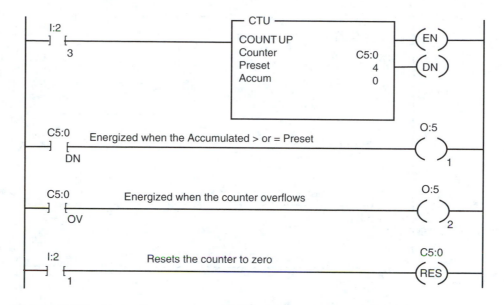

Figure 5-18 Use of a count-up (CTU) counter in a ladder diagram.

one. The done bit of counter C5:0 (C5:0/DN) is being used to turn output O:5/1 on when the accumulated value is equal to the preset value (ACC = PRE). The overflow bit of counter C5:0 (C5:0/OV) is being used to set output O:5/2 on if the count ever reaches +32,767. The last rung uses input I:2/1 to reset counter C5:0's accumulated value to zero.

Count-Down Counter

Figure 5-19 shows the use of a count-down counter in a ladder diagram. Each time input I:2/3 makes a false-to-true transition, the counter ACC value is decremented by one. The done bit of counter C5:0 (C5:0/DN) is being used to turn output O:5/1 on when the accumulated value is equal to or exceeds the preset value (ACC = PRE). The accumulated value of counters is retentive. They are retained until a reset instruction is used. The underflow bit of counter C5:0 (C5:0/UN) is being used to set output O:5/2 on if the count ever underflows −32,768. Note the use of the reset instruction to reset the accumulated value of the counter to zero. The last rung uses input I:2/1 to reset counter C5:0's accumulated value to zero (Figure 5-19). Figure 5-20 shows the function of CTD bits.

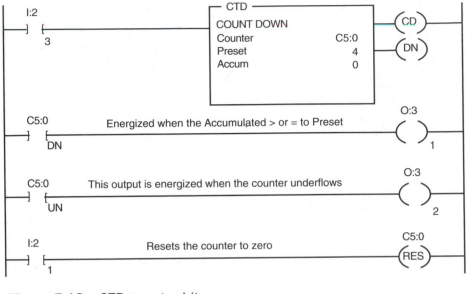

Figure 5-19 CTD counter bits.

Bit	Set When	Remains Set Till
Count-down underflow bit (bit 11 or UN)	Accumulated value wraps around to +32,768 (from −32,767) and continues counting down from there	A RES instruction that has the same address as the CTD instruction is executed or the count is incremented greater than or equal to +32,767 with a CTU instruction
Done bit (bit 13 or DN)	The accumulated value is equal to or greater than the preset value	The accumulated value becomes less than the preset
Count down enable bit (bit 14 or CD)	Rung conditions are true	Rung conditions go false or a RES instruction that has the same address as the CTD instruction is enabled

Figure 5-20 Use of a count-down (CTD) counter.

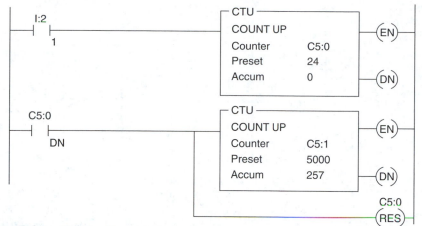

Figure 5-21 Cascading counters.

Cascading Counters

A counter's DN bit can be used to increment another counter. For example, in Figure 5-21 counter C5:0 is used to count 24 cans for each case. When C5:0 reaches 24, it increments C5:1 and resets its own counts to zero with the reset instruction. C5:1 is used to count the number of cases of 24 cans. In this example 257 cases have been produced. Sometimes applications require higher counts than one counter can accomplish. Cascading can also be used for this purpose.

QUESTIONS

1. What are the typical uses for timers?

2. Explain the two types of timers and how each might be used.

3. Describe the function of the TOF timer, especially the TT and DN bits.

4. What does the term *retentive* mean?

5. Draw a typical retentive timer and explain its operation.

6. What are the typical uses for counters?

7. In what way are counters and timers similar?

8. True or False? A RES instruction can be used with TON, TOF, and RTO timers.

9. What is cascading?

10. You have been asked to program a system that requires completed parts to be counted. The largest counter available in the PLC's instruction set can only count to 999. We must be able to count to 5000. Draw a ladder diagram that shows the method you would use to complete the task. *Hint:* Use two counters, one as the input to the other. The total count will involve looking at the total of the two counters.

Figure 5-22 Drawing of a heat-treat system.

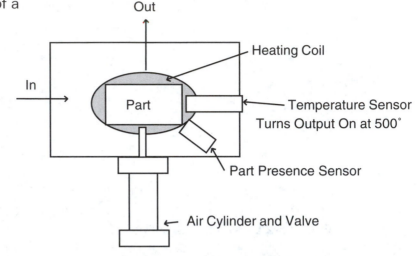

11. Figure 5-22 is a partial drawing of a heat-treat system. You have been asked by your supervisor to troubleshoot the system. The engineer who originally developed the system no longer works for your company. He never fully documented the system. A short description of the system follows. You must study the drawings and data and complete this assignment.

    A part enters this portion of the process. The temperature must then be raised from room temperature to 500°F. There is also a part presence sensor, and a sensor that turns on when the temperature reaches 500°F. The part must then be pushed out of the machine. The cycle should take about 25 seconds. If it takes an excessive amount of time and the temperature has still not been reached, an operator must be informed and must reset the system. Study the system drawing, and then complete the I/O chart (Figure 5-23) by

Figure 5-23 I/O table.

System I/O	
1:2/3	Part presence sensor
1:2/20	Operator reset
O:3/5	
O:3/8	
T4:1	
T4:9	
C5:1	
C5:2	

writing short comments that describe the purpose of each input, output, timer, and counter. Make your comments clear and descriptive so that the next person to troubleshoot the system will have an easier task. Then refer to Figure 5-24 and answer the following questions.

a. What is the purpose of counter T4:1?
b. What is the purpose of input I:2/3?

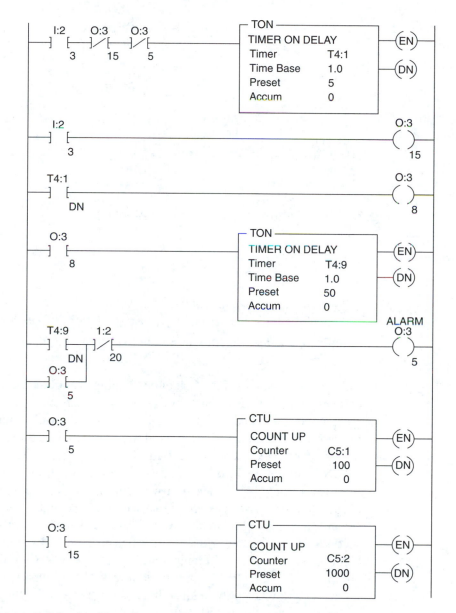

Figure 5-24 Ladder diagram for Exercise 11.

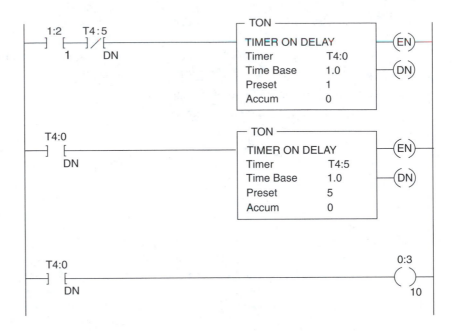

Figure 5-25   Ladder diagram for Question 12.

    c. What is the purpose of input I:2/20?

    d. What is the purpose of counter C5:2?

    e. What is the purpose of contact O:3/15?

    f. Part of the logic is redundant. Identify that part and suggest a change.

12. Examine the ladder diagram in Figure 5-25. Assume that input I:2/1 is always true. What will this ladder logic do?

13. You have been assigned the task of developing a stoplight application. Your company thinks there is a large market in intelligent street corner control. Your company is going to develop a PLC-based system in which lights will adapt their timing to compensate for the traffic volume. Your task is to program a normal stoplight sequence to be used as a comparison to the new system.

    Note in Figure 5-26 the two sets of lights. The north and south lights must react exactly alike. The east-west set must be the complement of the north-south set. Write a program that will keep the green light on for 25 seconds and the yellow light on for 5 seconds. The red will then be on for 30 seconds. You must also add a counter, because the bulbs are replaced at a certain count for preventive maintenance. The counter should count complete cycles. *Hint:* To simplify your task, do one small task at a time. Do not try to write the entire application at once. Write ladder logic to get one

Figure 5-26 Stoplights.

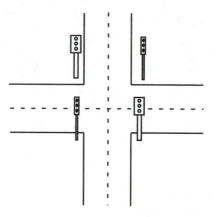

light working, then the next, then the next, before you even worry about the other stoplight. When you get one set done, the other is a snap. Remember: A well-planned job is half done.

Write the ladder diagram. Thoroughly document the ladder with labels and rung comments.

PROGRAMMING PRACTICE

RSLogix Relay Logic Instructions

The following exercises utilize the LogixPro software included with this book. Go to the LogixPro Student Exercises and Documentation portion of the CD. Remember that the Rockwell Automation instruction help is also on the CD.

1. This exercise involves PLC timers. Complete the introductory exercise called Traffic Control.
2. Complete the PLC Counters introductory exercise.

EXTRA CREDIT

This exercise will cover the topic of cascading timers. Complete the exercise called Applying Cascading TON Timers.

Input/Output Modules and Wiring

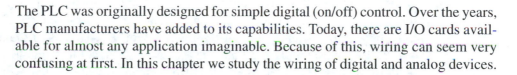

The PLC was originally designed for simple digital (on/off) control. Over the years, PLC manufacturers have added to its capabilities. Today, there are I/O cards available for almost any application imaginable. Because of this, wiring can seem very confusing at first. In this chapter we study the wiring of digital and analog devices.

OBJECTIVES

Upon completion of this chapter, you will be able to:

1. List at least two I/O cards that can be used for communication
2. Describe at least five special-purpose I/O cards
3. Define such terms as *resolution, high density, discrete* and *TTL.*
4. Choose an appropriate I/O module for a given application
5. Understand and be able to wire analog and discrete I/O modules

I/O MODULES

PLCs were originally used to control one simple machine or process. The changes in American manufacturing have required much more capability. The increasing speed of production and the demand for higher quality require closer control of industrial processes. PLC manufacturers have added modules to meet these new requirements.

Special modules have been developed to meet almost any imaginable need, including control processes. Temperature control is one example.

Industry is beginning to integrate its equipment so that data can be shared. Modules have been developed to allow the PLC to communicate with other devices such as computers, robots, and machines.

Velocity and position control modules have been developed to meet the needs of accurate high-speed machining. These modules also make it possible for entrepreneurs to start new businesses that design and produce special-purpose manufacturing devices such as packaging equipment, palletizing equipment, and various other production machinery.

These modules are also designed to be easy to use. They are intended to make it easier for the engineer to design an application. In the balance of this chapter we examine many of the modules that are available.

DIGITAL (DISCRETE) MODULES

Digital modules are also called discrete modules because they are either on or off. A large percentage of manufacturing control can be accomplished through on/off control. Discrete control is easy and inexpensive to implement.

DIGITAL INPUT MODULES

Digital input modules accept either an on or off state from the real world. The module inputs are attached to devices such as switches or digital sensors. The modules must be able to buffer the CPU from the real world. Assume that the input is 250 VAC. The input module must change the 250 VAC level to a low-level DC logic level for the CPU. The modules must also optically isolate the real world from the CPU. Input modules usually have fuses for module protection.

Input modules typically have light emitting diodes (LEDs) for monitoring the inputs. There is one LED for every input. If the input is on, the LED is on. Some modules also have fault indicators. The fault LED turns on if there is a problem with the module. The LEDs on the modules are useful for troubleshooting.

Most modules also have plug-on wiring terminal strips. All wiring is connected to the terminal strip, which is plugged into the actual module. If there is a problem with a module, the entire strip is removed, a new module inserted, and the terminal strip is plugged into the new module. Note that there is no rewiring. A module can be changed in minutes or less. This aspect is vital considering the huge cost of a system being down (unable to produce product).

Input modules usually need to be supplied with power. (Some of the small PLCs are the exception.) The power must be supplied to a common terminal on the module, through an input device, and back to a specific input on the module. Current must

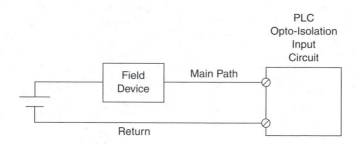

Figure 6-1 Typical I/O current path.

Figure 6-2 Typical shared return path (common).

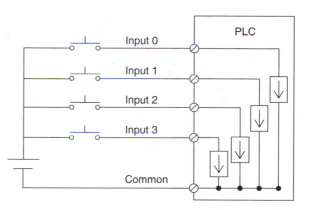

enter at one terminal of the I/O module and exit at another terminal (Figure 6-1). The figure shows a power supply, field input device, the main path, I/O circuit, and the return path. Unfortunately this would require two terminals for every I/O point. Most I/O modules provide groups of I/O that share return paths (commons). Figure 6-2 shows the use of a common return path.

WIRING

One of the easier ways to figure out how to wire is to simplify the circuit and get it on paper first, where most people can better visualize the whole picture. Imagine that we have a system with many inputs to wire. Let us say we worry about one input first. If we can figure out the first one, the rest will be easy. Figure 6-3 shows an example of one input, a power supply, and wiring terminals for a sinking input module. Input and output circuits almost always come down to three things: power, a device, and two terminals. Figure 6-4 shows how we would wire this simple circuit. It is easy to see the current path.

Lets now add the second input. Figure 6-5 shows the addition of one more input device. This device must be wired the same as the first. Positive must be

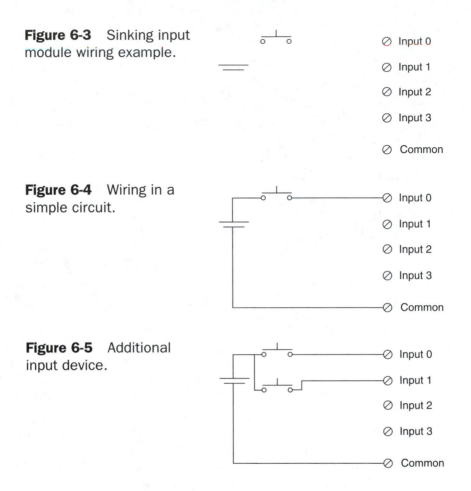

Figure 6-3 Sinking input module wiring example.

Figure 6-4 Wiring in a simple circuit.

Figure 6-5 Additional input device.

connected to one side of the switch, and the other side of the switch must be connected to the second input terminal.

Obviously this is a simple yet powerful technique. If you can figure out the wiring for the first device, the rest are easy. As stated, planning it on paper first will simplify the task of wiring.

Figure 6-6 shows a three-wire sensor that must be connected to an input. The sensor has a positive lead, a negative lead, and an output lead. The sensor is a sourcing sensor, so the output is positive. Figure 6-7 shows how this circuit was wired. The sensor had to be wired to + and − voltage to power the sensor. The + output was then connected to an input, and − from the supply was connected to the common on the sinking module.

Some modules provide multiple commons to allow the user to mix voltages on the same module (Figure 6-8). These commons can be jumpered together if desired (Figure 6-9).

Figure 6-6 Three-wire sensor example.

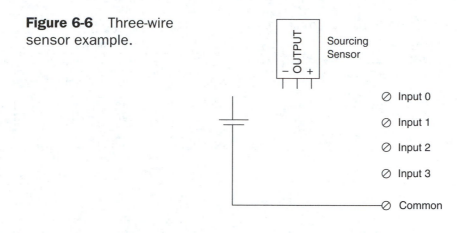

Figure 6-7 Complete wired circuit.

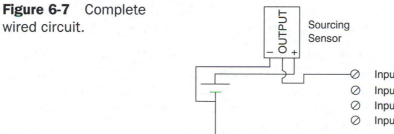
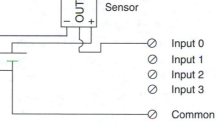

Figure 6-8 Input module with dual commons allows the user to mix input voltages.

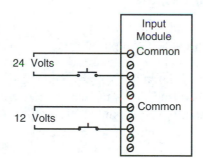

Figure 6-9 How dual commons can be wired together. All inputs would use the same voltage.

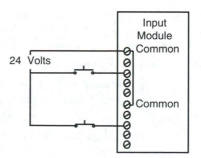

Figure 6-10 Example of
SLC DC input module
wiring. *(Courtesy Rockwell
Automation Inc.)*

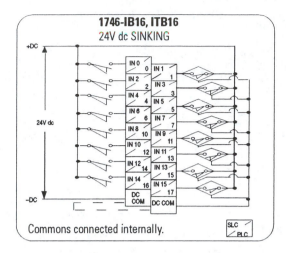

Figure 6-10 shows an input module for a Rockwell Automation SLC. Note that
the commons are connected internally for this module. Note also that the negative
side of the DC voltage must be connected to the common. The positive voltage
from the power supply is brought through the input devices and back to the input
terminal. This is a sinking module.

Input Wiring

Lets first look at what the module in Figure 6-10 requires for power before we consider the actual input wiring. There is no direct connection terminal on the module
for + power from the power supply. There is a direct connection from the negative
side of the power supply. The negative is connected to one of the commons. The
dashed line shows us that the two commons are internally connected. Next let us
look at the actual inputs. The inputs on the left are the equivalent of a switch or a
two-wire sourcing sensor. Consider the top left switch. The left side of the switch
is connected to the + side of the power supply. The other side of the switch is connected directly to the desired input terminal. As you can see, all of the switches' left
sides were commoned to the + side of the power supply. The right side of each
switch was connected to an individual input terminal. Imagine that the first switch
closes. We have a complete path from the positive side of the supply through the
switch to input terminal 0. The input would be on.

Next consider the right side of the input module. Three-wire sensors were used on
this side. A three-wire sensor requires two wires for power and another for the output
lead. Consider the first one. The negative power lead of the sensor (see bottom of the
sensor in Figure 6-10) was connected to the common (−) on the module. The positive
from the power supply was connected to the positive lead on the sensor. The output

Figure 6-11 Use of a
bleeder resistor.

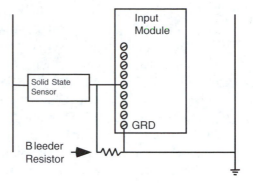

lead of the sensor was connected to the input terminal. Lastly, note that all of the negative leads on the three-wire sensors were connected to the − common on the module. All of the positive leads were connected to the + side of the power supply. The output side of each three-wire sensor was connected to the individual input terminal.

When two-wire sensors are used there is always a small leakage current that is necessary for the operation of the sensor, but this is not normally a problem. In some cases, however, this leakage current is enough to trigger the input of the PLC module. In this case, a resistor can be added that will "bleed" the leakage current to ground (Figure 6-11). When a bleeder resistor is added, most of the current goes through it to common, to ensure that the PLC input turns on only when the sensor is really on.

DISCRETE OUTPUT MODULES

Discrete output modules are used to turn real-world output devices either on or off. Discrete output modules can be used to control any two-state device. Output modules are available in AC and DC versions, and in various voltage ranges and current capabilities. Output modules can be purchased with transistor output, triac output, or relay output. The transistor output would be used for DC outputs. There are various voltage ranges and current ranges available, as well as transistor-transistor logic (TTL) output. Triac outputs are used for AC devices.

The current specifications for a module are normally given as an overall module current and as individual output current. The specification may rate each output at 1A. If it is an eight-output module, one might assume that the overall current limit would be 8A (8 × 1), but this is normally not the case. The overall current limit will probably be less than the sum of the individuals. For example, the overall current limit for the module might be 5A. The user must be careful that the total current to be demanded does not exceed the total that the module can handle. Normally the user's outputs will not each draw the maximum current, nor will they normally all be on at the same time. The user should consider the worst case when choosing an appropriate output module.

Output modules are normally fused, and this fuse is normally intended to provide short-circuit protection for wiring only to external loads. If there is a short circuit on an output channel, it is likely that the output transistor, triac, or relay associated with that channel will be damaged. In that case, the module must be replaced or the output moved to a spare channel on the output module. The fuses are normally easily replaced. Check the technical manual for the PLC to find the exact procedure. Figure 6-12 shows the fuse location and jumper setting for a Rockwell SLC module. Note that by choosing the jumper location, the user can choose whether the processor faults or continues in the event of a fuse blowing.

Some output modules provide more than one common terminal, to allow the user to use different voltage ranges on the same card (Figure 6-13). These multiple

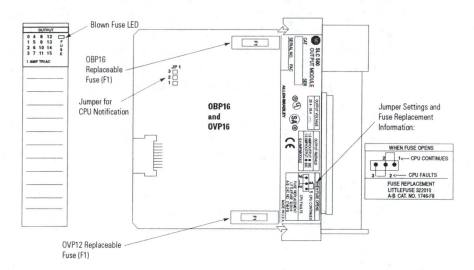

Figure 6-12   Fuse and jumper settings for a Rockwell SLC. Check the technical manual for your PLC to find the exact procedure. *(Courtesy Rockwell Automation Inc.)*

Figure 6-13   Use of a dual-common output module.

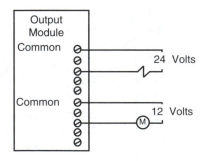

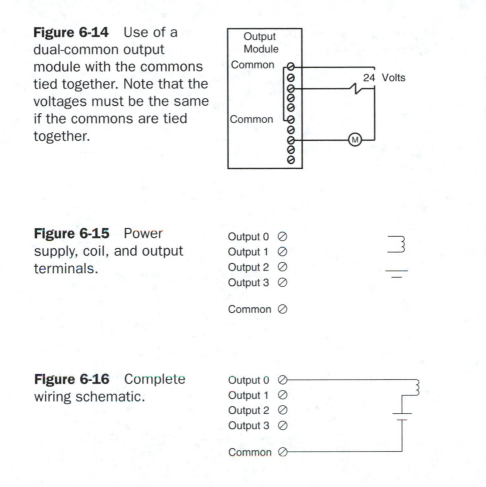

Figure 6-14 Use of a dual-common output module with the commons tied together. Note that the voltages must be the same if the commons are tied together.

Figure 6-15 Power supply, coil, and output terminals.

Figure 6-16 Complete wiring schematic.

commons can be tied together if the user desires. All outputs would be required to use the same voltage, however (Figure 6-14).

Output Wiring

Output wiring is similar in concept to input wiring. There are normally three things: power, a device, and output module terminals. Drawing a diagram before wiring can ease the task. Imagine a system that has many outputs. Let us first figure out one output circuit, then add more. Figure 6-15 shows an example of a power supply, a coil, and output terminals.

The wiring is shown completed in Figure 6-16. It is easy to see the current path. If the ladder logic turns on output 0, output terminal 0 will be internally connected to common and there will be a complete current path.

Figure 6-17   Additional output wiring example.

Figure 6-18   Complete wiring diagram.

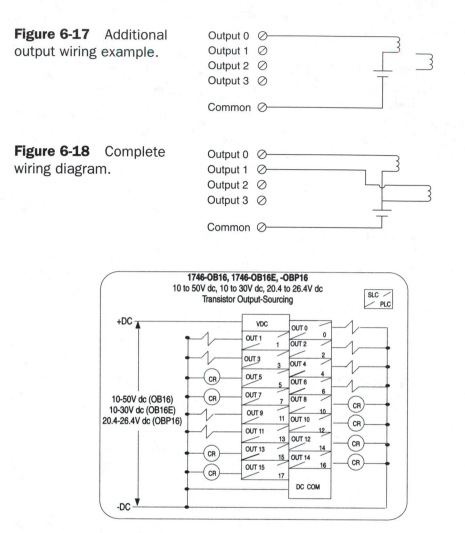

Figure 6-19   Example of SLC DC output module wiring. *(Courtesy Rockwell Automation Inc.)*

Next lets add another output (Figure 6-17). The output wiring should be the same for the output coil shown. One side of the coil must go to the output terminal and the other must be connected to the positive side of the power supply. Figure 6-18 shows the complete wiring diagram. It is difficult for most people to envision a complete wiring diagram, especially when many devices are involved. A simple paper drawing can ease the task.

Figure 6-19 shows a DC output module for a Rockwell Automation SLC. Note also that the positive side of the DC voltage must be connected to the VDC termi-

Figure 6-20 Example of SLC AC output module wiring. Note that these are triac outputs. *(Courtesy Rockwell Automation Inc.)*

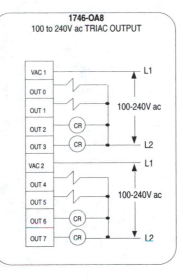

nal. The output devices are connected to an output terminal and then to the negative side of the power supply. The negative side of the supply must also be connected to the DC common.

Figure 6-20 shows a wiring diagram for a Rockwell AC triac output module. Note that L1 is connected to VAC 1 and VAC 2. L2 is connected through the actual output and then to the output module terminal.

Figure 6-21 shows the wiring of a Rockwell relay output module. First let us look at what the module requires for power before we consider the actual output wiring. There is a direct connection terminal on the top terminal of the module for +AC or DC power from the power supply. There is no direct connection for the – side of the power supply. Next let us look at the actual outputs. The outputs are the equivalent of coils. Consider the top left output. The left side of the output is connected to L2 or the –DC side of the power supply. The other side of the output is connected directly to the desired output terminal. As you can see, all of one side of the outputs are commoned to L2 or the –DC side of the power supply. The other side of each output was connected to an individual output terminal. Imagine that the ladder logic turns on the first output. We have a complete path and the output would in turn be energized.

Note that the top and bottom half of the wiring diagrams are separate, to allow the user to use different voltages for outputs 1 through 7 and 10 through 17; or the user could use AC for half and DC for the other half. Relay outputs can be protected with a diode to prolong contact life (Figure 6-22).

Some applications require connecting a PLC output to the solid state input of a device, usually to provide a low-level signal, not to power an actuator or coil.

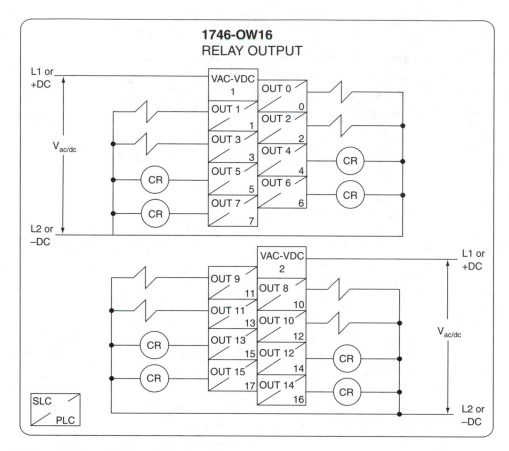

Figure 6-21 Wiring of a relay output module.
(Courtesy Rockwell Automation Inc.)

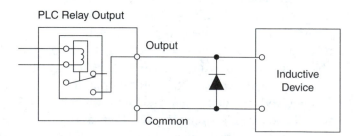

Figure 6-22 The use of a diode to help prolong contact life.

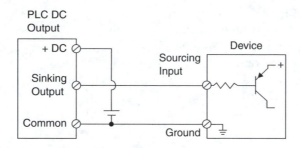

Figure 6-23 A PLC sinking output connected to a solid state sourcing input on an output device.

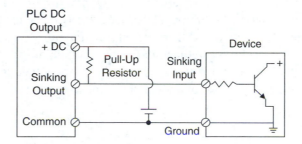

Figure 6-24 A PLC sinking output connected to a solid state sinking input on an output device.

Figure 6-25 The formula for calculating the correct size of pull-up resistor.

$$I_{INPUT} = \frac{V_{INPUT\ TURN\text{-}ON\ VOLTS}}{R_{INPUT}}$$

$$P_{PULL\text{-}UP} = \frac{V_{SUPPLY}^2}{R_{PULL\text{-}UP}}$$

$$R_{PULL\text{-}UP} = \frac{V_{SUPPLY} - 0.7}{I_{INPUT}} - R_{INPUT}$$

Figures 6-23 and 6-24 show how sinking and sourcing solid state devices can be connected to a PLC sinking output. It is important to size the pull-up resistor properly. Figure 6-25 shows the formula for calculating the proper size resistor.

Solid state modules can leak small unwanted current from output module outputs. If this is a problem, a bleeder resistor may be the solution. Figure 6-26 shows the use of a bleeder resistor to "bleed off" unwanted leakage through an output module. This leakage can occur with the solid state devices used in output modules.

Figure 6-26 Use of a bleeder resistor to bleed off unwanted leakage through an output module.

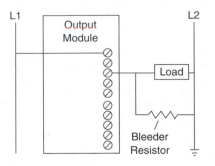

High-Density I/O Modules

High-density modules are digital I/O modules. A normal I/O module has eight inputs or outputs. A high-density module may have up to thirty-two inputs or outputs. The advantage is that there are a limited number of slots in a PLC rack. Each module uses a slot. With the high-density module, it is possible to install thirty-two inputs or outputs in one slot. The only disadvantage is that the high-density output modules typically cannot handle as much current per output.

ANALOG MODULES

Computers (PLCs) are digital devices. They do not work with analog information. Analog data such as temperature must be converted to digital information before the computer can work with it.

ANALOG INPUT MODULES

Cards have been developed to take analog information and convert it to digital information. These are called analog-to-digital (A/D) input cards. There are two basic types available: current sensing and voltage sensing. These cards will take the output from analog sensors (such as thermocouples) and change it to digital data for the PLC.

Voltage input modules are available in two types: unipolar and bipolar. *Unipolar modules* can take only one polarity for input. For example, if the application requires the card to measure only 0 V to +10 V, a unidirectional card will work. The bipolar module will take input of positive and negative polarity. For example, if the application produces a voltage between –10 V and +10 V, a bidirectional input card is required, because the measured voltage could be negative or positive. Analog input modules are commonly available in 0 V to 10 V models for the unipolar and −10 V to +10 V for the bipolar model.

Analog models are also available to measure current. These typically measure from the smallest input value of 4 milliamperes (mA) to the largest input value of 20 mA.

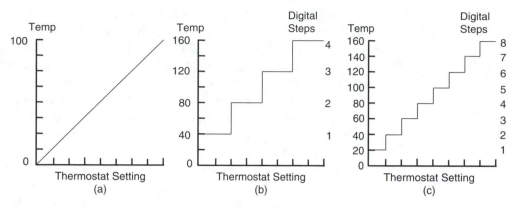

Figure 6-27 Graphs of temperature versus thermostat setting. (a) represents a linear relationship of temperature versus setting. In reality, when analog control is used, the analog is a series of steps (resolution). (b) shows how a four-step system would look. The resolution would be 40° per step. (c) shows an eight-step system. The resolution is 20°.

Many analog modules can be configured by the user. Dip switches or jumpers are used to configure the module, to accommodate different voltages or current. Some manufacturers make modules that will accept voltage or current for input. The user simply wires to either the voltage or the current terminals, depending on the application.

Resolution in Analog Modules

Resolution can be thought of as how closely a quantity can be measured. Imagine a 1 foot ruler. If the only graduations on the ruler were inches, the resolution would be 1 inch. If the graduations were every 1/4 inch, the resolution would be 1/4 inch. The closest we would be able to measure any object would be l/4 inch.

That is the basis for the measure of an analog signal. The computer can only work with digital information. The A/D card changes the analog source into discrete steps.

Examine Figure 6-27A. Ideally, the PLC would be able to read an exact temperature for every setting of the thermostat. Unfortunately, PLCs work only digitally. Consider Figure 6-27B. The analog input card changes the analog voltage (temperature) into digital steps. In this example, the analog card changed the temperature from 40° to 160° in four steps. The PLC would read a number between 1 and 4 from the A/D card. A simple math statement in the ladder could change the number into a temperature. For example, assume that the temperature was 120°. The A/D card would output the number 3. The math statement in the PLC would take the number and multiply by 40 to get the temperature. In this case, it would be 3 × 40°, or 120°. If the PLC read 4 from the A/D card, the temperature would be 4 × 40° or 160°. Assume now that the temperature is 97°. The A/D card would output the number 2. The PLC would read 2 and multiply by 40. The PLC would believe the temperature to be 80°. The closest the PLC can read the temperature is about 20° if four steps are used. (The temperature that the PLC calculates will always be in a range from 20° below the actual temperature to 20° above the measured temperature.) Each step is 40°. This is called *resolution*. The smallest temperature increment is 40°, the resolution would be 40.

Consider Figure 6-27C. This A/D card has eight steps. The resolution would be twice as fine, or 20°. For a temperature of 67°, the A/D would output 3. The PLC would multiply 3 × 20° and assume the temperature to be 60°. The largest possible error would be approximately 10°. (The PLC calculated temperature would be within 10° below the actual temperature to 10° above the actual temperature.)

Industry requires very fine resolution. Typically, an industrial A/D card for a PLC would have 12-bit binary resolution, which means that there would be 4096 steps. In other words, the analog quantity to be measured would be broken into 4096 steps—very fine resolution—although there are cards available with even finer resolution than this. The typical A/D card is 12 bits (4096 steps) or 14 bits (16,384 steps).

Analog modules are available that can take between one and eight individual analog inputs.

Input modules have user-selectable dip switch settings to choose whether each input will be a current or voltage input.

Figure 6-28 shows the wiring for an analog input module. Note the shield around the signal wires, and that it is grounded only at one end. It is normally grounded to the chassis at the control end. Note that each analog source has two leads to the module inputs. None are commoned together. This is called *differential wiring*. Note also that unused inputs are jumpered.

Input Resolution

Figure 6-29 shows the resolution for several analog input modules. Pay particular attention to the input ranges. Depending on which range the user selects, the second column of the table shows the range of decimal numbers that will appear

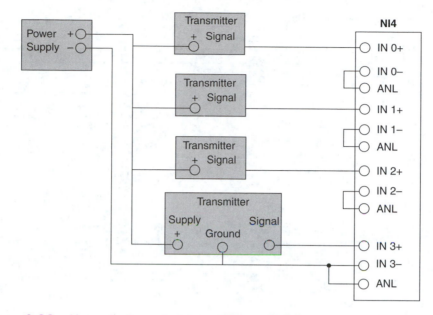

Figure 6-28 How single-ended (non-differential) input connections are made. *(Courtesy Rockwell Automation Inc.)*

NI4, NIO4I, & NIO4V Input Range	Decimal Range (input image table)	Number of Significant Bits	Nominal Resolution
±10V dc − 1 LSB	−32,768 to + 32,767	16	305.176µV/LSB
0 to 10V dc − 1 LSB	0 to 32,767	15	
0 to 5V dc	0 to 16,384	14	
1 to 5V dc	3,277 to 16,384	13.67	
±20 mA	±16,384	15	1.22070 µA/LSB
0 to 20 mA	0 to 16,384	14	
4 to 20 mA	3,277 to 16,384	13.67	

Figure 6-29 Resolution for various analog input modules. *(Courtesy Rockwell Automation Inc.)*

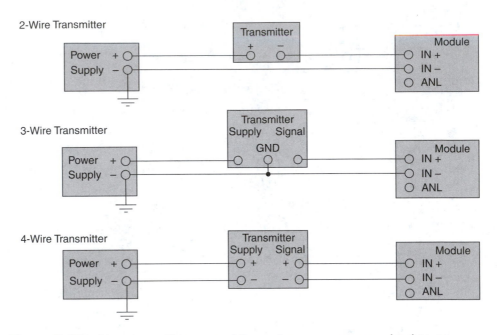

Figure 6-30   How two-, three-, and four-wire sensors are wired to an analog input module. *(Courtesy Rockwell Automation Inc.)*

in the input image table. The third column shows the number of significant bits that are used. The fourth column shows the resolution in microvolts or microamps per bit.

Figure 6-30 shows how two-, three-, and four-wire sensors are wired to an analog input module.

Special-purpose A/D modules are also available. One example would be thermocouple modules. These are simply A/D modules that have been adapted to meet the needs of thermocouple input. These modules are available to make it easy to accept input from various types of thermocouples. Thermocouples output tiny voltages. To use the entire range of the module resolution, a thermocouple module amplifies the small output from the thermocouple so that the entire 12-bit resolution is used. The modules also provide cold junction compensation. Figure 6-31 shows how a Rockwell Automation thermocouple input module is wired.

Figure 6-32 shows a tank filling application. There is a level sensor measuring the level in the tank. If it is empty, the sensor outputs 0 V. If the tank is full, it outputs 10 V. The output is linear between 0 level (0 V) and full (10 V). The output from the sensor becomes an input to an analog input module.

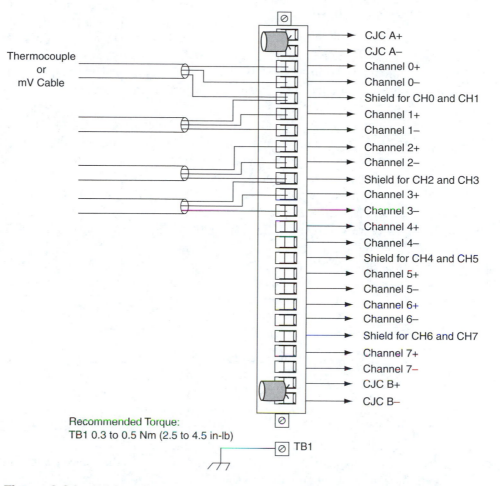

Figure 6-31 Wiring diagram for a Rockwell Automation thermocouple input module. *(Courtesy Rockwell Automation Inc.)*

Figure 6-32 A tank filling system.

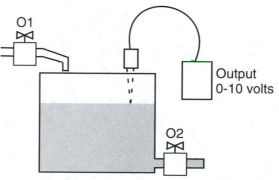

ANALOG OUTPUT MODULES

Analog output modules are also available. The PLC works in digital, so the PLC outputs a digital number (step) to the D/A converter module. The D/A converts the digital number from the PLC to an analog output. Analog output modules are available with voltage or current output. Typical outputs are 0 V to 10 V, −10 V to +10 V, and 4 mA to 20 mA.

Imagine a bakery. A temperature sensor (analog) in the oven could be connected to an A/D input module in the PLC. The PLC could read the voltage (steps) from the A/D card. The PLC would then know the temperature. The PLC can then send digital data to the D/A output module, which would control the heating element in the oven. This would create a fully integrated, closed-loop system to control the temperature in the oven.

Figure 6-33 shows the wiring for an analog output module. Note the shield around the signal wires. Note also that it is grounded only at one end—normally the output end. Unused outputs cannot be jumpered. Note that on this module the user can select whether to use an external 24 V supply or to use power from the backplane of the module.

Output Resolution

Figure 6-34 shows the resolution for several analog output modules. Pay particular attention to the output ranges for each module. The second column of the table shows the output range of current or voltage. The third column shows the range of decimal numbers that can be used in the output image table. The fourth column shows the number of significant bits that are used. The fifth column shows the resolution in micro amps or millivolts per bit.

Rethink the tank system in Figure 6-32. An analog output would be used to control the variable inlet valve to the tank. A second output could be used to control the variable valve that controls the outflow from the tank.

REMOTE I/O MODULES

Special modules are available for some PLCs that allow the I/O module to be positioned separately from the PLC. In some processes it is desirable (or necessary) to position the I/O at a different location. In some cases the machine or application is spread over a wide physical area. In these cases it may be desirable to position the I/O modules away from the PLC. Figure 6-35 shows an example of the use of an Allen-Bradley remote I/O adapter module.

Twisted pair wiring is a common method for connecting the remote module to the processor. Two wires are twisted around each other and connected between the PLC and the remote I/O. Twisting reduces the possibility of electrical interference (noise) as any noise acts on both conductors equally. Twisted pair connections can transmit data thousands of feet.

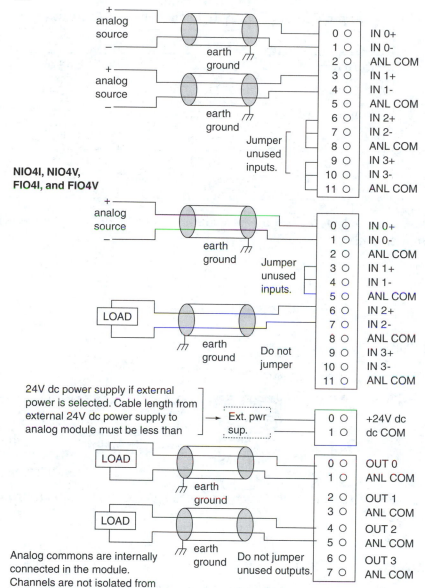

NI4

+ analog source −

earth ground

+ analog source −

earth ground

Jumper unused inputs.

0 ○	IN 0+
1 ○	IN 0-
2 ○	ANL COM
3 ○	IN 1+
4 ○	IN 1-
5 ○	ANL COM
6 ○	IN 2+
7 ○	IN 2-
8 ○	ANL COM
9 ○	IN 3+
10 ○	IN 3-
11 ○	ANL COM

**NIO4I, NIO4V,
FIO4I, and FIO4V**

+ analog source −

earth ground

Jumper unused inputs.

LOAD

earth ground

Do not jumper

0 ○	IN 0+
1 ○	IN 0-
2 ○	ANL COM
3 ○	IN 1+
4 ○	IN 1-
5 ○	ANL COM
6 ○	IN 2+
7 ○	IN 2-
8 ○	ANL COM
9 ○	IN 3+
10 ○	IN 3-
11 ○	ANL COM

24V dc power supply if external power is selected. Cable length from external 24V dc power supply to analog module must be less than

Ext. pwr sup.

| 0 ○ | +24V dc |
| 1 ○ | dc COM |

LOAD

earth ground

LOAD

earth ground

Analog commons are internally connected in the module. Channels are not isolated from

Do not jumper unused outputs.

0 ○	OUT 0
1 ○	ANL COM
2 ○	OUT 1
3 ○	ANL COM
4 ○	OUT 2
5 ○	ANL COM
6 ○	OUT 3
7 ○	ANL COM

Figure 6-33 Wiring diagram for a Rockwell Automation analog output module. *(Courtesy Rockwell Automation Inc.)*

Module	Output Range	Decimal Range (output image table)	Significant Bits	Resolution
FIO4I NIO4I NO4I	0 to 21 mA − 1 LSB	0 to 32,764	13 bits	2.56348 µA/LSB
	0 to 20 mA	0 to 31,208	12.92 bits	
	4 to 20 mA	6,242 to 31,208	12.6 bits	
FIO4V NIO4V NO4V	±10V dc − 1 LSB	−32,768 to + 32,764	14 bits	1.22070 mV/LSB
	0 to 10V dc − 1 LSB	0 to 32,764	13 bits	
	0 to 5V dc	0 to 16,384	12 bits	
	1 to 5V dc	3,277 to 16,384	11.67 bits	

Figure 6-34 Output resolution for various output modules. *(Courtesy Rockwell Automation Inc.)*

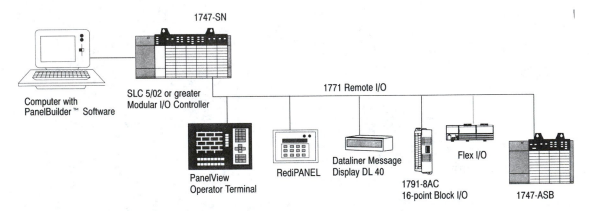

Figure 6-35 Example of the use of remote I/O modules. *(Courtesy Rockwell Automation Inc.)*

OPERATOR I/O DEVICES

As systems become more integrated and automated, they become more complex. Operator information becomes crucial. There are many devices available for this information interchange.

Operator Terminals

Many PLC makers now offer their own operator terminals, from simple to highly complex. The simpler ones are able to display a short message. The more complex

Figure 6-36 Operator display terminal. *(Courtesy Rockwell Automation Inc.)*

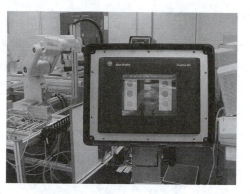

models are able to display graphics and text in color while taking operator input from touch screens (Figure 6-36), bar codes, keyboards, and so on. These display devices can cost from a couple hundred dollars to several thousand dollars. If we remember that the PLC has most of the valuable information about the processes it controls in its memory, we can see that the operator terminal can be a window into the memory of the PLC.

The greatest advances have been in the ease of use. Many PLC manufacturers have software available that runs on an IBM personal computer. The software essentially writes the application for the user. The user draws the screens and decides which variables from the PLC should be displayed. The user also decides what input is needed from the operator. When the screens are designed, they are downloaded to the display terminal.

These smart terminals can store hundreds of pages of displays in their memory. The PLC simply sends a message that tells the terminal which page and information to display. This helps reduce the load on the PLC. The memory of the display is used to hold the display data. The PLC only requests the correct display, and the terminal displays it.

The PLC needs only update the variables that may appear on the screen. The typical display would include graphics showing a portion of the process, variables showing times or counts, and any other information that might aid an operator in the use or maintenance of a system.

QUESTIONS

1. What voltages are typically available for I/O modules?

2. If an input module was sensing an input from a load-powered sensor when it should not, what might be the possible problem, and what is a possible solution?

3. What types of output devices are available in output modules? List at least three.

4. Explain the purpose of A/D modules and how they function.

5. Explain the purpose of D/A modules and how they function.

6. What type of module could be used to communicate with a computer?

7. Explain the term *resolution.*

8. If a 16-bit input module is used to measure the level in a tank, and the tank can hold between 0 and 15 feet of fluid, what is the resolution in feet?

9. What are remote I/O modules?

10. List three reasons why operator I/O devices are becoming more prevalent.

chapter 7

Math Instructions

Arithmetic instructions are vital in the programming of systems. They can simplify the task of the programmer. In this chapter we look at compare, add, subtract, multiply, divide, and other instructions of several brands of PLCs.

OBJECTIVES

Upon completion of this chapter, you will be able to:
1. Describe typical uses for arithmetic instructions
2. Explain the use of compare instructions
3. Explain the use of typical arithmetic instructions
4. Write ladder logic programs involving arithmetic instructions

INTRODUCTION

Many times contacts, coils, timers, and counters fall short of what the programmer needs, and many applications require mathematical computation. For example, imagine a furnace application that requires the furnace to be between 250° and 255° (Figure 7-1). If the temperature variable is between 250° and 255°, we might turn off the heater coil. If the temperature is below 250° we would turn on the heater coil. If the temperature is between 250° and 255°, we turn on a green indicator

115

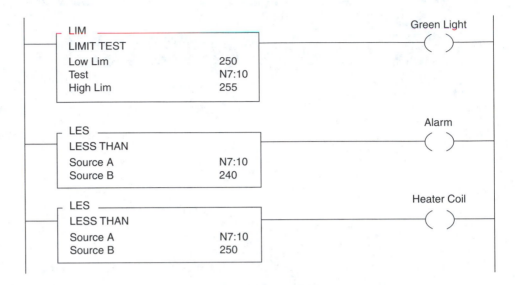

Figure 7-1 How comparison instructions could be used to program a simple application. In this application, an integer (N7:10) contains the current temperature. The instructions are being used to compare the current temperature (N7:10) to process limits. In the first rung, the green indicator lamp is on if the temperature is between 250° and 255°. In the second rung, an alarm sounds if the temperature drops below 240°. In the third rung, the heater coil will be on if the temperature is below 250°.

lamp. If the temperature falls below 240°, we might sound an alarm. (*Note:* Industrial temperature control is normally more complex than this. See chapters 12 and 13 for complex process control.

This simple application requires the use of relational operators (arithmetic comparisons). The application involves tests of limits (250°–255°) and less than concepts. The use of arithmetic statements makes this an easy application to write. Many of the small PLCs do not have arithmetic instructions available. All of the larger PLCs offer a wide variety of such instructions.

In additional cases, numbers may need to be manipulated, for example, added, subtracted, multiplied, or divided. There are PLC instructions to handle all of these computations. For example, we may have a system to control the temperature of a furnace. In addition to controlling the temperature, we would like to convert the Celsius temperature to degrees Fahrenheit for display to the operator. If the temperature was to rise too high, an alarm would be triggered. Arithmetic instructions could do this process easily.

ROCKWELL AUTOMATION ARITHMETIC INSTRUCTIONS

There are a multitude of arithmetic instructions available in the PLC-5 and SLC-500 controllers. We will cover a few in this section. Figure 7-2 shows the arithmetic functions that are available.

Instruction	Function	Description of Operation and Use
ADD	Add	Adds source A to source B and stores the result in the destination.
SUB	Subtract	Subtracts source B from source A and stores the result in the destination.
MUL	Multiply	Multiplies source A by source B and stores the result in the destination.
DIV	Divide	Divides source A by source B and stores the result in the destination and the math register.
DDV	Double Divide	Divides the contents of the math register by the source and stores the result in the destination and the math register.
CLR	Clear	Sets all bits of a word to zero.
SQR	Square Root	Calculates the square root of the source and places the integer result in the destination.
SCP	Scale with Parameters	Produces a scaled output value that has a linear relationship between the input and scaled values.
SCL	Scale Data	Multiplies the source by a specified rate, adds to an offset value, and stores the result in the destination.
ABS	Absolute	Calculates the absolute value of the source and places the result in the destination.
CPT	Compute	Evaluates an expression and stores the result in the destination.
SWP	Swap	Swaps the low and high bytes of a specified number of words in a bit, integer, ASCII, or string file.
LN	Natural Log	Takes the natural log of the value in the source and stores the result in the destination.
LOG	Log to the Base 10	Takes the log base 10 of the value in the source and stores the result in the destination.
XPY	X to the power of Y	Raises a value to a power and stores the result in the destination.

Figure 7-2   A sample of the Rockwell Automation math instructions.

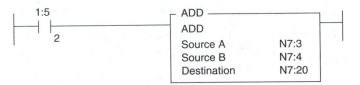

Figure 7-3 Use of an ADD instruction.

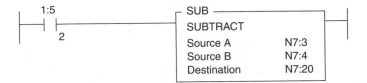

Figure 7-4 Use of a SUB instruction.

Add

The add (ADD) instruction is used to add two values (source A + source B). The result is put in the destination address. Figure 7-3 shows an example of an ADD instruction. If contact I:5/2 is true, the ADD instruction will add the number from source A (N7:3) and the value from source B (N7:4). The result will be stored in the destination address (N7:20).

Subtraction

The subtraction (SUB) instruction is used to subtract two values. The SUB instruction subtracts source B from source A. The result is stored in the destination address. Figure 7-4 shows the use of a SUB instruction. If contact I:5/2 is true, the SUB instruction is executed. Source B is subtracted from source A; the result is stored in destination address N7:20.

Multiply

The multiply (MUL) instruction is used to multiply two values. The first value, source A, is multiplied by the second value, source B. The result is stored in the destination address. Source A and source B can be either values or addresses of values. Figure 7-5 shows the use of a MUL instruction. If contact I:5/2 is true, source A (N7:3) is multiplied by source B (N7:4) and the result is stored in destination address N7:20.

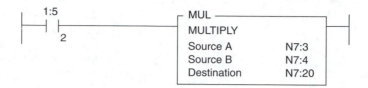

Figure 7-5 Use of a MUL instruction.

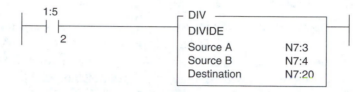

Figure 7-6 Use of a DIV instruction.

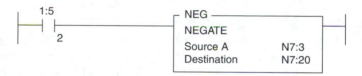

Figure 7-7 Use of a NEG instruction.

Divide

The divide (DIV) instruction is used to divide two values. Source A is divided by source B and the result is placed in the destination address. The sources can be values or addresses of values. Figure 7-6 shows the use of a DIV instruction. If contact I:5/2 is true, the DIV instruction will divide the value from source A (N7:3) by the value from source B (N7:4). The result is stored in destination address N7:20.

Negate

The negate (NEG) instruction is used to change the sign of a number. If it is used on a positive number, it makes it a negative number. If it is used on a negative number, it will change it to a positive number. Remember that this instruction will execute every time the rung is true. Use transitional contacts if needed. The use of a NEG instruction is shown in Figure 7-7. If contact I:5/2 is true, the value in source A (N7:3) will be given the opposite sign and stored in destination address N7:20.

Figure 7-8 Use of a SQR instruction.

Square Root

The square root (SQR) instruction is used to find the square root of a value. The result is stored in a destination address. The source can be a value or the address of a value. Figure 7-8 shows the use of a SQR instruction. If contact I:5/2 is true, the SQR instruction will find the square root of the value of the number found at the source address F8:3. The result will be stored at destination address F8:20.

Average

The average (AVE) instruction (PLC-5 processors only) is a file instruction. It is used to find the average of a set of values. The AVE instruction calculates the average using floating-point value regardless of the type specified for the file or destination. If an overflow occurs, the CPU aborts the calculation. In that case the destination remains unchanged.

The position points to the element that caused the overflow. When the ER bit is cleared, the position is rezeroed and the instruction is recalculated. Every time there is a low-to-high transition, the value of the current element is added to the next element. The next low-to-high transition causes the current element value to be added to the next element, and so on. Every time another element is added, the position field and the status word are incremented.

Figure 7-9 shows how an AVE instruction is used in a ladder diagram. The programmer must provide certain information. The file is the address of the first element to be added and used in the calculation. The destination is the address where the result will be stored. This address can be floating-point value or integer. The control is the address of the control structure in the control area (R) of CPU memory. The CPU uses this information to run the instruction. Length is the number of elements to be included in the calculation (0 to 1000). Position points to the element that the instruction is currently using.

Compute

The compute (CPT) instruction can be used to copy arithmetic logical and number conversion operations. The operations to be performed are defined by the user in

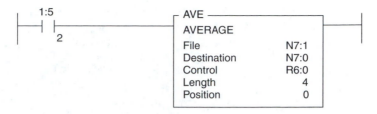

Figure 7-9   Use of an AVE instruction.

Order	Operation	Description
1	**	Exponential (x to the power of y)
2	-	Negate
	NOT	Bitwise Complement
3	*	Multiply
	/	Divide
4	+	Add
	−	Subtract
5	AND	Bitwise AND
6	XOR	Bitwise Exclusive OR
7	OR	Bitwise OR

Figure 7-10   Precedence (order) in which math operations are performed. When precedence is equal, the operations are performed left to right. Parentheses can be used to override the order.

the expression and the result is written in the destination. Operations are performed in a prescribed order. Operations of equal order are performed left to right. Figure 7-10 shows the order in which operations are performed. The programmer can override precedence order by using parentheses.

Figure 7-11 shows the use of a CPT instruction. The mathematical operations are performed when contact I:5/2 is true. In this case, two floating-point numbers (F8:1 and F8:2) are added to each other. Then the square root is calculated and stored in the destination address (F8:10).

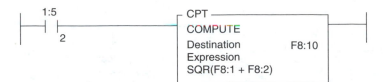

Figure 7-11   Use of a CPT instruction.

Instruction	Function	Description of Operation and Use
EQU	Equal	Used to test whether two values are equal.
NEQ	Not Equal	Used to test whether two values are not equal.
LES	Less Than	Used to test whether one value (source A) is less than another (source B).
LEQ	Less Than or Equal	Used to test whether one value (source A) is less than or equal to another (source B).
GRT	Greater Than	Used to test whether one value (source A) is greater than another (source B).
GEQ	Greater Than or Equal	Used to test whether one value (source A) is greater than or equal to another (source B).
MEQ	Masked Comparison for Equal	Used to compare data at a source address with data at a compare address.
LIM	Limit Test	Used to test for values within or outside a specified range.

Figure 7-12   Rockwell Automation relational operators.

RELATIONAL OPERATORS

Figure 7-12 shows Rockwell Automation relational instructions.

Equal

The equal (EQU) instruction is used to test if two values are equal. The values tested can be actual values or addresses that contain values. An example is shown in Figure 7-13. Source A is compared with source B to test if they are equal. If the value in N7:5 is equal to the value in N7:10, the rung will be true and output O:5/01 will be turned on.

Figure 7-13 Use of an EQU instruction.

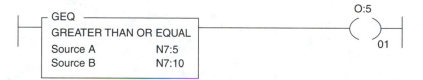

Figure 7-14 Use of a GEQ instruction.

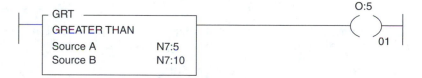

Figure 7-15 Use of a GRT instruction.

Greater Than or Equal

The greater than or equal (GEQ) instruction is used to test two sources to determine whether source A is greater than or equal to source B. The use of a GEQ instruction is shown in Figure 7-14. If the value of source A (N7:5) is greater than or equal to source B (N7:10), output O:5/01 will be turned on.

Greater Than

The greater than (GRT) instruction is used to see if a value from source A is greater than the value from source B. An example of the instruction is shown in Figure 7-15. If the value of source A (N7:5) is greater than the value of source B (N7:10), output O:5/01 will be set (turned on).

Less Than

The less than (LES) instruction is used to see if a value from source A is less than the value from source B. An example of the LES instruction is shown in

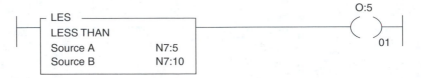

Figure 7-16 Use of a LES instruction.

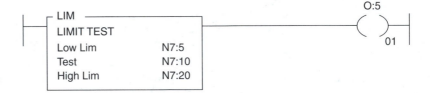

Figure 7-17 Use of a LIM instruction.

Figure 7-16. If the value of source A (N7:5) is less than the value of source B (N7:10), output O:5/01 will be set (turned on).

Limit

The limit (LIM) instruction is used to test a value to see if it falls in a specified range of values. The instruction is true when the tested value is within the limits. This could be used, for example, to see if the temperature of an oven was within the desired temperature range. In this case the instruction would be testing to see if an analog value (a number in memory representing the actual analog temperature) was within certain desired limits.

The programmer must provide three pieces of data to the LIM instruction when programming: a low limit, a test value, and a high limit. The low limit can be a constant or an address that contains the desired value. The address will contain an integer or floating-point value of 16 bits. The test value is a constant or the address of a value that is to be tested. If the test value is within the range specified, the rung will be true. The high limit can be a constant or the address of a value.

Figure 7-17 shows the use of a LIM instruction. If the value in N7:10 is greater than or equal to the lower limit value (N7:5) and less than or equal to the high limit (N7:20), the rung will be true and output O:5/01 will be turned on.

Not Equal

The not equal (NEQ) instruction is used to test two values for inequality. The values tested can be constants or addresses that contain values. An example is shown

Figure 7-18 Use of a NEQ instruction.

in Figure 7-18. If source A (N7:3) is not equal to source B (N7:4), the instruction is true and output O:5/01 is turned on.

LOGICAL OPERATORS

There are several logical operator instructions available that can be useful to the innovative programmer. They can be used, for example, to check the status of certain inputs while ignoring others.

And

The AND instruction is used to perform an AND operation using the bits from two source addresses. The bits are ANDed and a result occurs. Figure 7-19 shows the results of the four possible combinations. An AND instruction requires two sources (numbers). These two sources are ANDed and the result is stored in a third address (Figure 7-20). Figure 7-21 shows an example of an AND instruction. Addresses N7:3 and N7:4 are ANDed. The result is placed in destination address N7:5. Examine the bits in the source addresses to better understand how the AND produced the result in the destination.

Figure 7-19 Results of an AND operation on the four possible bit combinations.

Source A	Source B	Result
0	0	0
1	0	0
0	1	0
1	1	1

Source A N7:3	0	0	0	0	0	0	0	0	1	0	1	0	1	0	1	0
Source B N7:4	0	0	0	0	0	0	0	0	1	1	1	0	1	0	1	1
Destination N7:5	0	0	0	0	0	0	0	0	1	0	1	0	1	0	1	0

Figure 7-20 Result of an AND on two source addresses. The ANDed result is stored in address N7:5.

Figure 7-21　Use of an AND instruction. If input I:5/2 is true, the AND instruction executes. The number in address N7:3 is ANDed with the value in address N7:4. The result of the AND is stored in address N7:5.

Figure 7-22　Results of a NOT instruction on bit states.

Source	Result
0	1
1	0

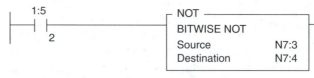

Figure 7-23　Use of a NOT instruction. If input I:5/02 is true, the NOT instruction executes. The number in address N7:3 is NOTed (1's complemented). The result is stored in destination address N7:4.

Source A N7:3	0	0	0	0	0	0	0	0	1	0	1	0	1	0	1	0
Destination N7:4	1	1	1	1	1	1	1	1	0	1	0	1	0	1	0	1

Figure 7-24　What would happen to the number 0000000010101010 if a NOT instruction were executed? The result is shown in destination address N7:4.

Not

NOT instructions are used to invert the status of bits. A 1 is made a 0 and a 0 is made a 1. See Figures 7-22, 7-23, and 7-24.

Or

Bitwise OR instructions are used to compare the bits of two numbers. Figures 7-25, 7-26, and 7-27 show examples of how the instruction functions.

Figure 7-25 Result of an OR instruction on bit states.

Source A	Source B	Result
0	0	0
1	0	1
0	1	1
1	1	1

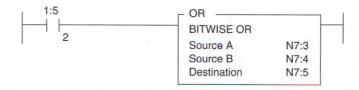

Figure 7-26 How an OR instruction can be used in a ladder diagram. If input I:5/2 is true, the OR instruction executes. Source A (N7:3) is ORed with source B (N7:4). The result is stored in the destination address (N7:5).

Source A N7:3	0	0	0	0	0	0	0	0	1	0	1	0	1	0	1	0
Source B N7:4	0	0	0	0	0	0	0	0	1	1	1	0	1	0	1	1
Destination N7:5	0	0	0	0	0	0	0	0	1	1	1	0	1	0	1	1

Figure 7-27 Result of an OR instruction on the numbers in address N7:3 and address N7:4. The result of the OR is shown in the destination address N7:5.

SCALE WITH PARAMETERS INSTRUCTION

Another type of scale instruction is the scale with parameters (SCP) instruction. In this example, an SCP will be used to scale an input value so that an actual temperature can be displayed. In industrial control there are many applications in which a physical property such as temperature is measured. A temperature such as 72° is measured by a thermocouple, which converts the temperature to a voltage. The voltage is received by an analog input module and converted to a bit count. For example, a 14-bit module would convert an analog input to a number between 0 and 16,383. The user would rather see the actual temperature. A scale instruction can be used to convert the input bit count to a temperature.

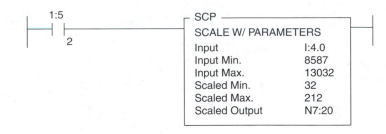

Figure 7-28   A SCP instruction.

The SCP instruction is shown in Figure 7-28. Imagine a system that will measure a temperature of between 32° and 212°F. Next imagine that the analog module shows 8587 for 32° and 13,032 for 212°. The user would like to display the
actual temperature on a touch screen. The user chose to use a SCP instruction to
accomplish the task. There are six values for the user to enter. The first value can
be an integer or the actual address of the input. In this example, the input will be
received from an analog input module. The address of the input is I:4.0 (input 0
on the analog module located in slot 4). The next two values to be entered are the
input minimum and input maximum values. These can be constants or addresses.
These are the minimum and maximum values from the analog input. The number 8587 was entered for the minimum input value and 13,032 was entered for
the maximum input value. The next two values are the scaled minimum and maximum values in our example 32 and 212. These can be constants or addresses.
The last value to be entered is the scaled output. The scaled output can be a word
address or an address of floating-point data elements. In this example the user
entered N7:20, which will contain a scaled value between 32 and 212 based on
the input value. The value of N7:20 could be displayed on the touch panel for an
operator.

QUESTIONS

1. Explain some of the reasons why arithmetic instructions are used in ladder
   logic.

2. What is the purpose of LIM instructions?

3. What is the purpose of comparison instructions?

4. Why might a programmer use an instruction that would change a number to
   a different number system?

5. Write a rung of ladder logic that would compare two values to see if the first is greater than the second. Turn an output on if the statement is true.

6. Write a rung of ladder logic that checks if one value is equal to a second value. Turn on an output if the statement is true.

7. Write a rung of ladder logic that checks if a value is less than 20 or greater than 40. Turn on the output if the statement is true.

8. Write a rung of ladder logic to check if a value is less than or equal to 99. Turn on an output if the statement is true.

9. Write a rung of ladder logic to check if a value is less than 75 or greater than 100 or equal to 85. Turn on an output if the statement is true.

10. Write a ladder logic program that accomplishes the following: A production line produces items that are packaged twelve to a pack. Your boss asks you to modify the ladder diagram so that the number of items and the number of packs are counted. There is a sensor that senses each item as it is produced. Use the sensor as an input to the instructions you will use to complete the task. (*Hint:* One way would be to use a counter and at least one arithmetic statement.)

11. Write a ladder diagram program to accomplish the following: A tank level must be maintained between two levels (Figure 7-29). An ultrasonic sensor is used to measure the height of the fluid in the tank. The output from the ultrasonic sensor is 0 V to 10 V (Figure 7-30). This directly relates to a tank level of 0 to 5 feet. It is desired that the level be maintained between 4.0 and 4.2 feet. Output 1 is the input valve. Output 2 is the output valve. The output from the sensor is an analog input to an analog input module.

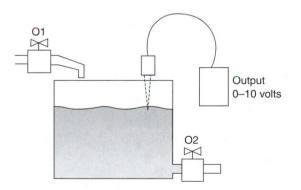

Figure 7-29   Tank level application.

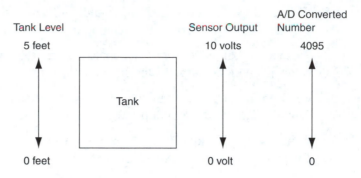

Figure 7-30 A comparison of tank level and A/D output.

PROGRAMMING PRACTICE

RSLogix Relay Logic Instructions

The following exercises utilize the LogixPro software included with this book. Go to the LogixPro Student Exercises and Documentation portion of the CD. Remember that the Rockwell Automation instruction set reference is also on the CD. It may be very helpful.

1. Complete the Word Compare Introductory exercise in LogixPro.
2. Complete Exercise 1—Traffic Control Utilizing 1 Timer in LogixPro software.

EXTRA CREDIT

Complete Exercise 2—Dealing with Pedestrians in LogixPro software.

chapter 8
Advanced Instructions

In this chapter we examine various instructions. We also learn about copying and moving memory, communicating between controllers, and other instructions that make the process of programming complex systems easier.

OBJECTIVES

Upon completion of this chapter, you will be able to:
1. Move and copy data utilizing SLC instructions
2. Utilize SLC communication instructions
3. Utilize special-purpose instructions such as copy, move, PID, and ramp
4. Write ladder logic using sequencers

COPY (COP) INSTRUCTION

A COP instruction is used to copy a range of memory to a different range of memory (Figure 8-1). The COP instruction has two values that must be entered: source and destination (Figure 8-2). The source is the beginning address of the file that you want to copy. The destination is the beginning address of the place where you would like the data copied. Length is the number of elements that you would like

131

Figure 8-1 A copy instruction copies data from one place in memory to another.

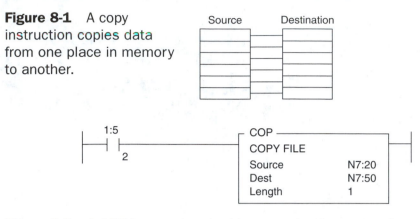

Figure 8-2 A COP instruction. In this example, the source is one element (word) from N7:20. This element will be copied to N7:50.

to copy. For example, if the address destination were a counter-type file (counters require three words per counter), then the maximum number you could copy would be 42. If copying words, the maximum would be 128. The entire source file is copied each program scan if the rung is true.

MOVE (MOV) INSTRUCTION

The MOV instruction is used to move the contents of one location to another location. This is a very useful instruction for many purposes. One example would be to change the preset value for a timer or counter. There are two values that must be entered by the programmer: source and destination (Figure 8-3). Source is a constant or the address of the data that you want to move. Destination is the address to which the data are moved. Note: If you want to move one word of data without affecting the arithmetic bits, use a COP instruction with a length of one word instead of a MOV.

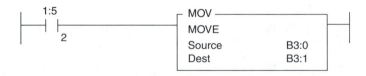

Figure 8-3 A MOV instruction. Note that in this example, word B3:0 was moved to destination B3:1. Note that a MOV instruction affects the math flags, a COP does not.

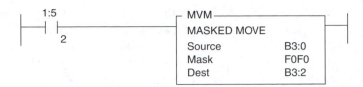

Figure 8-4 A MVM instruction.

MASKED MOVE (MVM) INSTRUCTION

The MVM instruction is similar to the MOV instruction, except that the source data are moved through a mask before being stored into the destination. There are three values that must be entered by the programmer: source, mask, and destination (Figure 8-4). For example, if we are moving an integer (N7:5) and the first 8 bits in the mask are 1s and the second half are 0s in the mask, only the first 8 bits of N7:5 will be moved to the destination. The second 8 bits will not be changed in the destination. They will remain in the same state as they were before the move.

FILE FILL (FLL) INSTRUCTION

The FLL instruction is used to fill a range of memory locations with a constant or a value from a memory address (Figure 8-5).

The FLL instruction has two values that must be entered: source and destination (Figure 8-6). The source is the constant or the element address. The destination is the beginning address of the file you would like to fill. Length is the number of elements that you would like to fill. For example, if the address destination were a

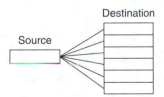

Figure 8-5 A FLL instruction copies data from one location in memory to multiple locations.

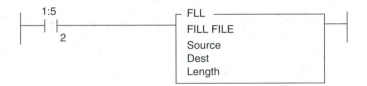

Figure 8-6 A FLL instruction.

counter-type file (counters require three words per counter), the maximum number you could copy would be 42. If copying words, the maximum would be 128. The entire file fills each program scan if the rung is true.

MESSAGE (MSG) INSTRUCTIONS

The MSG instruction is used to communicate between PLCs. The length limit is 103 words.

The SLC 5/03 (OS301 and higher) and the SLC 5/04 processors service up to four message instructions per channel, for a maximum of eight message instructions. If you consistently enable more MSG instructions than the buffers and queues can accomodate, the order in which MSG instructions enter the queue is determined by the order in which they are scanned. This means MSG instructions closest to the beginning of the program enter the queue regularly and MSG instructions later in the program may not enter the queue.

The MSG instruction initiates reads and writes through RS232 channel 0 when configured for the following protocols:

- DF1 Full-Duplex (Point-to-Point)
- DF1 Half-Duplex Master/Slave (Point-to-Multipoint)
- DH485 initiates reads and writes through
- DH485 channel 1 (SLC 5/03 processors only)
- DH+ channel 1 (SLC 5/04 processors only)

To invoke the MSG instruction, toggle its rung from false to true. Do not toggle the rung again until the MSG instruction has successfully or unsuccessfully completed the previous message, indicated by the processor setting either the DN or ER bit.

Following are some of the status bits available for the programmer.

Error (ER) bit (bit 12) is set when message transmission has failed. The ER bit is reset the next time the associated rung goes from false to true. Do not set or reset this bit. It is informational only.

Done (DN) bit (bit 13) is set when the message is transmitted successfully. The DN bit is reset the next time the associated rung goes from false to true. Do not set or reset this bit. It is informational only.

Start (ST) bit (bit 14) is set when the processor receives acknowledgment (ACK) from the target device. The ST bit is reset when the DN, ER, or TO bit is set. Do not set or reset this bit. It is informational only. For SLC 5/05 Ethernet (channel 1) communications, the ST bit indicates internally that the Ethernet daughterboard has received a command and it is acceptable for a transmission attempt. The command has not yet been transmitted.

Figure 8-7 MSG
instruction.

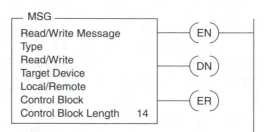

Enable (EN) bit (bit 15) is set when rung conditions go true and there is space available in either the MSG buffer or MSG queue. It remains set until message transmission is completed and the rung goes false. You may reset this bit once either the ER or DN bit is set in order to retrigger a MSG instruction with true rung conditions on the next scan. Do not set this bit.

Entering Parameters

After you place the MSG instruction on a rung, specify whether the message is to be a read or write. Then specify the target device and the control block for the MSG instruction. Figure 8-7 shows a MSG instruction.

Read/write Read indicates that the local processor (processor in which the instruction is located) is receiving data; write indicates that the processor is sending data.

Target device identifies the type of device that will receive data. More information about communicating with specific devices is included in the SLC instruction manual on the CD.

Control block is an integer file address that you select. It is a seven-element file, containing the status bits, target file address, and other data associated with the message instruction.

Control block length is fixed at seven elements. The MSG control block length increases from seven to fourteen words when changing from a SLC 5/02 to a SLC 5/03, SLC 5/04 (channel 0, DH485), or SLC 5/05 (channel 0, DH485) processor program. You must make sure that there are at least seven unused words following each MSG control block in your program.

BLOCK TRANSFER INSTRUCTIONS

The two block transfer instructions are block transfer read (BTR) and block transfer write (BTW). A block transfer instruction can be used with later models of 5/03,

Figure 8-8   A BTR instruction.

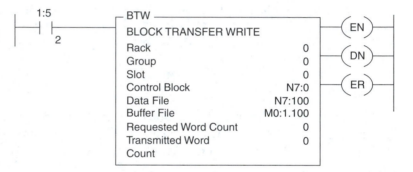

Figure 8-9   A BTW instruction.

5/04, and 5/05. Block transfer instructions can be used to transfer up to sixty-four words of memory to/from a remote device over a remote I/O link. A false-to-true transition initiates a BTW or BTR instruction. Figures 8-8 and 8-9 show BTR and BTW instructions.

The BTW instruction tells the processor to write data stored in the BTW data file to a device at the specified remote I/O (RIO) rack/group/slot address. The BTR instruction tells the processor to read data from a device at the specified RIO rack/group/slot address and store it in the BT data file. The data file may be any valid integer, floating point, or binary data file. A total of thirty-two block transfer buffers are available. Each buffer is 100 consecutive words.

Entering the Parameters for BTW and BTR Instructions

Data file is the address in the SLCs data file containing the BTW or BTR data. Bit integer or floating-point types can be used.

BTR/BTW buffer file is the file address used for the transfer buffer. For example, in M0:e.x00, *e* is the slot number of the scanner and *x* is the buffer number.

The range of buffer numbers is 1 to 32. Each BTR and BTW instruction uses both the M1 and M0 files for a specific file number. M0 is used for BTR control and for BTW data. M1 is used for BTW status and BTR data.

Control block is an integer file address that stores block transfer control and status information. The control block is three words in length. You should provide the following information for the control structure:

- Rack—the I/O rack number 0–3 of the I/O chassis in which the target I/O module exists
- Group—the I/O group number (0–7) of the position of the target module in the I/O chassis
- Slot—the slot number (0 or 1) within the group. If you are using two-slot addressing, the left slot is 1 and the right slot is 0. If you are using one-slot addressing, the slot is always 0.
- Requested word count—the number of words to transfer. If the length is set to 0, the processor reserves sixty-four words for transfer. The block transfer module transfers the maximum words that the adapter can handle. If you set the length from one to sixty-four, the processor transfers the number of words specified.

TIME STAMP INSTRUCTIONS

There are two instructions that can be used together to time events. These can be used in newer 5/03, 5/04, and 5/05 processors. The read high-speed clock (RHC) instruction is used to move the value of an internal 10-microsecond clock counter to either an integer (low 16 bits) or floating-point data location. The second instruction is the time difference (TDF) instruction. The TDF instruction is used to input two previously captured 10-microsecond clock values and return the elapsed time between them. This allows the user to time an event to within 10 microseconds. The user could utilize one event to trigger one RHC instruction to capture the counter time to N7:20, for example. A second RHC could be used to capture the time from a different event to address N7:21 (Figure 8-10). A TDF could then be used to compute the difference between the two events and store the difference in memory (N7:22 in this case). Figure 8-11 shows the use of a TDF instruction.

Figure 8-10   A RHC instruction.

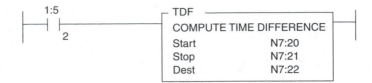

Figure 8-11 A TDF instruction.

RAMP INSTRUCTION

The ramp (RMP) instruction can be used to control motor speed or for valve position control. The RMP instruction allows the user to input time duration, beginning and ending output values, and a curve type (e.g., linear, acceleration, de-acceleration, and S-curve).

FILE BIT COMPARISON AND DIAGNOSTIC DETECT INSTRUCTIONS

The file bit comparison and diagnostic detect instructions can be used to compare large blocks of data. For example, they could be used for diagnostic data. The file bit comparison (FBC) instruction compares values in a bit file with values in a reference data file. The diagnostic detect (DDT) instruction is similar to the FBC except that when it finds a difference between the input file and the reference file, it changes the reference file. The user could develop a list of conditions for the process under operation. These can then be compared with actual conditions for diagnostics and troubleshooting. The FBC could be used to ensure that the actual conditions are the same as the desired conditions. The DDT could be used to record the actual conditions in the reference file for diagnostics.

PROPORTIONAL, INTEGRAL, DERIVATIVE INSTRUCTION

The proportional, integral, derivative (PID) instruction is used to control processes. It can be used to control physical properties such as pressure, temperature, level, concentration, density, and flow rate. The PID instruction is straightforward: It takes one input and controls one output. The input normally comes from an analog input module. The output is normally an analog output, but it can be a time proportioning on/off output to drive a heating or cooling unit.

The PID instruction is used to keep a process variable at a desired setpoint. Figure 8-12 shows a tank level example, in which a level sensor outputs an analog signal between 4 and 20 mA. It outputs 4 mA if the tank is 0% full and 20 mA if the tank is 100% full. The output from this sensor becomes an input to an analog input module in the PLC. There is a variable valve on the tank to control the inflow to the tank. The valve is 0% open if it receives a 0% signal and 100% open if it receives 20 mA. The PLC outputs an analog signal to the valve, and takes the input from the level sensor and uses the PID equation to calculate the proper output to control the valve.

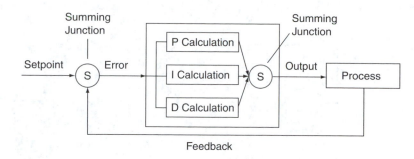

Figure 8-12 A block diagram showing a PID instruction.

Figure 8-12 shows how the PID system functions. The setpoint is set by the operator and is an input to a summing junction. The output from the level sensor becomes the feedback to the summing junction. The summing junction sums the setpoint and the feedback and generates an error. The PLC then uses the error as an input to the PID equation. There are three gains in the PID equation. The P gain is the proportional function and is the largest gain. It generates an output that is proportional to the error signal. If there is a large error, the proportional gain generates a large output. If the error is small, the proportional output is small. The proportional gain is based on the magnitude of the error, but it cannot completely correct an error.

The I gain is the integral gain, which is used to correct for small errors that persist over time. The P gain cannot correct for tiny errors, so the I gain is left to do the job.

The D gain is the derivative gain, and is used to correct for very rapidly changing errors. The derivative looks at the rate of change in the error. When an error occurs, the proportional gain attempts to correct for it. If the error is changing rapidly (e.g., maybe someone opened a furnace door), the P gain is insufficient to correct the error and the error continues to increase. The derivative would "see" the increase in the rate of the error and add a gain factor. If the error is decreasing rapidly, the D gain will damp the output. The derivative's damping effect enables the P gain to be set higher for quicker response and correction.

As you can see from Figure 8-12, the output from each of the P, I, and D equations is summed and an error (output) is generated. The output is used to bring the process back to setpoint.

Figures 8-13 and 8-14 show a block diagram of the whole system. As shown, the feedback from the process (tank level) is an input to an analog input module in the PLC. This input is used by the CPU in the PID equation and an output is generated from the analog output module. This output is used to control a variable valve that controls the flow of liquid into the tank. Note that there are always disturbances that

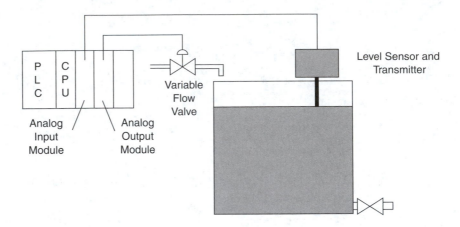

Figure 8-13 A level control system.

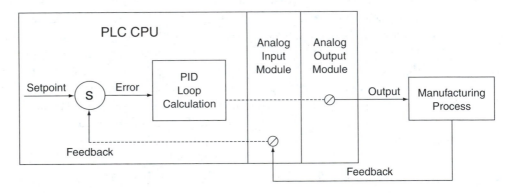

Figure 8-14 Block diagram of the use of a PLC and PID instruction to control a process.

affect the tank level. The temperature of the level affects the inflow and outflow. The outflow varies also due to density, atmospheric pressure, and many other factors. The inflow varies because of pressure of the fluid at the valve, density of the fluid, and many other factors. The PID instruction is able to account for disturbances and setpoint changes and control processes accurately.

Figure 8-15 shows the PID instruction. The user must provide some parameters. The first parameter is the control block. The control block is the file that will store the data used to operate the instruction. This file will occupy twenty-three words of memory. The user must enter the first address to be used. For example, if the user enters N7:10, the instruction will occupy addresses N7:0 through N7:22. Take care to use memory that is not used by other parts of the logic.

Figure 8-15 A PID
instruction.

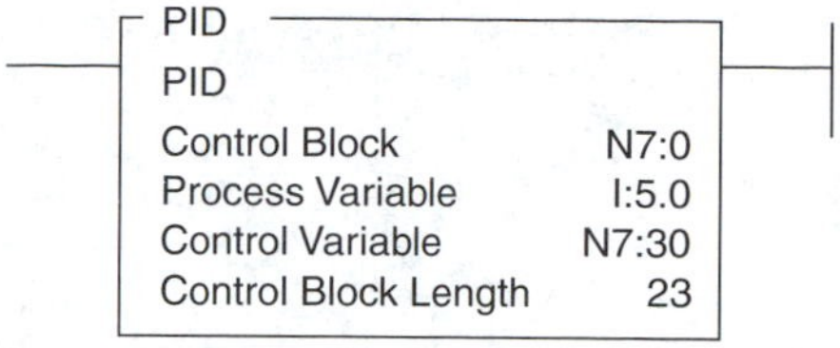

```
┌─ PID ──────────────────────────────────┐
│   PID                                   │
│   Control Block              N7:0       │
│   Process Variable           I:5.0      │
│   Control Variable           N7:30      │
│   Control Block Length       23         │
└─────────────────────────────────────────┘
```

The second parameter that must be entered is the process variable (PV). Think of this as the feedback from the process. It is usually the address of an analog input, although it could be an integer address if you want to scale the real-world input from the analog module and store it in an integer. In this case, the user entered I:5.0 for the address of the analog input.

The third parameter is the control variable (CV). Think of this as the output to the process. The output ranges from 0 to 16,383. Output 16,383 is the 100% on value, which is normally an integer value, so that the user can scale the PID output range to the range needed for your application. In this case, the user entered N7:30 for the address.

Next the user must enter the rest of the PID parameters. Clicking on the setup screen in the instruction brings up another parameter screen (Figure 8-16).

The first parameter is used to choose the automatic or manual mode. If the bit is set, the instruction functions in manual mode. The user enters it here and it is located in word 0, bit 1 of the control register file that you specified. In manual mode, the user is setting the output value. When you are tuning, it is suggested that you make changes in manual mode and then return to the auto mode. Note that if you set an output limit, it is applied in the manual and auto mode.

The second parameter is the time mode (TM). The user can choose between timed and STI. The user enters it here and it is located in word 0, bit 0 of the control register file that you specified. Timed means that the PID updates its output at the rate the user specifies in the loop update parameter. Note that the scan time of your ladder logic should be at least 10 times faster than your loop update time for the instruction to be accurate.

In the STI mode, the PID updates its output every time it is scanned. If you choose the STI mode, the PID instruction should be programmed in an STI subroutine, and the STI subroutine should have a time interval equal to the loop update parameter. The STI period is set in word S:30.

The next parameter is the control mode (CM) parameter. The control can be used to toggle between two modes: E=SP-PV (error = setpoint − present value) and E=PV-SP (error = present value − set point). E=PV-SP (direct acting) causes the output to

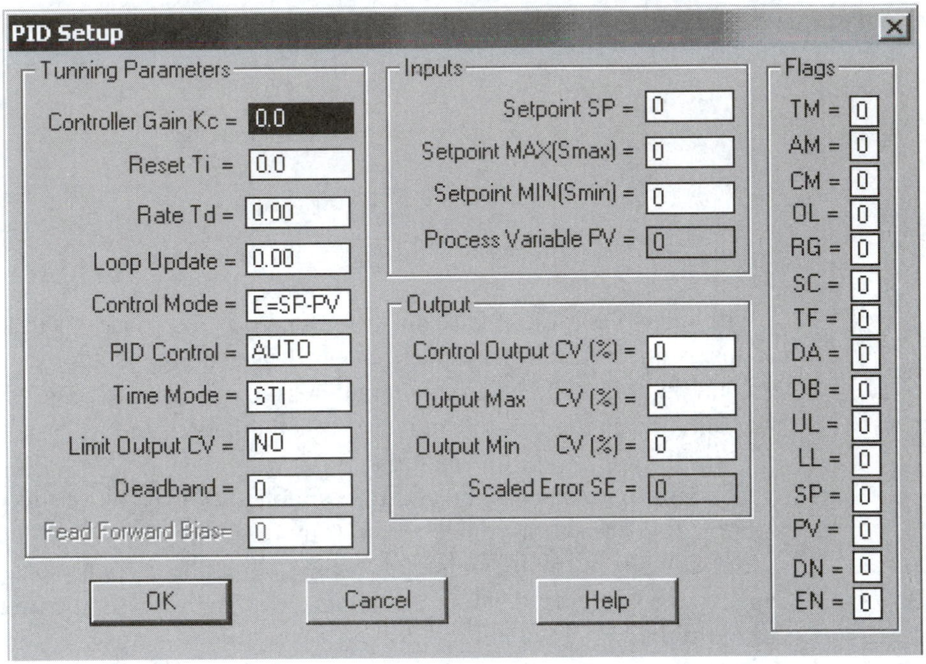

Figure 8-16 PID setup screen. *(Courtesy Rockwell Automation Inc.)*

increase when the input present value is larger than the setpoint. A cooling application might use direct acting. The other mode (E=SP-PV) is reverse acting. The output will increase when the input (PV) is less than the setpoint (SP). The user enters the choice here and it is located in word 0, bit 2 of the control register file that you specified.

The next parameter is the setpoint (SP). The setpoint is located in word 2 of the control register that you specified. You normally change this value with instructions in your ladder diagram. Your logic would move the desired value to word 3 of your control block. For example, if you had chosen N7:10 for the start address of your control register, you would move the desired setpoint value to N7:12. If you do not scale the range, this value is 0 to 16,383.

Gain (Kc) is located in word 3. It is the proportional gain, ranging from 0 to 3276.7 in most SLCs. A rule of thumb is to set the proportional gain to one-half the value that causes the output to oscillate when the reset (integral) and rate (derivative) are zeroed.

Reset (Ti) is located in word 4. It is the integral gain, with a valid range of values between −0 and 3276.7 minutes/repeat for most SLCs. A rule of thumb is to set the value equal to the natural period that is measured in the proportional gain calibration. Note that a value of 1 is the minimum integral term possible in the PID equation.

Rate (Td) is located in word 5. The rate is the derivative term, with a range of values from 0 to 3276.7 minutes for most SLCs. A rule of thumb is to set the value to one-eighth of the integral gain.

Maximum scaled (Smax) is located in word 7. If the setpoint is to be read in engineering units, this value corresponds to the value of the setpoint in engineering units when the control input is 16,383. In most SLCs the valid range is between −32,767 and +32,767.

Minimum scaled (Smin) is located in word 8. If the setpoint is read in engineering units, this parameter corresponds to the engineering value of the setpoint when the control output is 0. The valid range of values is between −32,767 and +32,767 for most SLCs.

Deadband (DB) is located in word 9. It must be a nonnegative value. The deadband extends above and below the value you enter. The deadband is entered at the zero crossing point of the PV and the SP. The deadband is only in effect after the PV enters the deadband and passes through the SP. The valid range is 0-scaled maximum or 0 to 16,383 if no scaling is done.

The loop update (word 13) is the time interval between PID calculations. The value is entered in 0.01-second intervals. The rule of thumb is to enter an update time 5 to 10 times faster than the natural period of the load. The natural period can be determined by setting the rate and reset parameters to 0 and then increasing the gain until the output begins to oscillate. If you are using the STI mode, this value must be equal to the STI time value. The valid range is between 0.01 and 10.24 seconds for most SLCs.

The next parameter is the scaled process (PV). It is located in word 14. This is the scaled value of the analog input PV. If not scaled, the value can be between 0 and 16,383.

Scaled error is only used for display. It is located in word 15. It is the scaled error as selected by the control mode parameter (E=SP-PV or E=PV=SP). The range is between −32,768 and +32,767. Errors smaller or larger than this cannot be represented.

Output CV% is located in word 16. This will display the actual output in terms of a percentage between 0 and 100. If you are in auto mode, this is only for display. If you are in manual mode, you can change the output percentage.

Output (CV) limit (OL) is located in word 0, bit 3. This parameter is used to toggle between yes and no. You would select yes if you want the output limited to the minimum and maximum values that you specify. The minimum output percentage is entered in the output (CV) minimum. The maximum output percentage is entered in the output (CV) maximum value.

The right column of parameters displays various flags associated with the PID instruction.

The TM bit (word 0, bit 0) specifies the PID mode. It is a 1 when the timed mode is selected and a 0 when the STI mode is in effect. You can set or clear this bit with your ladder logic.

The auto/manual (AM) bit is located in word 0, bit 1. This bit can be set or cleared by your ladder logic. If it is 0, the mode will be auto; if it is 1, the mode will be manual.

The CM bit is located in word 0, bit 2. If it is 1, the mode will be E= PV-SP; if it is 0, the mode will be E=SP-PV.

The output limiting enabled (OL) bit is in word 0, bit 3. It will be set if you have selected to limit the control variable. This bit can also be set or cleared in your ladder logic.

The reset and gain range enhancement (RG) bit is located in word 0, bit 4. If this bit is set, it causes the rest minute/repeat value and the gain multiplier to be enhanced by a factor of 10.

The scale setpoint flag (SC) bit is located in word 0, bit 5. It is cleared when setpoint scaling factors are specified.

The loop update time too fast (TF) bit is located in word 0, bit 6. It is set by the PID algorithm if the specified loop update time cannot be achieved because of scan time limitations.

The derivative (rate) action (DA) bit is located in word 0, bit 7. When this bit is set, it causes the derivative calculation to be evaluated based on the error instead of the PV. If the bit is clear, the derivative calculation is performed using the PV.

The DB, set when error in DB bit is located in word 0, bit 8. This bit is set when the process variable is within the deadband range.

The output alarm, upper limit (UL) bit is located in word 0, bit 9. This bit is set when the calculated control output CV exceeds the CV limit.

The output alarm, lower limit (LL) bit is located in word 0, bit 10. This bit is set when the calculated control output CV is less than the lower CV limit.

The setpoint out of range (SP) bit is located in word 0, bit 11. This bit is set when the setpoint exceeds the maximum scaled value or is less than the minimum scaled value.

The process var out of range (PV) bit is located in word 0, bit 12. It is set when the unscaled process variable exceeds 16,383 or is less than 0.

The PID done (DN) bit is located in word 0, bit 13. It is set on scan where the PID algorithm is computed. It is computed at the loop update rate.

The PID enabled (EN) bit is set when the rung of the PID instruction is enabled.

Applications involving transport lags may require that a bias be added to the CV output in anticipation of a disturbance. This bias can be accomplished using the processor by writing a value to the feed forward bias element, the seventh element (word 6) in the control block file. Figure 8-17 shows a block diagram of how the feedforward gain is added. The value you write is added to the output, allowing a feedforward action to take place. You may add a bias by writing a value between −16,383 and +16,383 to word 6 with your ladder logic or directly from the computer or handheld programmer.

The instruction set manual on the CD has a PID tuning procedure in the section on the PID instruction.

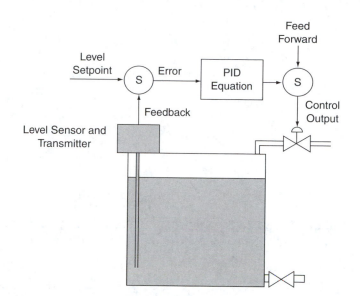

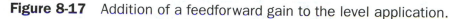

Figure 8-17   Addition of a feedforward gain to the level application.

SEQUENCERS

Before PLCs there were many innovative ways to control machines. One of the earliest control methods for machines was punched cards. These date back to the earliest automated weaving machines. Punched cards controlled the weave. Until just a few years ago, the main method of input to computers was punched cards.

Most manufacturing processes are highly sequential, meaning that they process a series of steps, from one to the next. Imagine a sequential bottling line: Bottles enter the line, are cleaned, filled, capped, inspected, and packed. Many of our home appliances work sequentially. The home washer, dryer, dishwasher, breadmaker, and so on, are examples of sequential control. Plastic injection molding, metal molding, packaging, and filling are a few examples of industrial processes that are sequential.

Many of these machines were (and some still are) controlled by a device called a drum controller. A drum controller functions just like a player piano. The player piano is controlled by a paper roll with holes punched in it. The holes represent the notes to be played. Their position across the roll indicates which notes should be played, and when they are to be played. A drum controller is the industrial equivalent. It is a cylinder with holes around the perimeter and pegs placed in the holes (Figure 8-18). The pegs hit switches as the drum turns. Each peg then turns, closing the switch that it contacts and turning on the output to which it is connected. The speed of the drum is controlled by a motor. The motor speed can be controlled, but each step must take the same amount of time. If an output must be on longer than one step, then consecutive pegs must be installed.

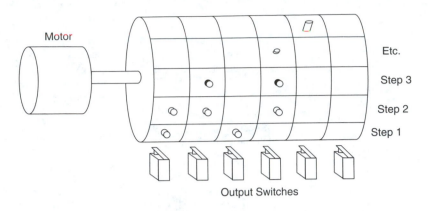

Figure 8-18   Drum controller. Note the pegs that activate switches as the drum is turned at slow speed by the motor. Figure 8-19 shows the output conditions for the steps.

Step #	Input Pump	Heater	Add Cleaner	Sprayer	Output Pump	Blower
1	On		On			
2	On	On		On		
3		On		On		
4				On		
5					On	

Figure 8-19   Output conditions for the drum controller shown in Figure 8-18.

The drum controller has several advantages. It is simple to understand, which makes it easy for a plant electrician to operate. It is also easy to maintain and program. The user makes a simple chart that shows which outputs are on in which steps (Figure 8-19). The user then installs the pegs to match the chart.

Many of our home appliances are also controlled with drum technology. Instead of a cylinder some utilize a disk with traces (Figure 8-20). Think of a washing machine. The user chooses the wash cycle by turning the setting dial to the proper position. The disk is then moved slowly as a synchronous motor turns. Brushes make contact with traces at the proper times and turn on output devices such as pumps and motors. Many home appliances utilize a control that works like the one shown in Figure 8-18, except that a series of camlike disks are used that activate switches to control the sequence.

Although there are many advantages to the drum type of control, it also has some major limitations. The time for individual steps cannot be controlled individually. The sequence is set and it does not matter if something goes wrong. The drum will continue

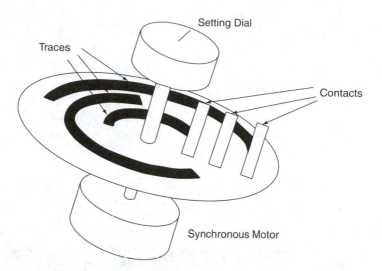

Figure 8-20   Disk-type drum controller. Some home appliances use these. Note that when you turn the dial you are actually turning the disk to its starting position.

to turn, and turn devices on and off. In other words, it would be nice if the step would not occur until certain conditions are met. PLC instructions have been designed to accomplish the good traits of drum controllers and also to overcome the weaknesses.

SEQUENCER INSTRUCTIONS

Sequencer instructions can be used for processes that are cyclical in nature. They can be used to monitor inputs to control the sequencing of the outputs, and can make programming many applications a much easier task. The sequencer is similar to the drum controller.

Processes with defined steps can be easily programmed with sequencer instructions.

There are three main instructions available in Rockwell Automation PLCs: sequencer output (SQO), sequencer compare (SQC), and sequencer load (SQL).

Imagine a sequential process of six steps. We could write the states of the outputs for every step (Figure 8-21). Note that in step 1, output 0 is on. In step 2, output 0 stays on and output 1 turns on.

This would be a good application for a sequencer instruction—a SQO instruction would be used. Figure 8-22 shows a simple ladder diagram with a timer and SQO instruction.

The first entry you need to make in the SQO is the file number to be used. File is the starting location in memory for our output conditions for each step. In this example, the starting file address is N7:0. The output states for each step are entered next, starting at N7:0 (Figure 8-23). This process has six steps, so they would be

Step #	Output 5	Output 4	Output 3	Output 2	Output 1	Output 0
1						On
2					On	On
3				On		On
4			On			
5		On		On		
6	On			On		

Figure 8-21 Table showing which outputs are on in which steps.

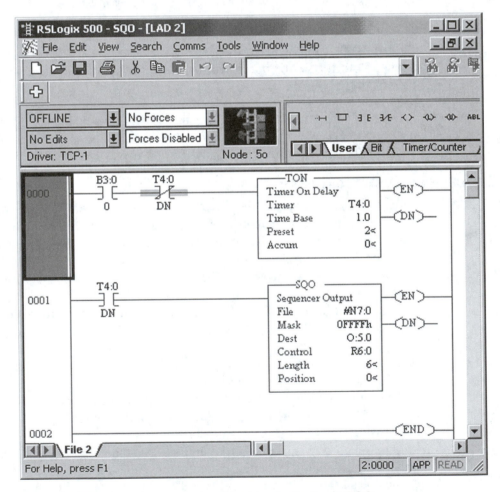

Figure 8-22 Simple example of ladder logic for a SQO.

RSLogix 500 - SQCNEW

File   Edit   View   Search   Comms   Tools   Window   Help

OFFLINE   No Forces
No Edits   Forces Disabled
Driver: TCP-1   Node : 7o

User   Bit   Timer/C

Data File N7 (bin) -- INTEGER

Offset	15	14	13	12	11	10	9	8	7	6	5	4	3	2	1	0
N7:0	0	0	0	0	0	0	0	0	0	0	0	0	0	0	0	1
N7:1	0	0	0	0	0	0	0	0	0	0	0	0	0	0	1	1
N7:2	0	0	0	0	0	0	0	0	0	0	0	0	0	1	0	1
N7:3	0	0	0	0	0	0	0	0	0	0	0	0	1	0	0	0
N7:4	0	0	0	0	0	0	0	0	0	0	0	1	0	1	0	0
N7:5	0	0	0	0	0	0	0	0	0	0	1	0	0	1	0	0
N7:6	0	0	0	0	0	0	0	0	0	1	0	1	0	0	0	0

N7:0/0   Radix: Binary
Symbol: Columns: 16
Desc:
N7   Properties   Usage   Help

For Help, press F1   0:0000   APP   READ

Figure 8-23   How desired output conditions are stored in memory.

located in words N7:0, N7:1, N7:2, N7:3, N7:4, N7:5, and N7:6. Note that this is actually seven words in memory. The first word used is for step 0. Step 0 is not actually part of our six operational steps. SQOs always start at step 0 the first time. When the SQO reaches the last step, however, it will reset to step 1 (position 1).

Next we would enter a mask. The mask can be a file in memory or one word (16 bits) in memory. If an address is entered for the mask value, the mask will be a list of values starting at the address specified in the mask value. For example, if the user enters N7:20, then N7:20 through N7:25 would be the location of the mask values for each of the six steps. The user would have to fill these locations with the

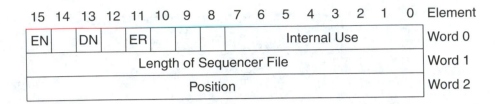

Figure 8-24   Memory organization for a SQO control memory.

desired mask values. In this example there are six steps, so each of the six mask values would correspond to one step.

A constant can also be used. If so, the SQO will use the constant as a mask for all of the steps. In our example, a hex number was entered (Figure 8-24). The four hex digits represent 16 bits. Each bit corresponds to one output in our SQO. If the bit is a 1 in the mask position, then the output is enabled and will turn on if the step condition tells it to be on. In other words, the bit conditions for the active step are ANDed with the mask. If the bit in the step is a 1 and the corresponding mask bit is a 1, the output will be set.

The destination is the location of the outputs. In this example the outputs are in O:5.0 (the output module in slot 5). This means that output 0 would be O:5/0, output 1 would be O:5/1, and so on.

Remember that the output states for each step are located in N7:1 through N7:6. When the ladder diagram is in the first step, output 0 will be on. In the next step, outputs 0 and 1 will be on. In the next step, outputs 0 and 2 will be on, and so it continues.

A file location must also be entered for control (Figure 8-22). Control is where the SQO stores status information for the instruction. A SQO or SQC uses three words in memory (Figure 8-24). The three bits are EN, DN, and ER bits. Word 1 contains the length of the sequencer (number of steps). Word 2 contains the current position (step in the sequence).

Length is the number of steps in the process starting at position 1. The maximum length is 255 words. Position 0 is the startup position. The first time the SQO is enabled it moves from position 0 to position 1. The instruction resets to position 1 at the end of the last step.

Position is the word location (or step) in the sequencer file from/to which the instruction moves data. In other words, position shows the number of the step that is currently active.

The enable (EN) bit (bit 15) is set by a false-to-true rung transition and indicates that the SQO instruction is enabled.

The done (DN) bit (bit 13) is set by the SQO instruction after it has operated on the last word in the sequencer file. It is reset on the next false-to-true rung transition after the rung goes false.

The error (ER) bit (bit 11) is set when the processor detects a negative position value or a negative or zero length value. This results in a major error if not cleared before the END or TND instruction is executed.

Let us see how this process would work. First, assume that it is a simple process and every step takes 2 seconds. A 2-second timer is used as the input condition to the SQO instruction. Every time the timer accumulated value reaches 2 seconds, the timer done bit forces the SQO instruction to move to the next step. That step's outputs are turned on for 2 seconds until the timer done bit enables the SQO again. The SQO then moves to the next step and sets any required outputs. Note that the timer done bit also resets the accumulated time in the timer to zero and the timer starts timing to 2 seconds again. When the SQO is in the last step and receives the enable again, the SQO will return to step 1 (note that the first time the ladder is executed the SQO will start at step 0).

In the last example, every step was the same length of time, but we are not always that fortunate. In most applications we would have specific input conditions that need to be met before we could move to the next step of the process. We can use any logic we would like to enable the SQO. It can get quite complex to set up all of the different conditions in logic. Fortunately, Rockwell Automation PLCs have a sequential compare (SQC) instruction that can make the task easy. If we make a list of the input conditions we need for every step, we can use those as a way to trigger the SQO (Figure 8-25).

Note that in the SQC in Figure 8-22 we had to give the instruction for the starting file number. In this example, N7:10 was entered as the starting address. The desired input conditions to move from step 1 to step 2 are entered into N7:11 (Figure 8-26). Remember that the sequencer will initially begin with step 0, and the actual program steps begin in step 1. The rest of the desired input conditions are entered as shown in Figure 8-27.

Figure 8-27 shows a SQC. File is the location of the first word of input conditions. Our example is a six-step process, so we would have six input words.

Step #	Input 3	Input 2	Input 1	Input 0
1		On		On
2		On	On	
3	On			
4			On	
5		On		
6	On			On

Figure 8-25 Input condition table. Note that if we are presently in step 2, we would need inputs 1 and 2 to be true to move to step 3.

RSLogix 500 - SQCNEW

File   Edit   View   Search   Comms   Tools   Window   Help

OFFLINE   No Forces
No Edits   Forces Disabled
Driver: TCP-1   Node : 7o

User Bit Timer/C

Data File N7 (bin) -- INTEGER

Offset	15	14	13	12	11	10	9	8	7	6	5	4	3	2	1	0
N7:10	0	0	0	0	0	0	0	0	0	0	0	0	0	0	0	0
N7:11	0	0	0	0	0	0	0	0	0	0	0	0	0	1	0	1
N7:12	0	0	0	0	0	0	0	0	0	0	0	0	0	1	1	0
N7:13	0	0	0	0	0	0	0	0	0	0	0	0	1	0	0	0
N7:14	0	0	0	0	0	0	0	0	0	0	0	0	0	0	1	0
N7:15	0	0	0	0	0	0	0	0	0	0	0	0	0	1	0	0
N7:16	0	0	0	0	0	0	0	0	0	0	0	0	1	0	0	1

N7:0/0   Radix: Binary

Symbol: Columns: 16

Desc:

N7   Properties   Usage   Help

For Help, press F1   0:0000   APP   READ

Figure 8-26   Desired input conditions in integer memory.

The mask is used just like it is with the SQO. The mask can be a file in memory or one word (16 bits) in memory. In our example, a constant will be used, but an address can be entered for the mask value. If an address is entered, the mask will be a list of values starting at the address specified in the mask value. For example, if the user enters N7:30, then N7:30 through N7:35 would be the locations of the mask values for each of the six steps. The user would have to fill these locations with the desired mask values. Each mask value would correspond to a step in the sequence. This example has six steps, so each of the six mask values would correspond to one step.

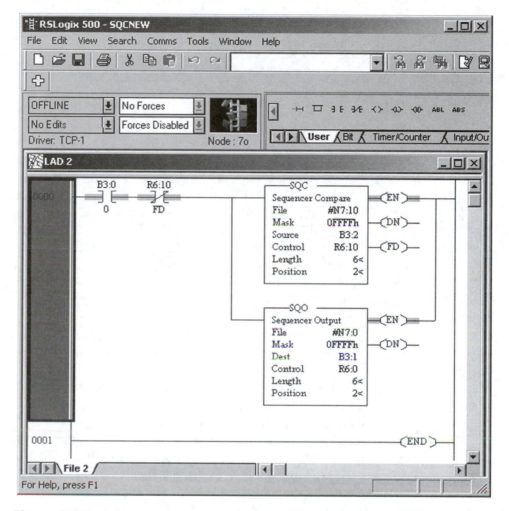

Figure 8-27 Ladder logic showing the use of a SQC and a SQO.

Otherwise a constant can be used. In our case, a hex constant is entered. The four hex digits correspond to 16 bits. If the bit is a 1 in the mask, that input is enabled. The source word (usually real-world input conditions) is ANDed with the mask value and compared with the current step (word) in the file. In this case, our input mask is 000FH. In this application, we are only interested in the states of the first four inputs. The 000FH (H = HEX) means the first four inputs are used and that the last sixteen are ignored (0000 0000 0000 1111).

Next the source must be entered. The source is the address of the real-world inputs. In this example, they are at I:4.0. The address I:4.0 would be sixteen inputs in the module in slot 4. The states of these real-world inputs will be compared with the desired inputs in the present step. If they are the same, the SQC position value

15	14	13	12	11	10	9	8	7	6	5	4	3	2	1	0	Element
EN		DN		ER			FD				Internal Use					Word 0
Length of Sequencer File																Word 1
Position																Word 2

Figure 8-28 Control register memory addressing for a SQC instruction.

is incremented to the next step and the FD bit is set in the control register. The FD bit (R6:10/FD in this case) was used to trigger the SQO to transition to the next step. This means that our desired input conditions can be used to control the transition from step to step in our process.

A file location must also be entered for control. Control is the location where the SQC stores status information for the instruction. A SQC uses three words in memory (Figure 8-28). The four bits that can be used are EN, DN, ER, and FD bits.

The enable (EN) bit (bit 15) is set by a false-to-true rung transition and indicates that the SQC instruction is enabled.

The done (DN) bit (bit 13) is set by the SQC instruction after it has operated on the last word in the sequencer file. It is reset on the next false-to-true rung transition after the rung goes false.

The error (ER) bit (bit 11) is set when the processor detects a negative position value or a negative or zero length value. This results in a major error if not cleared before the END or TND instruction is executed.

The found (FD) bit (bit 8) is set when the status of all nonmasked bits in the source address match those of the corresponding reference word. This bit assessed each time the SQC instruction is evaluated while the rung is true.

Word 1 contains the length of the sequencer (number of steps). Word 2 contains the current position.

Length must also be entered. Length is the number of steps in the process starting at position 1. The maximum length is 255 words. Position 0 is the startup position. The first time the SQO is enabled, it moves from position 0 to position 1. The instruction resets to position 1 at the end of the last step.

Position is the word location (or step) in the sequencer file from/to which the instruction moves data. In other words, position is the step that is currently active.

Sequencer Load Instruction

The sequencer load (SQL) instruction can be used to store source information (words) into memory. For example, input conditions could be stored into integer memory every time the SQL instruction sees a false-to-true transition. When it gets to the last position, it will transition back to step 1 when it sees the last false-to-true transition.

Station #	1	2	3	4	5	6	7	8
Part Present	1	0	0	0	1	0	0	1

Figure 8-29   What a shift register might look like when monitoring whether or not parts are present at processing stations. A 1 in the station location would be used to turn an output on and cause the station to process material. In this case, the PLC would turn on outputs at stations 1, 5, and 8. After processing has occurred, all bits would be shifted to the right. A new 1 or 0 would be loaded into the first bit, depending on whether a part was or was not present. The PLC would then turn on any stations that had a 1 in their bit. In this way, processing occurs only when parts are present.

Shift Resister Programming

A shift register is a storage location in memory. These storage locations can typically hold 16 bits of data, that is, 1s or 0s. Each 1 or 0 could be used to represent good or bad parts, presence or absence of parts, or the status of outputs (Figure 8-29). Many manufacturing processes are linear in nature. Recall the bottling line example used earlier. The bottles are cleaned, filled, capped, and so on, which is a linear process. There are sensors along the way to sense for the presence of a bottle, to check fill, and other steps. All of these conditions could easily be represented by 1s and 0s.

Shift registers essentially shift bits through a register to control I/O. In the bottling line are many processing stations, each represented by a bit in the shift register. We want to run the processing station only if there are parts present. As the bottles enter the line, a 1 is entered into the first bit. Processing takes place. The stations then release their product and each moves to the next station. The shift register also increments. Each bit is shifted one position. Processing takes place again. Each time a product enters the system, a 1 is placed in the first bit. The 1 follows the part all the way through production to make sure that each station processes it as it moves through the line. Shift register programming is applicable to linear processes.

QUESTIONS

1. What instruction could be used to fill a range of memory with the same number?

2. What instruction could be used to move an integer in memory to an output module?

3. What instruction could be used to make a copy of a range of memory and then copy it to a new place in memory?

4. What instruction could be used to move data if desired to mask some of the bits?

5. What does PID stand for?

6. What does the proportional gain do?

7. What does the integral gain do?

8. What does the derivative gain do?

9. Draw a PID instruction and set it up to use input 1 on an analog module in slot 3 and analog output 0 on an analog module in slot 4. Use appropriate addressing.

10. Describe the operation of an SQO.

11. Describe the operation of an SQC.

12. What are at least two advantages of SQO/SQC instructions over the traditional mechanical drum controller?

PROGRAMMING PRACTICE

RS Logix Relay Logic Instructions

These exercises utilize the LogixPro software included with this book. Go to the LogixPro Student Exercises and Documentation portion of the CD. Remember that the Rockwell Automation instruction set reference on the CD may be very helpful.

1. Complete the Word Compare Introductory exercise in LogixPro.
2. Complete Exercise 1—Traffic Control utilizing 1 Timer in LogixPro software.

EXTRA CREDIT

Complete Exercise 2—Dealing with Pedestrians in LogixPro software.

chapter

Industrial Sensors

In this chapter we examine types and uses of industrial sensors. Topics include digital and analog sensors and the wiring of sensors.

OBJECTIVES

Upon completion of this chapter, you will be able to:
1. Describe at least two ways in which sensors can be classified
2. Choose an appropriate sensor for a given application
3. Describe the typical uses of digital sensors
4. Describe the typical uses of analog sensors
5. Explain common sensor terminology
6. Explain the wiring of load- and line-powered sensors
7. Explain how field-effect sensors function
8. Explain the principle of operation of thermocouples
9. Explain such common thermocouple terms as *types* and *compensation*

THE NEED FOR SENSORS

Sensors have become vital in industry, because manufacturers are moving toward integrating pieces of computer-controlled equipment. In the past, operators were the brains of the equipment. The operator was the source of all information about

157

the operation of a process. The operator knew if parts were available, which parts were ready, if they were good or bad, if the tooling was okay, if the fixture was open or closed, and so on. The operator could sense problems in the operation through sight, sound, touch (vibration, etc.), and even smell.

Industry is now using computers (in many cases PLCs) to control the motions and sequences of machines. PLCs are much faster and more accurate than an operator at these tasks, but they cannot see, hear, feel, smell, or taste processes alone. Industrial sensors equip industrial controllers with these capabilities.

Simple sensors can be used by the PLC to check if parts are present or absent, to size the parts, even to check if the product is empty or full. The use of sensors to track processes is vital for the success of the manufacturing process and to ensure the safety of the equipment and operator.

Sensors, in fact, perform simple tasks more efficiently and accurately than people do. Sensors are much faster and make far fewer mistakes.

Studies have been done to evaluate how effective human beings are in tedious, repetitive inspection tasks. One study examined people inspecting table tennis balls. A conveyor line was set up to bring table tennis balls past a person. White balls were considered good, black balls were considered scrap. The study showed that people were 70 percent effective at finding the defective balls. Certainly people can find all of the black balls, but they do not perform mundane, tedious, repetitive tasks well. People become bored and make mistakes, whereas a simple sensor can perform simple tasks almost flawlessly.

SENSOR TYPES

Contact versus Noncontact

Sensors are classified in a number of ways. One common way is to divide sensors into two categories: contact and noncontact. If the device must contact a part to sense the part, then it would be called a *contact sensor.* A simple limit switch on a conveyor is an example. When the part moves the lever on the switch, the switch changes state. The contact of the part and the switch creates a change in state that the PLC can monitor.

Noncontact sensors can detect the product without touching the product physically. They are also called proximity sensors, which is a simple method of identification. Noncontact sensors do not operate mechanically (no moving parts). Mechanical devices are much less reliable than electronic devices. This means that noncontact sensors are less likely to fail. Speed is another consideration. Electronic devices are much faster than mechanical devices. Noncontact devices can perform at very high production rates. Another advantage of not touching the product is that you do not slow or interfere with the process. The remainder of the chapter focuses on noncontact sensors.

Digital versus Analog

Another way in which sensors can be classified is digital or analog. Digital sensors are the easiest to use. A computer actually works only with 1s or 0s (on or off). A digital sensor has two states: on or off. Most applications involve presence/absence and counting. A digital sensor meets this need perfectly and inexpensively.

Digital output sensors are either on or off. They generally have transistor outputs. If the sensor senses an object, then the output will turn on. The transistor turns on and allows current to flow. The output from the sensor is usually connected to a PLC input module.

Sensors are available with either normally closed or normally open output contacts. Normally open contact sensors are off until they sense an object. Normally closed contact sensors are on until they sense an object. When they sense an object, the output turns off.

When photo sensors are involved, the terms *light-on* and *dark-on* are often used. Dark-on means that the sensor output is on when there is no light returned to the sensor, similar to a normally closed condition. A light-on sensor's output is on when light is returned to the receiver, similar to a normally open sensor.

The current limit for most sensors' output is quite low. Usually output current must be limited to under 100 mA. Check the sensor before turning on the power. You must limit the output current or you will destroy the sensor! This is usually not a problem if the sensor is being connected to a PLC input, because the PLC input will limit the current to a safe amount.

Analog sensors are more complex but can provide much more information about a process. Analog sensors are also called *linear output sensors.*

Think about a sensor used to measure temperature. A temperature is analog information. The temperature in the Midwest is usually between 0° and 90° F. An analog sensor could sense the temperature and send a current to the PLC. The higher the temperature, the higher the output from the sensor. The sensor may, for example, output between 4 and 20 mA, depending on the actual temperature. There is an unlimited number of temperatures (and thus current outputs). Remember that the output from the digital sensor is either on or off. The output from the analog sensor can be any value in the range from low to high; thus, the PLC can monitor temperature accurately and control a process closely. Pressure sensors are also available in analog style. They provide a range of output voltage (or current) depending on the pressure.

A 4 to 20 mA current loop system can be used for applications in which the sensor needs to be mounted a long distance from the control device. A 4 to 20 mA loop is good to about 800 meters. A 4 to 20 mA sensor varies its output between 4 and 20 mA. There must be an adjustment on the sensor to adjust the range and sensitivity, so that the sensor can measure the required values of the characteristic of interest, such as temperature.

There are needs for both digital and analog sensors in industrial applications. Digital sensors are more widely used because of their simplicity and ease of use. Certain applications, however, require information that only analog sensors can provide.

DIGITAL SENSORS

Digital sensors come in many types and styles. Types of digital sensors are examined in this section.

Optical Sensors

Optical sensors use light to sense objects. All optical sensors function in approximately the same manner. There is a light source (emitter) and a photodetector to sense the presence or absence of light. LEDs are typically used for the light source. An LED is a semiconductor (PN type) diode that emits light. Forward-biased electrons from the N-type material enter the P-type material, where they combine with excess holes. When an electron and a hole combine, energy is released. These energy packets are called photons. Photons then escape as light energy. The type of material used for the semiconductor determines the wavelength of the emitted light.

LEDs are chosen because they are small, sturdy, efficient, reliable, and can be turned on and off at extremely high speeds. They operate in a narrow wavelength and are not sensitive to temperature, shock, or vibration. LEDs also have an almost endless life.

The LEDs in sensors are used in a pulsed mode. The emitter is pulsed (turned off and on repeatedly). The "on time" is extremely small compared with the "off time." LEDs are pulsed so that the sensor is unaffected by ambient light and so that the life (modulation) of the LED is increased.

The pulsed light is sensed by the photodetector. The photo emitter and photo receiver are both "tuned" to the frequency of the modulation. The photodetector essentially sorts out all ambient light and looks for only the correct frequency. The light sources chosen are typically invisible to the human eye. The wavelengths are chosen so that the sensors are not affected by other lighting in the plant. The use of different wavelengths allows some sensors, called color mark sensors, to differentiate between colors. Visible sensors are normally used for this purpose. The pulse method and the wavelength chosen make optical sensors very reliable.

Some applications utilize ambient light. Red-hot materials such as glass or metal emit infrared light. Photo receivers that are sensitive to infrared light can be used in these applications.

All the various types of optical sensors function in the same basic manner. The differences are in the way in which the light source (emitter) and receiver are packaged.

Light/Dark Sensing   Optical sensors are available in either light or dark sensing (light-on or dark-on). In fact, many sensors can be switched between light and dark modes. Light/dark sensing refers to the normal state of the sensor, whether its output is on or off in its normal state.

Light Sensing (Light-On)   The output is energized (on) when the sensor receives the modulated beam. In other words, the sensor is on when the beam is unobstructed.

Dark Sensing (Dark-On)   The output is energized (on) when the sensor does not receive the modulated beam. In other words, the sensor is on when the beam is blocked. Street lights are examples of dark-on sensors. When it gets dark outside, the street light turns on.

Timing Functions   Timing functions are available on some optical sensors. They are available with on-delay and off-delay. *On-delay* delays the turning on of the output by a user-selectable amount. *Off-delay* holds the output on for a user-specified time after the object has moved away from the sensor.

Types of Optical Sensors

Reflective Sensors   A common type of optical sensor is the reflective or diffuse reflective sensor. The emitter and receiver are packaged in the same unit. The emitter sends out light, which bounces off the product to be sensed. The reflected light returns to the receiver where it is sensed (Figure 9-1). Reflective sensors have less sensing distance (range) than other types of optical sensors because they rely on light reflected off the product.

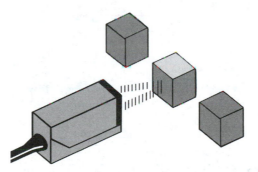

Figure 9-1   Reflective-type sensor. The light emitter and receiver are in the same package. When the light from the emitter bounces off an object, it is sensed by the receiver and the output of the sensor changes state. The broken-line style of the arrows represents the pulsed mode of lighting, which is used to ensure that ambient lighting does not interfere with the application. The sensing distance (range) of this style is limited by how well the object can reflect the light back to the receiver. *(Courtesy ifm efector, inc.)*

Polarizing Photo Sensors   The polarizing photo sensor is a special kind of sensor for shiny objects. This sensor uses a special reflector that consists of small prisms which polarize the light from the sensor. The sensor emits horizontally polarized light. The reflector vertically polarizes the light and reflects it back to the sensor receiver. Thus, if a very shiny object moves between the sensor and reflector and reflects light back to the sensor, it will be ignored because it is not vertically polarized (Figure 9-2).

Retroreflective Sensor   The retroreflective sensor is similar to the reflective sensor (Figure 9-3). The emitter and receiver are both mounted in the same package. The difference is that the retroreflective sensor bounces the light off a reflector instead of the product. The reflector is similar to those used on bicycles.

Retroreflective sensors have more sensing distance (range) than reflective (diffuse) sensors, but less sensing distance than that of a thru-beam sensor. They are a good choice when scanning can be done from only one side of the application, which can occur when space is an issue.

Figure 9-2 A polarizing photo sensor. Note the use of the special reflector.

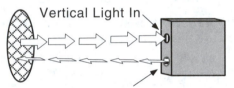

Vertical Light In

Horizontal Light Out

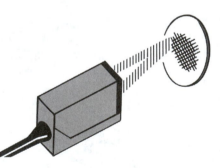

Figure 9-3 Retroreflective sensor. The light emitter and receiver are in the same package. The light bounces off a reflector (similar to the reflector on a bicycle) and is sensed by the receiver. If an object obstructs the beam, the output of the sensor changes state. The excellent reflective characteristics of a reflector give this sensor more sensing range than a typical diffuse style, where the light bounces off the object. The broken-line arrows represent the pulsed method of lighting that is used. *(Courtesy ifm efector, inc.)*

Figure 9-4 Thru-beam sensor. The emitter and receiver are in separate packages. The broken line symbolizes the pulsed mode of the light that is used in optical sensors. *(Courtesy ifm efector, inc.)*

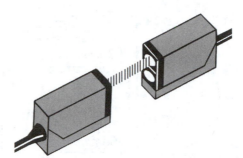

Figure 9-5 Fiber-optic sensor. *(Courtesy ifm efector, inc.)*

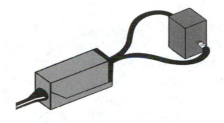

Thru-Beam Sensor   Another common sensor is the thru-beam (Figure 9-4). This mode can also be called the *beam break* mode. In this configuration, the emitter and receiver are packaged separately. The emitter sends out light across a space and the light is sensed by the receiver. If the product passes between the emitter and receiver, it stops the light from hitting the receiver and the sensor knows there is product present. This is probably the most reliable sensing mode for opaque (nontransparent) objects.

Fiber-Optic Sensors   Fiber-optic sensors are simply mixes of the other types. The actual emitter and receiver are the same, with fiber-optic cables attached to both the emitter and the receiver. Fiber-optic cables are small and flexible. They are transparent strands of plastic or glass fibers that are used as a "light pipe" to carry light.

The light from the emitter passes through the cable and exits from the other end. The light enters the end of the cable attached to the receiver, passes through the cable, and is sensed by the receiver. The cables are available in both thru-beam and reflective configuration (Figure 9-5).

ELECTRONIC FIELD SENSORS

Field sensors are used to sense objects. The two types include capacitive and inductive. Both types of field sensors produce an electromagnetic field. If the field is interrupted by an object, the sensor turns on. An inductive sensor creates a field that is sensitive to metal. A capacitive sensor is sensitive to any object. Special types of field sensors are available for various uses. Field sensors are a good choice in dirty

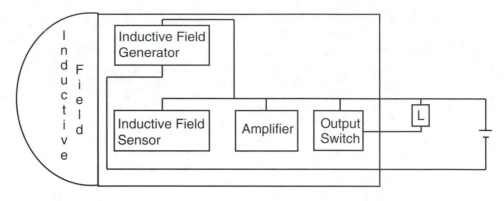

Figure 9-6   Block diagram of an inductive sensor. The inductive field generator creates an inductive field in front of the sensor. This field is monitored by the field sensor. When metal enters the field, the field is disrupted. The disruption in the field is sensed by the field sensor and the output of the sensor changes state. The sensing distance of these sensors is determined by the size of the field. This means that the larger the required sensing range, the larger the diameter of the sensor will be.

or wet environments, because a photo sensor can be affected by dirt, liquids, or air-borne contamination.

The two most common types of field sensors function in essentially the same way. They have a field generator and a sensor to sense interference. Imagine the magnetic field from a magnet; the field generator puts out a similar field.

Inductive Sensors

The inductive sensor is used to sense metallic objects by the principle of electro-magnetic induction (Figure 9-6). Inductive sensors function in a manner similar to the primary and secondary windings of a transformer. The oscillator and coil in the sensor produce a weak magnetic field. As an object enters the sensing field, small eddy currents are induced on the surface of the object. Because of the interference with the magnetic field, energy is drawn away from the oscillator circuit of the sensor. The amplitude of the oscillation decreases, causing a voltage drop. The detector circuit of the sensor senses the voltage drop of the oscillator circuit and responds by changing the state of the sensor.

Sensing Distance   Sensing distance (range) is related to the size of the inductor coil and whether the sensor coil is shielded or nonshielded (Figure 9-7). When the sensor coil is shielded, a copper band goes around the coil to prevent the field from extending beyond the sensor diameter. Note that this reduces the sensing distance.

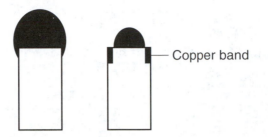

Figure 9-7 The use of a copper band in a shielded field sensor. Note that the sensing distance is reduced. It does allow the sensor to be mounted flush, however. If the unshielded sensor were mounted flush, it would detect the object in which it was mounted.

Figure 9-8 Example of hysteresis. Note that the on-point and off-point are different.

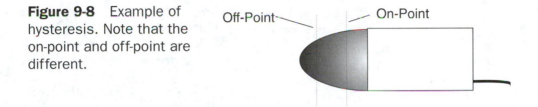

The shielded sensor has about half the sensing range of an unshielded sensor. Sensing distance also is affected by temperature, varying by about 5 percent due to changes in ambient temperature.

Hysteresis Hysteresis means that the object must be closer to turn a sensor on than to turn it off (Figure 9-8). Direction and distance are important. If the object is moving toward the sensor, it will have to move to the closer point to turn on. Once the sensor turns on (operation point or on-point), it will remain on until the object moves away to the release point (off-point). This differential gap, or travel, is caused by hysteresis. The principle is used to eliminate the possibility of "teasing" the sensor, which is either on or off.

Hysteresis is a built-in feature in proximity sensors which benefits us because it helps stabilize part sensing. Imagine a bottle moving down a conveyor line. Vibration causes the bottle to wiggle as it moves along the conveyor. If the on-point was the same as the off-point, and the bottle was wiggling as it went by the sensor, it could be sensed many times as it wiggles in and out past the on-point. When hysteresis is involved, however, the on-point and off-point are at different distances from the sensor.

To turn the sensor on, the object must be closer than the on-point. The sensor output will remain on until the object moves farther away than the off-point. This prevents multiple unwanted reads.

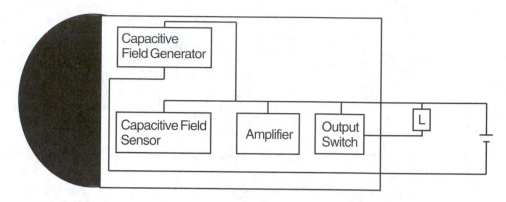

Figure 9-9 Block diagram of a capacitive sensor.

Figure 9-10 Capacitive sensors. *(Courtesy ifm efector, inc.)*

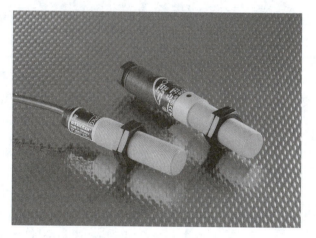

Capacitive Sensors

Capacitive sensors (Figures 9-9 and 9-10) can be used to sense both metallic and nonmetallic objects. They are commonly used in the food industry. Capacitive sensors can also be used to sense for product inside nonmetallic containers (Figure 9-11).

Capacitive sensors operate on the principle of electrostatic capacitance. They function in a manner similar to the plates of a capacitor. The oscillator and electrode produce an electrostatic field. (Remember that the inductive sensor produced an electromagnetic field.) The target (object to be sensed) acts as the second plate of a capacitor. An electric field is produced between the target and the sensor. As the amplitude of the oscillation increases, the oscillator circuit voltage increases and the detector circuit responds by changing the state of the sensor.

Almost any object can be sensed by a capacitive sensor. The object acts like a capacitor to ground. When the target (object) enters the electrostatic field, the DC

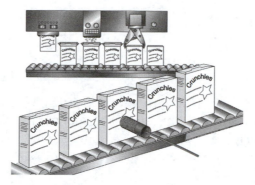

Figure 9-11   Use of a capacitive sensor to check inside boxes. They are also used to check fluid and solid levels inside tanks. An adjustment screw on some capacitive sensors allows them to be adjusted so that the container is not sensed, rather the material inside. *(Courtesy ifm efector, inc.)*

balance of the sensor circuit is disturbed. This starts the electrode circuit oscillation and maintains the oscillation as long as the target is within the field.

Sensing Distance   Capacitive sensors are unshielded, nonembedding devices (Figure 9-10), which means that they cannot be installed flush in a mount because they would then sense the mount. Conducting materials can be sensed farther away than nonconductors because the electrons in conductors are freer to move. The target mass affects the sensing distance: The larger the mass, the larger the sensing distance.

Capacitive sensors are more sensitive than inductive sensors to temperature and humidity fluctuation. Sensing distance can fluctuate as much as plus or minus 15 to 20 percent. Capacitive sensors are not as accurate as inductive sensors. Repeat accuracy can vary by 10 to 15 percent in capacitive sensors.

Some capacitive sensors are available with a sensitivity adjustment. This can be used to sense product inside a container (Figure 9-11). The sensitivity can be reduced so that the container is not sensed, but the product inside is.

SENSOR WIRING

The two basic wiring schemes for sensors are load powered and line powered. This applies to AC- and DC-powered sensors.

Sensors are available in two-wire and three-wire types. The most important consideration must be to limit the sensor's output current to an acceptable level. Output current refers to the sensor's output. The output device in the sensor is normally a transistor. If the output current exceeds the output current limit, then the sensor will fail. Check the specifications for the sensor. A sensor with a transistor output

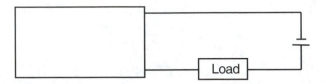

Figure 9-12 Two-wire sensor (load powered). The load represents whatever the technician will be monitoring the sensor output with. It is normally a PLC input. The load must limit the current to an acceptable level for the sensor, or the sensor output will be blown.

Figure 9-13 Leakage current versus supply voltage. *(Courtesy PLC Direct by Koyo.)*

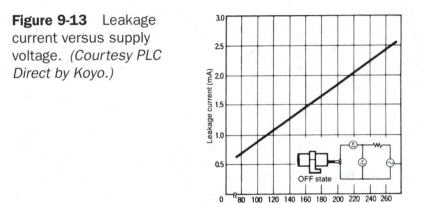

can generally handle up to about 100 mA. Sensors with a relay output can handle 1A or more.

Load-Powered Sensors

Two-wire sensors are called load-powered sensors. One wire is connected to power, the other wire is connected to a load wire (Figure 9-12). The other load wire is then connected to power. Wiring diagrams can usually be found on the sensor.

The current required for the sensor to operate must pass through the load. A load is anything that will limit the current of the sensor output. Think of the load as being an input to a PLC. The small current flow that allows the sensor to operate is called leakage current, or operating current.

This current is typically under 2.0 mA (Figure 9-13), which is enough current for the sensor to operate, but not enough to turn on the input of the PLC. (The leakage current is usually not enough current to activate a PLC input. If it is enough current to turn on the PLC input, it will be necessary to connect a bleeder resistor,

Figure 9-14 Use of a two-wire sensor (load powered). In this case the leakage current was enough to cause the input module to sense an input when there was none. A resistor was added to bleed the leakage current to ground so that the input could not sense it.

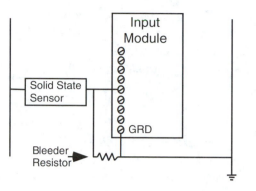

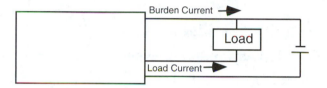

Figure 9-15 Three-wire (line-powered) sensor. Note the load—it must limit the current to an acceptable level.

as shown in Figure 9-14.) When the sensor turns on, it allows enough current to flow to turn on the PLC input.

Response time is the lapsed time between the target being sensed and the output changing state. Response time can be crucial in high-production applications. Sensor specification sheets will give response times.

Line-Powered Sensors

Line-powered sensors are usually the three-wire type (Figure 9-15), but there can be either three or four wires. There are two power leads and one output lead in the three-wire variety.

The sensor needs a small current, called burden current or operating current, to operate. This current flows whether the sensor output is on or off. The load current is the output from the sensor. If the sensor is on, there is load current. This load current turns the load (PLC input) on. The maximum load current is typically between 50 to 200 mA for most sensors. Make sure that you limit the load (output) current or the sensor will be ruined. Note that it is possible for the output LED on a sensor to function and the output still be bad.

Figure 9-16 A sourcing switch connected to a PLC input. *(Courtesy AutomationDirect, Inc.)*

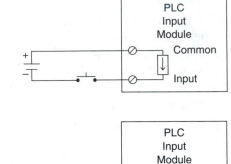

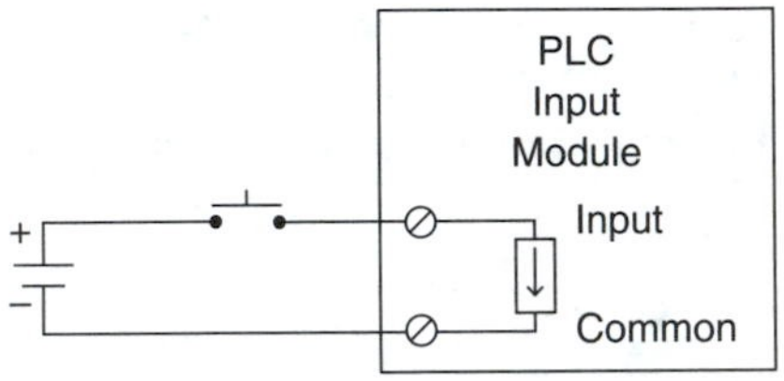

Figure 9-17 A sinking switch connected to a PLC input. *(Courtesy AutomationDirect, Inc.)*

SOURCING AND SINKING SENSORS

PNP Sensor (Sourcing Type)

Conventional current flow goes from plus to minus. When the sensor is off, the current does not flow through the load. In the case of a PNP, when there is an output current from the sensor, the sensor sources current to the load (sourcing type) (Figure 9-16).

NPN Sensor (Sinking Type)

When the sensor is off (nonconducting), there is no current flow through the load. When the sensor is conducting, there is a load current flowing from the load to the sensor (Figure 9-17). The choice of whether to use an NPN or a PNP sensor is dependent on the type of load. In other words, choose a sensor that matches the PLC input module requirements for sinking or sourcing.

Sinking = Path to supply ground $(-)$
Sourcing = Path to supply source $(+)$

ANALOG SENSORS

There are many types of analog sensors available. Many of the types already discussed are also available with analog output, including photo sensors and field sensors.

Analog Considerations

Analog sensors provide much more information about a process than do digital sensors. They provide an output that varies depending on the conditions being measured.

Accuracy, Precision, and Repeatability

Accuracy can be defined as how closely a sensor indicates the true quantity being measured. In a temperature measurement, accuracy would be defined as how closely the sensor indicates the actual temperature being measured.

Precision refers to a group of sensors. Precision is a measure of how closely each measures the same variable. For example, if we measured a given temperature, the output of each should be the same. This factor is vital to many applications (e.g., when we need to replace a sensor).

Repeatability is the ability of a sensor to repeat its previous readings. For example, in temperature measurement, the sensor's output should be the same every time it senses a given temperature.

Thermocouples

The thermocouple is one of the most common devices for temperature measurement in industrial applications. The principle of thermocouples was discovered by Thomas J. Seebeck in 1821. A thermocouple is a simple device: two pieces of dissimilar metal wire joined at one or both ends (Figure 9-18). The typical industrial thermocouple is joined at one end. The other ends of the wire are connected via compensating wire to the analog inputs of a control device such as a PLC. The principle of operation is that when dissimilar metals are joined, it produces a small voltage. The voltage output is proportional to the difference in temperature between the cold and hot junctions (Figure 9-19). Thermocouples are color-coded for polarity and also for type. The negative terminal is red and the positive terminal is a different color used to identify the thermocouple type. The cold junction is assumed to

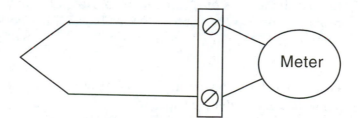

Figure 9-18 Common thermocouple connection. Note that the actual thermocouple wires are only connected to each other on one end. The other end of each is connected to copper wire, which in this case is connected to a meter. They are normally connected at a terminal strip. The terminal strip ensures that both ends remain at the same temperature (ambient temperature). The net loop voltage remains the same as the double-ended loop.

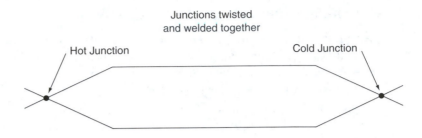

Figure 9-19   Simple thermocouple. A thermocouple can be made by twisting the desired type of wire together and silver soldering the end. To measure the temperature change, the wire would be cut in the middle and a meter inserted. The voltage would be proportional to the difference in temperature between the hot and cold junctions.

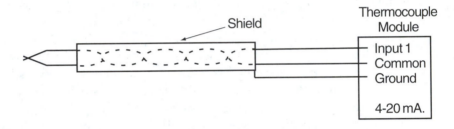

Figure 9-20   Thermocouple. Note that the wire connecting the thermocouple to the PLC module is twisted-pair (two wires twisted around each other) shielded cable. The shield around the twisted pair is to help eliminate electrical noise as a problem. Twisted-pair wiring also helps reduce the effects of electrical noise. Note also that the shielding is grounded only at the control device. Typical PLC modules would allow four or more analog inputs.

be at ambient temperature (room temperature). Figure 9-20 shows a thermocouple connected to an input module.

Industrial thermocouple tables use 75°F for the reference temperature. The thermocouple "types" identify the range of temperatures that can be measured (see Figure 9-21). Figure 9-22 shows a graph of voltage output versus temperature for two types of thermocouples. Note the range in which the output is linear.

In reality, temperatures vary considerably in an industrial environment. If the cold junction varies with the ambient temperature, the readings will be inaccurate. This would be unacceptable in most industrial applications. It is too complicated to maintain the cold junction at 75°F. Industrial thermocouples must therefore be

Type	Temperature (°F)	Temperature (°C)
J	−50 to +1400	−40 to +760
K	−100 to +2250	−80 to +1240
T	−200 to +660	−130 to +350
E	−200 to +680	−130 to +1250
R	0 to +3200	−20 to +1760
S	0 to +3200	−20 to +1760
B	+500 to +3200	+260 to +1760
C	0 to +4200	−20 to +2320

Figure 9-21 Temperature ranges for various types of thermocouples. Note the output for the difference in temperature between the hot and cold junctions. The table is based on a cold junction temperature of 75°F.

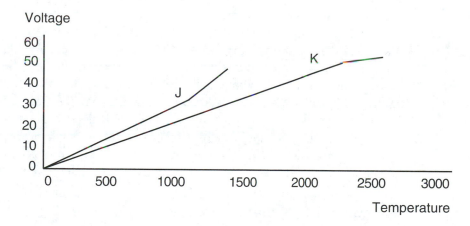

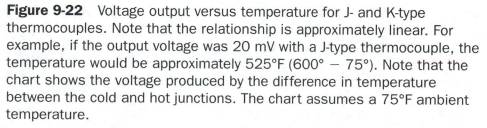

Figure 9-22 Voltage output versus temperature for J- and K-type thermocouples. Note that the relationship is approximately linear. For example, if the output voltage was 20 mV with a J-type thermocouple, the temperature would be approximately 525°F (600° − 75°). Note that the chart shows the voltage produced by the difference in temperature between the cold and hot junctions. The chart assumes a 75°F ambient temperature.

E	Nickel-Chromium vs. Copper-Nickel (Chromel-Constantan)
J	Iron vs. Copper-Nickel (Iron-Constantan)
K	Nickel-Chromium vs. Nickel-Aluminum (Chromel-Alumel)
T	Copper vs. Copper-Nickel (Copper-Constantan)
C	Tungsten 5% Rhenium vs. Tungsten 26% Rhenium
D	Tungsten vs. Tungsten 26% Rhenium
G	Tungsten 3% Rhenium vs. Tungsten 25% Rhenium
R	Platinum vs. Platinum 13% Rhodium
S	Platinum vs. Platinum 10% Rhodium
B	Platinum 6% Rhodium vs. Platinum 30% Rhodium

Figure 9-23   Composition of various thermocouple types.

compensated, normally with the use of resistor networks that are temperature sensitive. The resistors that are used have a negative coefficient of resistance: Resistance decreases as the temperature increases. This adjusts the voltage automatically so that readings remain accurate. PLC thermocouple modules automatically compensate for temperature variation.

The thermocouple is an accurate device. The resolution is determined by the device that takes the output from the thermocouple. The device is normally a PLC analog module. The typical resolution of an industrial analog module is 12 bits; 2^{12} is 4096; thus, if the range of temperature to be measured was 1200°F the resolution would be 0.29296875°/bit (1200/4096 = 0.29296875), which would mean that our PLC could tell the temperature to about 0.25°. This is reasonably good resolution—close enough for the vast majority of applications. Higher-resolution analog modules are available. Thermocouples are the most widely used temperature sensors, with various types available. Figure 9-23 shows the composition of some of the common thermocouples.

Resistance Temperature Device

A resistance temperature device (RTD) is a device that changes resistance with temperature. One of a metal's basic properties is that its electrical resistivity changes with temperature. Some metals have a predictable change in resistance for a given change in temperature. An RTD is basically a precision resistor. The chosen metal is made into a resistor with a nominal resistance at a given temperature. The change in temperature can then be determined by comparing the resistance at the unknown temperature to the known nominal resistance at the known temperature.

RTDs are made from a pure wire-wound metal that has a positive temperature coefficient. These are naturally occurring metals, which means that as the temperature increases, the resistance to current flow increases. There also is a very small change in resistance.

RTDs come in two configurations. One is a wire-wound construction. This coiled construction allows for a greater change in resistance for a given change in temperature. This increases the sensor's sensitivity and helps improve the resolution. The coil is wrapped around a nonconductive material such as ceramic to help the wire respond more quickly to temperature change. The coil is then covered by a sheath to protect it from abuse and the environment. The sheath is also filled with a dry, thermal conducting gas to increase the temperature conductivity. The sheath is constructed from materials that are very temperature conductive. Stainless steel is the usual choice.

There are tables available from manufacturers that show the temperature-resistance relationships for various metals used in RTDs.

Platinum is the most popular material for RTDs. Other materials include copper, nickel, balco, tungsten, and iridium. Platinum sensors are now being made with very thin film resistance elements that use a small amount of platinum. This makes platinum RTDs more competitive in price. Platinum has a very linear change in resistance versus temperature and has a wide operating range. Platinum is also a very stable element, which ensures long-term stability.

RTDs are connected like resistors. The most common resistance for an RTD is 100 ohms at 0°C. Other RTDs are available in the 50 to 1000 ohm range.

Wiring An RTD is really a two-wire device like a resistor. The lead wires from the RTD can affect the accuracy of the RTD, because of the additional uncompensated resistance. A third wire can be added to compensate for lead wire resistance.

Four-wire RTDs also are available but are generally only used in laboratory applications. A four-wire RTD can be used with a three-wire device, but it does not improve the accuracy over a three-wire RTD. A three-wire RTD, however, cannot be used with a four-wire device. It is best to use the appropriate RTD for the measurement device (Figure 9-24).

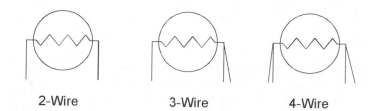

2-Wire   3-Wire   4-Wire

Figure 9-24 Three RTD wiring configurations.

The other RTD configuration is a thin film metal layer that has been deposited on a nonthermally conductive substrate (e.g., ceramic). These can be made very small and do not require an external sheath, because the ceramic serves as a protective sheath. Simple circuitry can be used to linearize RTDs, which are more accurate than thermocouples.

INSTALLATION CONSIDERATIONS

Electrical

The main consideration for sensors is to limit the load current. The output (load) current must be limited on most sensors to a very small output current, typically between 50 and 200 mA. If the load draws more than the sensor current limit, the sensor fails and you buy a new one. More sensors probably fail because of improper wiring than from use. It is crucial that you carefully limit current to a level that the sensor can handle. PLC input modules limit the current to acceptable levels. Some sensors are available with relay outputs. These can handle higher load currents (typically 3A).

If high-voltage wiring is run in close proximity to sensor cabling, the cabling should be run in a metal conduit to prevent the sensor from false sensing, malfunction, or damage. The other main consideration is to buy the proper polarity sensors. If the PLC module requires sinking devices, be sure to purchase them.

Mechanical

Sensors should be mounted horizontally when possible to prevent the buildup of chips and debris on the sensor which could cause misreads. In a vertical position, debris such as chips, dirt, and oil can gather on the sensing surface and cause the sensor to malfunction. In a horizontal position, the chips fall away. If the sensor must be mounted vertically, provision must be made to remove chips and dirt periodically. Air blasts or oil baths can be used.

Care should also be exercised that the sensor does not detect its own mount. For example, an inductive sensor mounted improperly in a steel fixture might sense the fixture. You must also be sure that two sensors do not mutually interfere. If two sensors are mounted too close together, they can interfere with each other and may cause erratic sensing.

TYPICAL APPLICATIONS

One common use of a sensor is in a product feeding situation. It may involve parts moving along a conveyor or in some type of parts feeder. The sensor is used to notify the PLC when a part is in position, ready to be used. This is typically called a presence/absence check.

The same sensor can also provide the PLC with additional information. The PLC can take the data from the sensor and use it to count the parts as they are sensed. The PLC can also compare the completed parts and elapsed time to compute cycle times.

This one simple sensor allowed the PLC to accomplish three tasks:

Are there parts present?

How many parts have been used?

What is the cycle time for each part?

Simple sensors can be used to decide which product is present. Imagine a manufacturer that produces three different-size packages on the same line. Now imagine the product sizes moving along a conveyor at random. When each package arrives at the end of the line, the PLC must know what size product is present. This can be done easily with three simple sensors. If only one sensor is on, the small product is present. If two sensors are on, it must be the middle-size product. If three sensors are on, the product must be the large size. The same information could then be used to track production for all product sizes and cycle times for each size.

Sensors can even be used to check whether containers have been filled. Imagine aspirin bottles moving along a conveyor with the protective foil and the cover on. There are simple sensors that can sense through the cap and seal and make sure that the bottle is full. One sensor would be set up to sense when there is a bottle present. This is often called a gate sensor. A gate sensor is used to show when a product is in place. The PLC then knows that a product is present and can perform further checks.

A second sensor would be set up to sense the aspirin in the bottle. If there is a bottle present, but the sensor does not detect the aspirin inside, the PLC knows that the aspirin bottle was not filled. The PLC can then make sure that no empty bottles leave the plant. The PLC can also track scrap rates, production rates, and cycle times.

Sensors can be used to monitor temperature. Imagine an oven used in a bakery. The PLC can control the heater element in the oven to maintain the ideal temperature, as monitored by the sensor.

Pressure is vital in many processes. Imagine a plastic injection machine. Heated plastic is forced into a mold under a given pressure. The pressure must be accurately maintained or the parts will be defective. Sensors can be used to monitor these pressures. The PLC can then monitor the sensor and control the pressure.

Flow rates are important in process industries such as papermaking. Sensors can be used to monitor the flow rates of fluids and other raw materials. The PLC can use these data to adjust and control the flow rate of the system. Think about your water supply at home. The water department monitors the flow of water to calculate your bill.

Figure 9-25 shows a temperature and flow application. The flow sensor on the upper left of the machine is used to monitor for the proper flow of cooling water into the chiller. A built-in display shows the flow setpoint and status. The sensor on the lower right of the machine is a temperature sensor. An operator can set the proper temperature and alarm point.

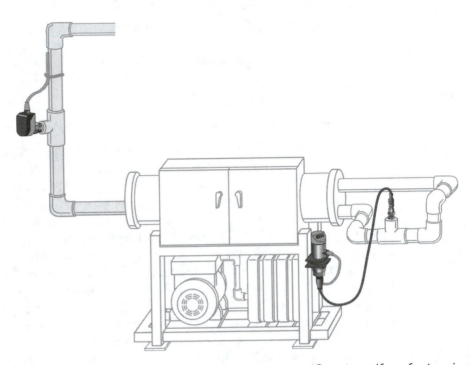

Figure 9-25   Temperature and flow application. *(Courtesy ifm efector, inc.)*

The applications discussed here are but a few of the simple uses to which sensors can be put. The innovative engineer or technician will invent many other uses. You should now be aware that the data from one sensor can be used to provide many different types of information (i.e., presence/absence, part count, cycle time).

When choosing the sensor for a particular application, you have several important considerations. The characteristics of the object to be sensed are crucial. Is the material plastic? Is it metallic? Is it a ferrous metal? Is the object clear, transparent, or reflective? Is it large or very small?

The specifics of the physical application are vitally important. Is there a large area available to mount the sensor? Are there problems with contaminants? What speed of response is required? What sensing distance is required? Is excessive electrical noise present? What accuracy is required?

Answering these questions will help narrow the available choices. A sensor must then be chosen based on such criteria as the cost of the sensor, the cost of failure, and reliability.

As systems become more automated they reduce the opportunity for human observation and intervention. Sensors must be used to sense problems in an auto-

Figure 9-26 Use of a sensor to sense empty and full level in a container. *(Courtesy ifm efector, inc.)*

Figure 9-27 An photo sensor can be used to sense for the proper capping of a container. *(Application concept courtesy Omron Electronics.)*

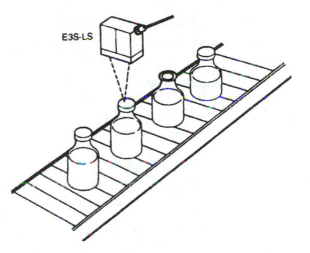

mated system. The cost of failure is usually the guide to how much sensing must be done. If the cost is high, then sensors should be used to notify the PLC.

Figure 9-26 shows a smart level sensor. The sensor's microprocessor and push button are used to teach the empty and full conditions of the container.

Figure 9-27 shows how a photo sensor can be used in a bottle capping application. The output from this sensor can be used to distinguish between those bottles that are capped and those that are not. Note that a field sensor can work in hostile environments.

Figure 9-28 shows three fiber-optic applications. In the first, the sensor checks for part presence. The second application uses a special fiber-optic head that spreads the beam. The third checks diameter in a tape winding application.

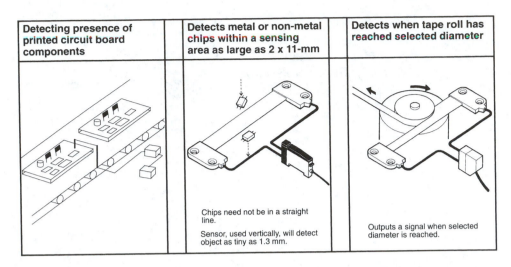

Detecting presence of printed circuit board components	Detects metal or non-metal chips within a sensing area as large as 2 x 11-mm	Detects when tape roll has reached selected diameter
	Chips need not be in a straight line. Sensor, used vertically, will detect object as tiny as 1.3 mm.	Outputs a signal when selected diameter is reached.

Figure 9-28 Small objects can be sensed by a laser sensor. *(Application concept courtesy Omron Electronics.)*

Figure 9-29 Transparent film can be detected. *(Application concept courtesy Omron Electronics.)*

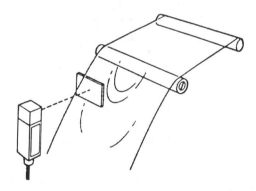

Figure 9-29 shows how transparent film can be detected. In this case, the sensor is mounted perpendicular to the film to maximize the reflected light to the receiver.

Figure 9-30 shows an example of an inductive sensor being used to check that screws have been correctly assembled. This inductive sensor provides digital outputs for high/pass/low detection. This could be used to pass or fail the parts into pass bins, too tall bins, and too short bins.

Figure 9-31 shows an application that utilizes a fiber-optic sensor because of the confined space.

Figure 9-32 shows how capacitive sensors can be used to check through a box and determine that all nine bottles have been loaded into the carton.

Figure 9-30 Small metal objects can be detected. *(Application concept courtesy Omron Electronics.)*

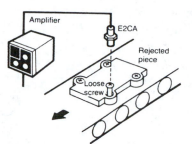

Figure 9-31 Fiber-optic application. *(Courtesy ifm efector, inc.)*

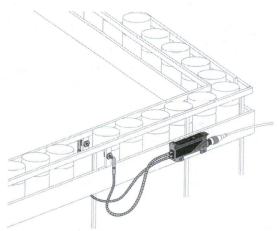

Figure 9-32 Capacitive sensor application. *(Courtesy ifm efector, inc.)*

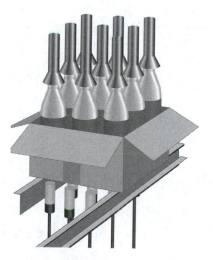

Figure 9-33 The inductive sensor is being used to sense each tooth as they pass. *(Courtesy ifm efector, inc.)*

Figure 9-33 shows an inductive sensor being used to sense gear teeth as the gear rotates. The user could tell position by the number of gear teeth that pass, or velocity of the number of teeth that pass the inductive sensor in a given amount of time.

Choosing a Sensor for a Special Application

Certain applications present special problems for the technician or engineer; for example, the sensor may fail to sense every part or fail randomly. In these cases a different type or different model of sensor may need to be chosen. Sales representatives and applications engineers from sensor manufacturers can be helpful in choosing a sensor to meet a specific need. They have usually seen the particular problem before and know how to solve it.

The types of sensors and the complexity of their use in solving application problems grow daily. New sensors are constantly being introduced to solve needs. There are almost as many sensor types available as there are applications. There are even magazines devoted to the topic of sensors.

The innovative use of sensors can help increase the safety, reliability, productivity, and quality of processes. The technician must be able to choose, install, and troubleshoot sensors properly.

QUESTIONS

1. Describe at least four uses of digital sensors.

2. Describe at least three analog sensors and their uses.

3. List and explain at least four types of optical sensors.

4. Explain how capacitive sensors work.

5. Explain how inductive sensors work.

6. Explain the term *hysteresis.*

7. Draw and explain the wiring of a load-powered sensor.

8. Draw and explain the wiring of a line-powered sensor.

9. What is burden current? Load current?

10. Why must load current be limited?

11. Explain the basic principle on which a thermocouple is based.

12. How are changes in ambient temperature compensated for?

13. What is the temperature range for a type J thermocouple?

14. Describe at least three electrical precautions as they relate to sensor installation.

15. Describe at least three mechanical precautions as they relate to sensor installation.

Communications, ControlLogix, and DeviceNet

10

This chapter will examine some of the newer technologies in communications and control. Topics include the three levels of industrial communications (information networks, control networks, and device networks), ControlLogix, and DeviceNet.

OBJECTIVES

Upon completion of this chapter, you will be able to:
1. Describe the three levels of industrial communications
2. Describe the purpose and capabilities of ControlLogix
3. Describe the purpose and capabilities of DeviceNet
4. Describe appropriate uses for ControlLogix and DeviceNet

INDUSTRIAL COMMUNICATIONS

The three main types of industrial networks are information networks, control networks, and device networks. Figure 10-1 shows the hierarchy for the three typical networks.

Figure 10-1   Industrial communications hierarchy.

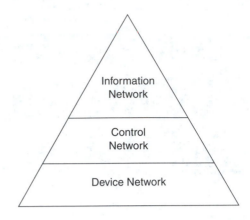

INFORMATION LEVEL NETWORK

The top level is the information network layer. This is the enterprise's computer network. It typically consists of Ethernet local area networks (LANs) that can exchange information between the enterprise's computers. It also serves as a link between the plant floor and the manufacturing software systems.

Ethernet

Ethernet is the most widely used protocol at the information systems level of communications. Computer networking has become increasingly more important as enterprises have integrated their computers and systems. Computers are linked to share enterprise data, e-mail, and other resources such as printers and data storage. These computers are connected through LANs.

Ethernet is popular because it is fast, inexpensive, and easy to install. The Institute for Electrical and Electronic Engineers (IEEE) defined a standard for Ethernet. It is known as IEEE Standard 802.3. Ethernet is the most prevalent personal computer networking standard. It is based on the carrier sense, multiple access/collision detect (CSMA/CD) access method. A computer must have some way to gain access to a network when it needs to communicate. If CSMA/CD is used, the computer "listens" to the access line (carrier) to see if it is being used or available (carrier sense). If available, the computer can talk. This, by the way, is similar to how telephone service once operated. Neighbors, especially in country areas, would share a line, called a party line. If you wanted to use the phone, you would pick it up and see if anyone else was talking on it. You were supposed to hang up if it was being used. If no one was on the line, you could call someone. (Party lines also provided entertainment for nosy neighbors.) CSMA/CD is similar. If the line is available, the computer can talk. Sometimes, however, the line is available, but two or more computers may try to talk at the same time, which can lead to a data collision. This explains why collision detection (CD) is necessary. The computers that had the collision of data would sense the collision and then wait to talk again. The wait is controlled by algorithms so that they do not attempt to talk again at exactly the same time. These collisions are minor and do not affect speed unless the line utilization is very high.

Ethernet also employs a bus structure, which makes for easy connections in a manufacturing or office environment. It is also easy to add additional length to a bus network as a company grows or expands a network.

Fast Ethernet A faster standard has also been established for Ethernet. IEEE has established the Fast Ethernet standard (IEEE 802.3u). This standard raises the Ethernet speed limit from 10 Megabits per second (Mbps) to 100 Mbps with only minor changes to the existing cable structure. There are three types of Fast Ethernet: 100BASE-TX for use with level 5 UTP cable, 100BASE-FX for use with fiber-optic cable, and 100BASE-T4 which utilizes an extra two wires for use with level 3 UTP cable. The 100BASE-TX standard has become the most popular due to its close compatibility with the 10BASE-T Ethernet standard. An enterprise's communications networks will have a combination of Ethernet and Fast Ethernet. The future promises even faster Ethernet standards.

LANs A network is any collection of computers that communicate with one another over a shared network. LANs can be small and link a few computers or can be huge and link hundreds of computers. An enterprise will often have many smaller LANs that are also interconnected. The standardization of protocols is what enables enterprises to make good use of LANs. This has certainly been the case with Ethernet. As more and more enterprises decide to use Ethernet, the prices of hardware and software have been dramatically reduced. Many medium and large organizations have sites that are not in close physical proximity. These enterprises often utilize wide area networks (WANs), so that the LANs in each site can communicate with the whole organization.

WANs WANs can integrate LANs that are geographically separate, by connecting the different LANs using dedicated leased phone lines, dial-up phone lines, data carrier services, or even satellite links. Wide area networking can be as simple as a modem and remote access server into which employees can dial, or it can be hundreds of branches linked over any geographic area.

CONTROL LEVEL NETWORK

The control level network is the level at which the controllers reside. This level would include the PLCs, personal computers, operator I/O devices, drives, motion controllers, robot controllers, and vision systems. Communication at this level is mainly between the devices; for example, we can share data among PLCs. Communication at this level must be dependable. Rockwell offers several protocols for this level. Data Highway+ (DH+) is one standard for connecting controllers at this level. ControlNet is another popular protocol at this level for communicating between controllers.

ControlNet

ControlNet was developed to provide a real-time, control-layer network to provide high-speed transport of both time-critical I/O data and messaging data, including upload/download of programming and configuration data and peer-to-peer messaging, on a single physical media link. ControlNet's access method is deterministic. Remember that Ethernet employs CSMA/CD, which is not deterministic because of collisions. ControlNet's access method is deterministic and repeatable. ControlNet's 5 Mbps control and data capabilities enhance I/O performance and peer-to-peer communications. ControlNet is highly deterministic and repeatable—critical requirements for manufacturing control and communication. Determinism is the ability to reliably predict when data will be delivered; repeatability ensures that transmit times are constant and unaffected by devices connecting to, or leaving, the network.

ControlNet's access method utilizes the producer/consumer model. ControlNet allows multiple controllers to control I/O on the same wire. Many other networks only allow one master controller on the wire. ControlNet also allows multicast of both inputs and peer-to-peer data, thus reducing traffic on the wire and increasing system performance.

ControlNet Characteristics

High bandwidth for I/O, peer-to-peer messaging, and programming

Network access from any node

Deterministic, repeatable performance for both discrete and process applications

Multiple controllers controlling I/O on the same link

Simple installation requiring no special tools to install or tune the network

Network access from any node

Flexibility in topology options (bus, tree, star) and media types (coax, fiber, other)

DEVICE LEVEL NETWORK

The device level network is the lowest level. It consists of plant-floor devices such as sensors, valves, and drives. There are many device-type networks available. One of the more common is DeviceNet. It is like a LAN for plant-floor devices. A device level network can connect many types of plant-floor devices.

Device level networks are becoming prevalent in industrial control. They are sometimes called field buses or industrial buses. These networks have many similarities to the conventional office computer network. Office networks allow many computers to communicate without being directly hooked to each other. Each computer has only one connection to the network. Imagine if every computer had to be physically connected to every other computer. Networks therefore minimize the amount of wiring that needs to be done. Networks also allow devices such as printers to be shared. Industrial networks share some of the same advantages.

Imagine a complex automated machine that has hundreds of I/O devices. Now imagine the time and expense of connecting each and every I/O device back to the controller. Conduit has to be bent and mounted as well as the hundreds of wires that need to be run. This can require hundreds of wires (or more) in a complex system and can involve long runs of wire. Typical devices such as sensors and actuators now require that two or more wires be connected at the point of use and then run to an I/O card at the control device. Industrial networks eliminate this need so only a single twisted-pair wire bus (generally two to four wires) needs to be used for communication. All devices can then connect directly to the bus. This could also be called distributed I/O. Figure 10-2 shows an example of two valve manifolds.

Figure 10-2   Two valve manifolds. The one on top is DeviceNet capable. *(Courtesy Parker Hannefin Inc.)*

Figure 10-3   Two communications modules that could be used with a valve manifold. The one on the left is a Profibus module and the one on the right is a DeviceNet module. *(Courtesy Parker Hannefin Inc.)*

P2S-EA162BP16A
Head & Tail Set with
Profibus-DP®

P2S-EA162BD16A
Head & Tail Set with
DeviceNet™

The top one has a DeviceNet module. This module could be plugged into a De-viceNet bus. The bottom one is not a bus type and would require many connections through a 25-pin connector.

Multiple devices can even share one connection with the bus in some cases. Several manufacturers have developed I/O blocks that allow multiple I/O points to share one connection to the bus. One example would be valve manifolds (Figure 10-3). This particular unit could have up to thirty-two valves and up to thirty-two I/O with only two connections. Wiring and installation costs are drastically reduced when industrial networks are used.

The cost of field bus devices is higher than that of conventional devices. The field bus devices gain a cost advantage when one considers the labor cost of installation, maintenance, and troubleshooting. The cost benefit received from using distributed I/O is really in the labor saved during installation and startup. There is also a material savings when one considers the wire that does not have to be run—there is a tremendous savings in labor when only a fraction of the number of connections need to be made and only a fraction of the wire needs to be run. A field bus system is also much easier to troubleshoot than a conventional system. If a problem exists, only one twisted-pair cable needs to be checked. A conventional system might require the technician to sort out hundreds of wires.

Field Devices

Sensors, valves, actuators, and starters are examples of I/O called field devices. The capabilities of field devices have increased rapidly as well as their ability to communicate. This has led to a need for a way to network them. Imagine what it would be like in your home if there was no electrical standard. Your television might use 100 volts at 50 cycles. Your refrigerator might use 220 at 60 cycles, and so on. Every device might use a different plug. It would be a nightmare to change any device to another brand, because the wiring and outlets would need to be changed. This has been the case in terms of communications between industrial devices.

Simple industrial digital devices such as sensors can be interchanged. They typically operate on 24 volts or 110 volts, and their outputs are digital, so any brand can be used. In other words, we could replace a simple digital photo sensor from one manufacturer with a different brand because it is only an on/off signal.

Figure 10-4 shows a simple industrial network with several field devices attached. Note the I/O block (I/O concentrator) and the valve manifold. Both are used to connect multiple devices to a network.

Industrial applications often need analog information such as temperature and pressure. These devices typically convert the analog signal to a digital form and then need to communicate that information to a controller. They may also be able to pass other information such as piece counts, cycle times, and error codes. Devices such as drives have also gained capability. Parameters such as acceleration and other drive parameters can be sent by a computer or PLC to alter the way a drive operates. Every device manufacturer has had different communication

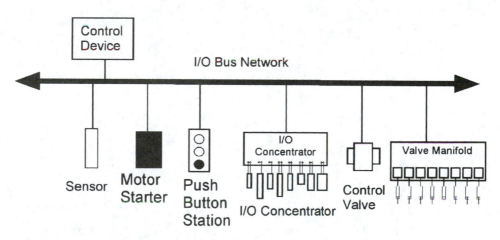

Figure 10-4   A simple industrial network.

protocols, until now, for that communication. This required a separate network for each brand of device.

TYPES OF INDUSTRIAL BUSES

The two basic categories of industrial bus networks are device and process. Device-type buses are intended to handle the transmission of short messages, typically a few bytes in length. Most devices in a device bus are discrete, such as sensors, push buttons, and limit switches. Many discrete buses can also utilize some analog devices. They would typically be devices that only require a few bytes of information transmission, for example, temperature controllers, some motor drives, and thermocouples. Since the transmission packets are small, device buses can transmit data packets from many devices in the same amount of time as it would take to transmit one large packet of data on a process bus.

Industrial buses range from simple systems that can control discrete I/O (device-type bus) to buses that could be used to control a whole plant (process bus). Figure 10-5 shows the capabilities of several common industrial buses. The left of the graph begins with simple discrete I/O control and increases in capability to plant control. Block I/O would be devices like manifolds that would have several valves on one block and only two to four wires would need to be connected to control all of the I/O. By using an industrial bus, only two to four wires would have to be run instead of a few dozen.

An example of a smart device would be a digital motor drive to which we could send parameters and commands serially. The peer level would be the capability for peer controllers to communicate with each other. The next levels are cell control, control of a line of cells, and overall plant control.

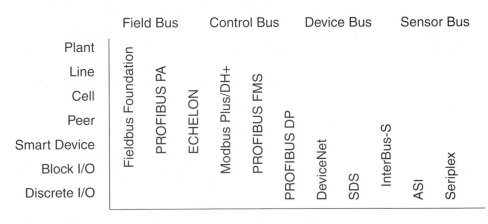

Figure 10-5   A comparison of common industrial buses.

Device Buses

Device buses have two categories: bit wide and byte wide. Byte-wide buses can transfer 50 or more bytes of data at a time. Bit-wide buses typically transfer 1 to 8 bits of information to/from simple discrete devices. Byte-type systems are excellent for higher level communication; and bit-type systems are best for simple, physical level I/O devices such as sensors and actuators.

Process Buses

Process buses are capable of communicating several hundred bytes of data per transmission. Process buses are slower because of their large data packet size. Most analog control devices do not require fast response times. Process controllers typically are smart devices that control analog types of variables such as flow, concentration, and temperature. These processes are typically slow to respond. Process buses are used to transmit process parameters to process controllers. Most devices in a process bus network are analog.

This chapter will focus on the device bus type. DeviceNet will be covered in detail later in the chapter.

EXAMPLE COMMUNICATIONS SYSTEM

Figure 10-6 shows an example of an industrial communications hierarchy, with three networks. There is the typical Ethernet LAN for the computers to communicate at the information systems level. Ethernet is the overwhelming choice at this level. The computers are networked with Ethernet. Rockwell Automation RSLinx software is running on each of the computers, so that they can communicate through the KTX card to any of the PLCs. If we have programming software on the computers, any of them can be used to program, upload/download, or monitor any PLC on the DH+ network. The KTX card in the one computer acts as a gateway so that the computer network can talk to the DH+ network. The use of RSLinx and the KTX card as a bridge between the Ethernet and DH+ networks allows any of the PLCs and computers to share information. For example, supervisory control and data acquisition (SCADA) software such as RSView32 or Wonderware could be used to gather information from floor-level devices and controllers and share it with the rest of the enterprise network.

At the controller level are several communications protocols available for communicating between controllers. Data Highway Plus (DH+) is one of them. DH+ can be used to program the controllers and to communicate between them. DH+ is easy to implement. It is simply a three-wire conductor that is daisy chained between

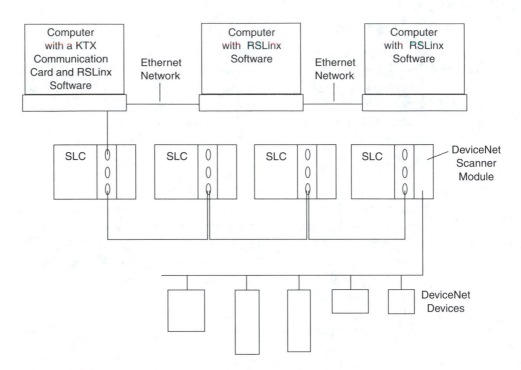

Figure 10-6   Example communications network.

controllers. Daisy chaining means that the wire comes into a controller and back out to the next. Figure 10-6 shows an example of PLCs that are daisy chained.

Our example has a DH+ network for the PLCs to communicate with each other at the control level. DH+ enables data to be exchanged between controllers and even enables one controller to control another's I/O.

Note that ControlNet or Ethernet could have been used instead of DH+ at this level to communicate between controllers. SLC 5/05s are Ethernet capable. They could be plugged into the Ethernet computer network as well. If we want to use ControlNet, we need to add a ControlNet module in each SLC. ControlNet is a controller communications standard developed by Rockwell Automation and then given to a user group to be an open standard.

DeviceNet was used at the device level. There is a DeviceNet scanner module in the fourth PLC. The DeviceNet network would network floor-level devices into the fourth PLC.

Next we will consider ControlLogix, another alternative to linking these levels and different protocols.

CONTROLLOGIX

Rockwell Automation ControlLogix (CL) is a new technology that can be used for control, communication, and integrating various types of networks.

Imagine a device that could be used for controlling any type of system or could be used as a gateway so that many different types of communications networks could communicate. Until now it has been relatively difficult to communicate between different protocols and systems. A device that can link different types of communications protocols so all can communicate with each other is called a gateway. Imagine a device that could do control or act as a communications gateway, or both, simultaneously.

Rockwell Automation developed a family of products to accomplish this task. The backbone of the system is a chassis that can house control modules, I/O modules, and communications modules.

A chassis with a control module and some I/O modules becomes a controller. A chassis with communications modules to integrate various protocols becomes a communications gateway to link various networks. A chassis with a control module and communications modules can act as a controller and a communications gateway.

ControlLogix is a modular platform for multiple types of control and communications. As a controller, the user can utilize a CL system for sequential, motion control, and process control in any combination. As a communications gateway, CL also enables multiple computers, PLCs, networks, and I/O communications to be integrated.

Control Choices

CL can integrate various types of control systems and communications systems into a seamless network of control (Figure 10-7). To make the task easier, there is a wide variety of software and hardware available.

A ControlLogix system can be a simple stand-alone controller. Programming is provided through RSLogix 5000. It is IEC 1131-3 compliant. IEC 1131-3 is an international standard for programming languages for PLCs. It allows the user to program in ladder logic, function block, and even symbolic programming with structures and arrays.

Figure 10-8 shows an example of a simple system. In this system a CL controller has been utilized with CL I/O modules. I/O would be wired directly to the modules. This system would look like a typical PLC system.

One or more controllers can be used in a chassis. Chassis sizes range from four to seventeen slots. Multiple controllers can read input values from all inputs. The controllers can address a large number of I/O points (128,000 digital maximum/4000 analog maximum).

Figure 10-7   A typical CL system. Note that a CL system is modular so the user can build it to meet the application needs for communication and control. *(Courtesy Rockwell Automation Inc.)*

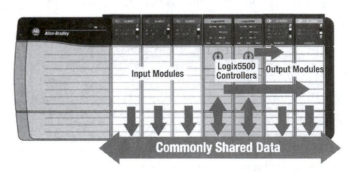

Figure 10-8   A simple CL system. *(Courtesy Rockwell Automation Inc.)*

I/O Modules for a CL Controller

There are a wide variety of I/O modules available. AC and DC input and output modules feature advanced diagnostic, fusing, and isolation capability. I/O modules with diagnostics can provide diagnostics to the point level on the module. Modules with electronic fusing have internal fusing to prevent too much current from flowing through the module. Modules are also available with individually isolated I/O.

Another, special-purpose, I/O module is a configurable flow meter module. It can be used to control metering applications for process control, and it can be used for high-speed frequency measurements for speed or rate control. The module has two outputs that can be triggered based on flow, frequency, or other states.

There is also a high-speed counter module available, which can be used with devices that provide a pulsed output such as sensors or encoders.

A programmable limit switch module is also available. This type of module is common in packaging operations. The module takes its input from a resolver. It can provide control of packaging operations up to 1500 parts per minute. It is based on controlling outputs, as based on the rotation of the resolver, and can detect to within 1.08 degrees of rotation at 1800 RPM.

There are a variety of wiring options for the I/O modules. Removable terminal blocks, similar to typical PLC terminal blocks, for wiring directly to the module are available in screw-clamp or spring-clamp types.

Interface modules can also be used to separate the terminations from the actual I/O module. They are mounted on DIN rails and connected to the actual I/O module by a cable.

If one needs to create a distributed I/O system, FlexLogix can be used to control and integrate Flex I/O modules

Motion Control

Figure 10-9 shows how a typical motion control system would be implemented in a CL system. Modules are chosen and installed in the chassis. RSLogix 5000 software would then be used to configure each axis of motion. RSLogix 5000 software is then used to develop the motion application; the application is then downloaded to the controller and can be run.

Figure 10-10 diagrams the development and operation of a motion application to control two axes. In the first panel RSLogix 5000 is used to configure and program the application. The second panel shows the ControlLogix control module running the program logic and communicating with the servo module. The third panel shows the servo module that actually controls the motor drives. In this case, two drives are being controlled.

There is an international open standard for multiaxis motion-synchronized motion control, called the Serial Real-time Communication System (SERCOS). It is designed to be a protocol over a fiber-optic medium. Modules that employ the SERCOS standard are also available. Figure 10-11 shows an example of a SERCOS. The SERCOS interface uses a ring topology with one master and multiple slaves (axes). The fiber-optic ring begins and ends at the master.

Analog modules are also available.

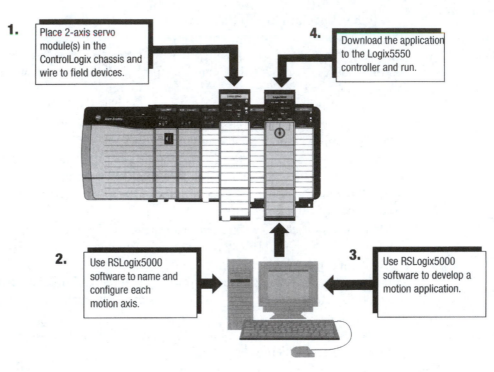

1. Place 2-axis servo module(s) in the ControlLogix chassis and wire to field devices.

4. Download the application to the Logix5550 controller and run.

2. Use RSLogix5000 software to name and configure each motion axis.

3. Use RSLogix5000 software to develop a motion application.

Figure 10-9 A typical CL motion control system. *(Courtesy Rockwell Automation Inc.)*

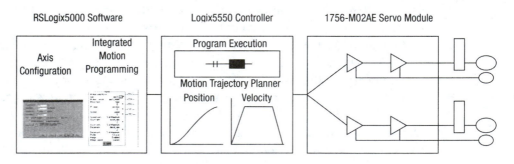

RSLogix5000 Software   Logix5550 Controller   1756-M02AE Servo Module

Axis Configuration   Integrated Motion Programming

Program Execution

Motion Trajectory Planner
Position   Velocity

Figure 10-10 The development and operation of a motion application. *(Courtesy Rockwell Automation Inc.)*

A CL system can also be used as a communications gateway. The user just adds the communications modules to connect to the required networks. This allows the CL to communicate with other PLC-based networks in multiple protocols. If the system is used for communications, the controller is not required. Protocols include Ethernet, ControlNet, DeviceNet, and others.

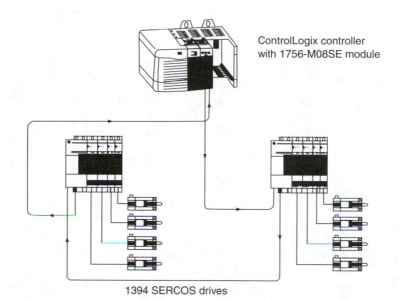

ControlLogix controller
with 1756-M08SE module

1394 SERCOS drives

Figure 10-11   A SERCOS drive system. Note that the communications network is a ring. *(Courtesy Rockwell Automation Inc.)*

Process Control

CL can be used for process control by utilizing ProcessLogix, a distributed control system (DCS) for process control. It can be used to control various types of process controllers and can utilize the FieldBus communications standard.

DeviceNet

We now take an in-depth look at DeviceNet. Device level networks must be installed and configured. It is likely that the technician will need to be actively involved with any device level network implementation.

Industrial networks are increasing in acceptance and use. DeviceNet is a communications link to connect industrial devices (such as limit switches, photo sensors, motor starters, drives, valves and valve manifolds, pushbuttons, bar code readers, panel displays, and operator interfaces) to a network, and at the same time eliminate costly and time-consuming hand wiring.

The basis of many device level networks is the controller area network (CAN) chip. The CAN chip was developed for the European automotive industry. Figure 10-12 shows a conceptual automobile network.

Note that the network has a bus configuration. Imagine one communication wire that runs from the front of the car to the back. Imagine that each device is plugged into the bus. At the back of the car the taillights are plugged in. The door locks and power windows also are plugged in. The CAN chip handles the communications to

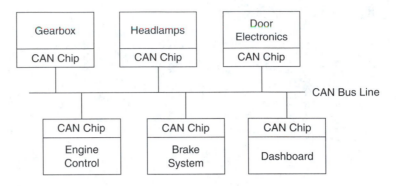

Figure 10-12 Automobile CAN network. *(Courtesy Rockwell Automation Inc.)*

other devices on the bus. The CAN chip is a smart communications front-end for each device. The CAN chip is a receiver/transmitter. If the driver hits the brakes, the computer senses the brake pressure and sends a message over the bus to turn on the brakes and brake lights.

This technology offers several advantages. First, it simplifies the car wiring. The large and complex wiring harness is no longer needed. Each device simply plugs into the bus. Second, the chips are quite inexpensive—over 40 million CAN chips are sold annually, at $3 each. A network can also simplify troubleshooting. CAN chip systems can have powerful diagnostic capabilities. A bus system also simplifies installation of the wiring.

Rockwell Automation used the CAN chip when it developed DeviceNet. DeviceNet is an open standard invented by Rockwell Automation in 1993. The network specifications and protocol are open, which means that vendors are not required to purchase hardware, software, or licensing rights to connect devices to a system. The DeviceNet standard is maintained by the Open DeviceNet Vendors Association (ODVA—www.odva.org). It is open to any manufacturer who wants to make and sell devices that are DeviceNet compatible. This means that you can buy DeviceNet devices from any manufacturer and they will work in your DeviceNet system.

Figure 10-13 shows an example of a DeviceNet networked system. Note that there is only one cable running to the PLC, and that all devices plug into the trunk line. The PLC has a scanning module that acts as the brains of the network.

DeviceNet Components

Figure 10-14 shows the typical components for a DeviceNet cable system. The trunk line is the backbone of the system. It is the one cable to which all devices attach. In DeviceNet terminology, a device that has an address would be called a node. There are two types of wire: thick and thin. Thick wire is used for the trunk

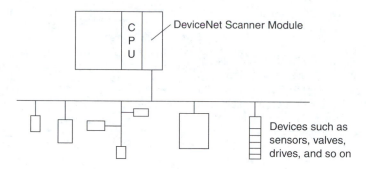

Figure 10-13 DeviceNet system. Note that there is only one cable running to the scanner for all of the I/Os.

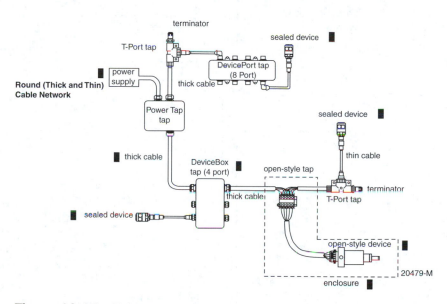

Figure 10-14 Typical components in a DeviceNet system. *(Courtesy Rockwell Automation Inc.)*

line. The wire that connects devices to the trunk lines is called a drop line. Drop lines usually utilize thin cable.

The most important device in a DeviceNet network is a scanner (Figure 10-15). For our sample system, the scanner is a module installed in the PLC rack. The scanner acts as an interface between the PLC CPU and the inputs and outputs in our system. The scanner reads inputs and writes to outputs in the system. The scanner also monitors the devices for faults and downloads configuration data to each device. The scanner may also be equipped with a readout to help with troubleshooting the

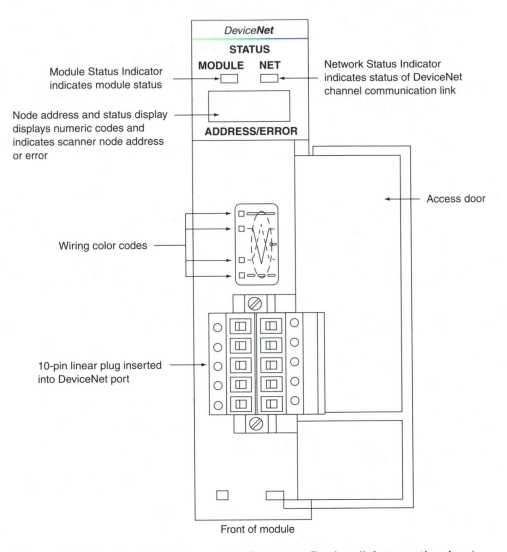

Module Status Indicator indicates module status

Network Status Indicator indicates status of DeviceNet channel communication link

Node address and status display displays numeric codes and indicates scanner node address or error

Access door

Wiring color codes

10-pin linear plug inserted into DeviceNet port

Front of module

Figure 10-15 DeviceNet scanner. *(Courtesy Rockwell Automation Inc.)*

network. A Rockwell Automation scanner will flash a number that represents the error code and the number of the node that has the problem.

Figure 10-16 shows an example of a typical DeviceNet system with several types of devices. Of the devices, many types of sensors are available. Lets look at a Rockwell Series 9000 photo sensor. This sensor has several important features. Normally we would have to stock light-on and dark-on sensors for various applications. This sensor can be configured to be light-on or dark-on, so that we only need to stock one type. It also features some troubleshooting capability. The sensor has a margin

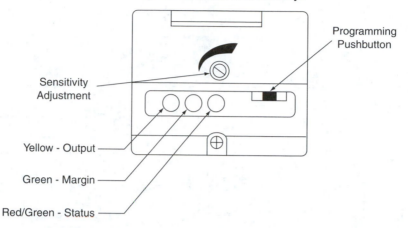

Top View of Series 9000 Photoeye

Programming
Pushbutton

Sensitivity
Adjustment

Yellow - Output

Green - Margin

Red/Green - Status

Figure 10-16 A Rockwell Series 9000 DeviceNet photo sensor. *(Courtesy Rockwell Automation Inc.)*

output. Imagine that the sensor transmits light to a reflector and then back to the sensor where it is sensed. The margin output from the sensor will turn on if the reflector gets dirty and does not reflect the amount of light the sensor expects. It would also turn on if the reflector or sensor is bumped out of alignment. We can use the margin output in our ladder logic for troubleshooting if so desired. The device must be configured with a node address. DeviceNet can have sixty-four nodes, of which one is the scanner, so that leaves sixty-three other potential node addresses. New devices come configured as node number 63. The sensor can be configured by switches on the sensor or by utilizing DeviceNet software and a PC. The sensor has LEDs on it for troubleshooting. Many manufacturers make DeviceNet sensors.

Another example of a DeviceNet device is a Rockwell Automation RediSTATION (Figure 10-17). This device features a start button, a stop button, and a red light. It requires one node address, but has two inputs (start and stop pushbuttons) and an output (red light).

Rockwell Automation also makes a device named DeviceLink for devices in a system that are not DeviceNet compatible. A DeviceLink can be used to connect a non-DeviceNet digital device to a DeviceNet network. The DeviceLink is connected to the network and given an address. The device (a limit switch, for example) is connected to the DeviceLink, which can transmit its state (on or off) to the scanner. Each DeviceLink requires one node address.

A motor drive is another example of a DeviceNet device. Figure 10-17 shows a Rockwell Automation 160 AC drive with DeviceNet capability. It is possible with this setup for the scanner to send speed, accell/decell, direction, and so on, to the drive. It is also possible for the scanner to read operating information from the drive.

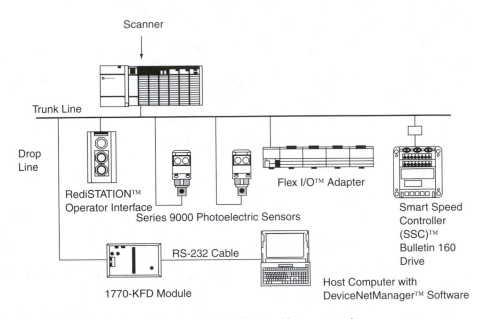

Figure 10-17   A simple conceptual DeviceNet network.
(Courtesy Rockwell Automation Inc.)

Thus far we have looked at devices that basically have one device per node address. Let us examine a few that can have multiple devices with only one node address. Rockwell Automation Flex I/O is a way to connect many I/O devices and only use one node address. The I/O that is connected to the modules does not have to be DeviceNet capable. Any digital or analog I/O can be connected to the modules. Flex I/O modules are available for multiple inputs or outputs in digital or analog. Up to eight modules can be plugged together, meaning that up to 128 discrete devices or sixty-four analog channels could be connected to a DeviceNet network using a FLEX I/O system. All these devices could be connected and use only one node address. The modules are then attached to a DeviceNet communications module that is connected to the network. Flex I/O is very appropriate for connecting non-DeviceNet devices to a DeviceNet network and also when a large number of devices may be concentrated in one area of a machine away from the controller.

Pneumatic components are also available for DeviceNet. Several manufacturers make multiple valve arrangements with a DeviceNet communications module. Thirty-two or more valves can be utilized with only one node address.

We also need a way to connect to a DeviceNet network with a computer. Rockwell utilizes a communications module between the computer and the network. A Rockwell 1770-KFD module plugs into the computer serial port. The other side of

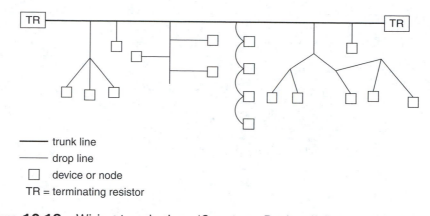

— trunk line
— drop line
☐ device or node
TR = terminating resistor

Figure 10-18　Wiring topologies. *(Courtesy Rockwell Automation Inc.)*

the KFD module plugs into a DeviceNet device for configuration or to the actual network. DeviceNet configuration software is run on the computer. Rockwell calls its software DeviceNet Manager. Other DeviceNet manufacturers have their own versions of software. DeviceNet Manager software can be used online or offline to build a network. The software can also be used to configure individual devices; for example, we can plug a Rockwell 9000 series photo sensor into the KFD module and utilize the computer and software to set the sensor's node address (remember that new devices come with a default address of 63). We can also set operation parameters such as light-on or dark-on.

Wiring

Let us take a closer look at wiring a DeviceNet system. Figure 10-18 shows a simple, generic network. Note that the trunk line is thick cable, which is capable of handling 8A, although National Electric Code (NEC) only allows 4A. Thin cable is normally used for drop lines. Thin cable can handle up to 3A of power. Both thick and thin cable have power and communication lines, which is important because many devices can be powered directly from the DeviceNet thick or thin cable. Two wires supply 24 volts to the network; two other wires are used for communication. The ends of the trunk line must be terminated with 121 ohm resistors. Terminating resistors should never be used on drop lines.

DeviceNet is quite flexible in wiring layout. Figure 10-18 shows several possible topologies for wiring. Devices are shown as circles. The left-most example shows a tree-type structure. Next we see a single device attached through a drop line to the trunk line, a daisy chain topology, and then a bus-type topology.

There is a maximum allowable drop line length of 20 feet (Figure 10-19), and a maximum cumulative drop line length, which varies by the network speed: The

Network Speed	Maximum Drop Line Length	Maximum Cumulative Drop Line Length
125 K Baud		512 Feet
250 K Baud	20 Feet	256 Feet
500 K Baud		128 Feet

Figure 10-19 Allowable line lengths for DeviceNet network speeds.

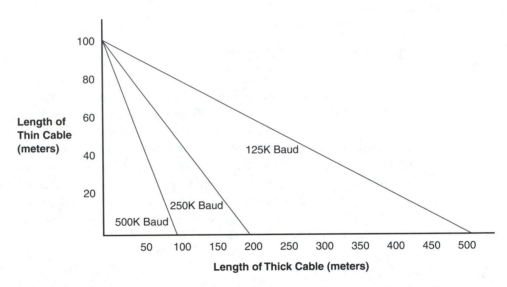

Figure 10-20 Graph of allowable line length. *(Courtesy Rockwell Automation Inc.)*

slower the speed, the longer the line length allowed; the faster the network, the less drop line length allowed. The maximum drop line length is based on the cumulative drop line length. Figure 10-19 shows the maximum cumulative line length for the three network speeds allowed in a DeviceNet system.

Figure 10-20 shows approximate line lengths for combinations of thick and thin cable at the three speeds. For example, if we assume a speed of 125 K baud we could only have a line length of 300 feet if all thin cable was used. If all thick cable was used, we could have a line length of approximately 1500 feet; or we could choose any point along the graph of the 125 K speed. For example, assume we will use thick cable for the trunk line. The trunk needs to be 300 feet long. Look for the 300-foot point on the horizontal line of the graph. Look directly above the 300-foot point and you will see that approximately 270 feet of thin cable could still be used.

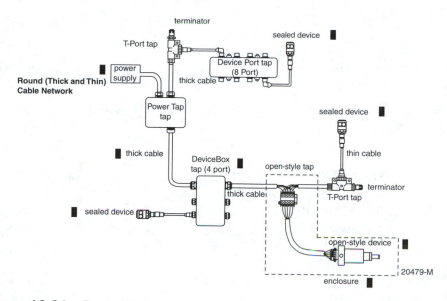

Figure 10-21 DeviceNet connectors. *(Courtesy Rockwell Automation Inc.)*

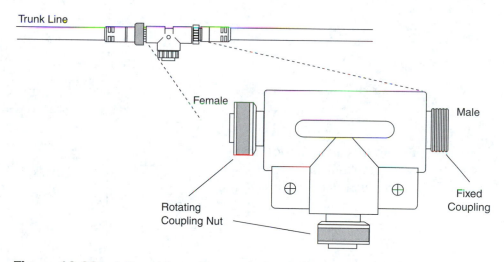

Figure 10-22 A T-port tap. *(Courtesy Rockwell Automation Inc.)*

Connections

Figure 10-21 shows examples of connection devices that can be used. The trunk line is attached to the left and right sides of the T-port tap. The drop line would be connected to the third port of the T-port tap (Figure 10-22). These are screw-type connections. A DevicePort tap (Figure 10-23) can be used to connect up to seven devices to the trunk line. The trunk line is connected to one port on the DevicePort

Figure 10-23 A DevicePort tap. *(Courtesy Rockwell Automation Inc.)*

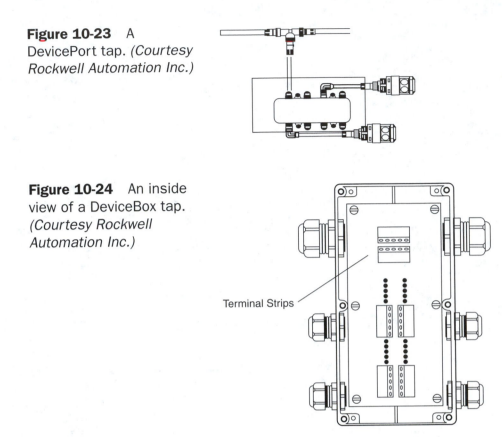

Figure 10-24 An inside view of a DeviceBox tap. *(Courtesy Rockwell Automation Inc.)*

Terminal Strips

Inside View of a DeviceBox tap

Figure 10-25 A DeviceBox tap. *(Courtesy Rockwell Automation Inc.)*

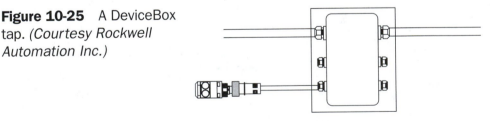

and up to six other devices can be connected to the other ports. These are also screw-type connections. A DeviceBox tap is very similar except these are compression-type fittings. The top is removed from the box and the wires are individually connected to terminals (Figure 10-24). The trunk line (thick cable) is attached to the larger compression fittings on the top left and top right, and up to four devices are connected through the four compression-type fittings (Figure 10-25). The compression fittings grip the cord and also seal the cable entry. DeviceBox taps are available in two-port, four-port, and eight-port configurations.

Figure 10-26 An open-style connector. *(Courtesy Rockwell Automation Inc.)*

Open Connection

The third type of connector (Figure 10-26) is an open-style connector. Three lines can be connected with this device.

A box called a PowerTap is used to connect 24 volt DC power to the network. Two lines are used for the trunk line (compression style) and the third is used to run a power line into the box. There are two fuses in the PowerTap—one for the left side of the network and the other for the right side of the network. One can be removed so that the power supply only powers one side of the network (you will see why this might be done later). Even if the fuse is removed, the communications lines run to both sides of the network. The fuse is just used to protect the 24 volt power supply.

Attaching a Computer to a DeviceNet Network

Figure 10-27 shows a typical network with a computer attached. Note the Rockwell Automation KFD module. The purpose of this module is to be an interface between the serial port of a computer and the DeviceNet protocol of the network.

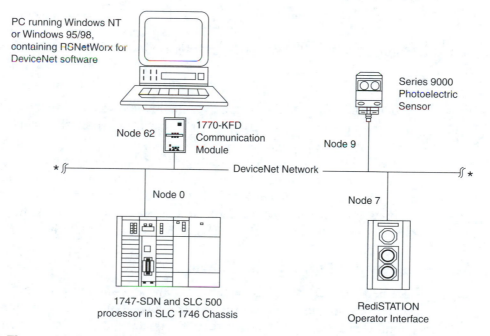

Figure 10-27 Typical computer connection. *(Courtesy Rockwell Automation Inc.)*

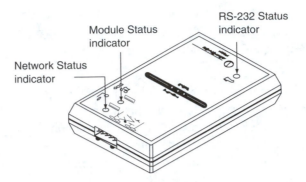

Figure 10-28   KFD module and troubleshooting status indicators. *(Courtesy Rockwell Automation Inc.)*

If the RS232 Status Indicator is:	Then:
Off	No Activity—Link OK
Flickering Green	Activity—Link OK
Solid Red	Link Failed—Critical Fault
Flashing Red	Link Failed—Noncritical Fault

Figure 10-29   RS232 status indicator conditions.

Note that power must be supplied to the module through the power supply connector on the side or directly from a DeviceNet network. The switch on the side is used to choose the proper source of power.

KFD modules have three LEDs for troubleshooting (Figure 10-28). The RS232 status LED is used to troubleshoot the serial connection between the module and the computer. The module status LED is used to troubleshoot the module. The network status indicator is used to troubleshoot the DeviceNet network. Figures 10-29 through 10-31 show how the LEDs can be used for troubleshooting.

Supplying Power to the Network

Remember that a DeviceNet network handles communications, but it also provides the 24 volt DC power to operate many devices. It is very important to design the system so that current limits are not exceeded. One important consideration is that NEC does not allow over 4A on the trunk line. Drop lines also limit the amount of allowable current. Figure 10-32 shows the current lim-

If the Module Status Indicator is:	Then:
Off	No Power
Solid Green	Device OK
Flashing Green	Not Configured
Solid Red	Critical Fault
Flashing Red	Noncritical Fault

Figure 10-30 KFD module status indicator conditions.

If the Network Status Indicator is:	Then:
Off	Offline
Solid Green	Online—Communicating
Flashing Green	Online
Solid Red	Link Failed—Critical Fault

Figure 10-31 Network status indicators.

Drop Line Length	Maximum Allowable Current
5 Feet	3A
6.6 Feet	2A
10 Feet	1.5A
15 Feet	1A
20 Feet	0.75A

Figure 10-32 Allowable drop line current for various lengths.

its for various drop line lengths. Note that the longer the drop line is, the lower the current limit.

Figure 10-33 is a chart that can be used to determine maximum currents for given network lengths. For example, if your network is 525 feet long, the current limit would be approximately 1.9A. Note that any current on the chart above 4A is not allowed under NEC guidelines.

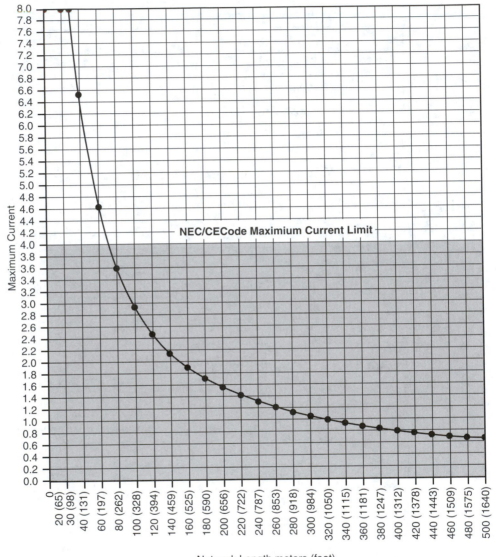

Figure 10-33 Maximum current chart. *(Courtesy Rockwell Automation Inc.)*

Let us look at a few examples of power supply calculation. Figure 10-34 shows a simple system. The network is 450 feet long. If we add the device currents, we find that the total current draw is 2.0A. Our network length is 450 feet. (If we go to the chart in Figure 10-33 we see that we are allowed approximately 2.1A.) Since our total draw is 2.0A, we are within the limits.

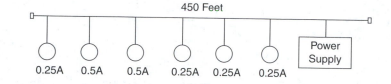

Figure 10-34   Simple DeviceNet System.

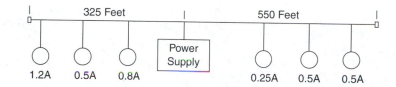

Figure 10-35   Network with power supply in the middle of the network.

Note that device current is based on how much current the device will draw from the DeviceNet network. Some devices require external power. A drive, for example, will require an external supply and may draw very little current from the network. Base your current calculations on how much the devices draw from the network.

Let us consider another example (Figure 10-35). In this case, the power supply has been placed in the middle of the network. There is a distinct advantage to putting the power supply somewhere in the middle instead of on the end of the network. In this case we have 2.5A total current on the left leg of the network and 1.5A of current on the right. Consider the left side first. The length of the left side of the network is 450 feet. If we look at Figure 10-33 we see that for 325 feet we are allowed approximately 2.9A. Our total draw for this side of the network is 2.5A. The actual draw is less than the allowable draw, so the left side is within limits. The total current draw for the system is under 4A, so this system is within NEC guidelines.

The right side of the network is 550 feet long. (The allowable current for a 550-foot length from Figure 10-33 is approximately 1.8A.) The actual current is 1.25A, so the current draw for each side is within the limits. The total draw for the system is 2.5A + 1.25A, or 3.75A. The total of 3.75A does not exceed the code of 4A, so the whole network is within specifications.

Figure 10-36 shows an example in which the total current draw exceeds the NEC 4A limit. If we add the current draws we get a total of 6.25A. We can construct this network if we split the network into two segments and utilize two power supplies. Note that the dotted lines between the segments represent the communications lines. They are connected over the whole network. The power lines are not, however. If you recall the PowerTap allowed us to power one side or both sides of the network. In this case, the first power supply powers only the left side of the

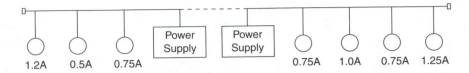

Figure 10-36 Note that two power supplies are used to keep power under 4A on each side of the network. Note also that the communications line connects both sides; only the power lines are separate for each side.

network. The second power supply powers the right segment. Remember, however, that the communications lines are connected over the whole length. The left side only draws 2.5A and the right side draws 3.75A. Both segments are under 4A, so this network is within the limits.

Communication Flow in a DeviceNet Network

The scanner card (or master) coordinates and controls all communication in a DeviceNet system. Figure 10-37 shows a typical system. The information that a scanner receives or transmits is stored in its memory. The CPU (processor) of the SLC can utilize this information in ladder logic. The CPU can receive or transmit information in

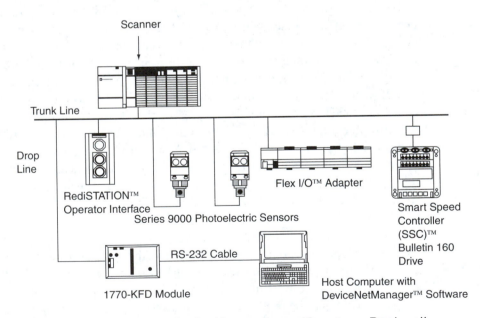

Figure 10-37 Typical DeviceNet system. *(Courtesy Rockwell Automation Inc.)*

two modes. One of the modes is I/O. I/O messaging is used for time-critical, control-oriented data exchange. The second mode is explicit messaging, which enables the CPU to transmit/receive a minimum of six words, up to a maximum twenty-six words.

Explicit messaging could be used to transmit and receive information for a device like a drive. The ladder diagram in the CPU could determine speeds, acceleration/deceleration, and so on. It would then use an explicit message to the scanner module (master). The scanner would then transmit the message to the drive as a block of information. The CPU could also request drive information from the scanner. The scanner would then request the information from the drive and make it available to the CPU. As you can see, the scanner handles all communications with the devices and makes the information available to the CPU. In a Rockwell system, explicit messaging is initiated by an instruction in the ladder. A write from the processor to the scanner module would utilize the M0 file in the scanner. A write from the processor utilizes the M1 file of the scanner. These reads and writes are only performed when they are called by the CPU. The programmer should be careful to only make these calls when they are needed. They should not be called every scan, as they are time intensive.

I/O messaging is almost transparent to the user. The user can access I/O like regular I/O in the rung, utilizing the slot and bit number of the particular I/O in the scanner.

Configuring the Scanner

Let us assume for this example that the DeviceNet scanner is in slot 1 of the SLC. Remember that this is the physical address (slot 1) for the scanner. The scanner will also have a node address for DeviceNet communications.

Scanners need to be configured. Configuration is done with a computer and software attached to the network. Rockwell's software is called RSNetworx. First node addresses would need to be set on individual devices. Remember that new devices come with an address of 63. Some devices can be configured manually, whereas others might have to be connected individually to the computer and RSNetworx software used for configuring the device and setting its node address.

Consider an imaginary application. We will go through the steps to create a DeviceNet network. Note that this example will not include every step, but it is intended to give an overview of the process. There is one photo sensor, a drive, one limit switch, and the scanner. First we connect to the scanner module and set the node address to 0. It is desirable to have the scanner at the lowest address. The rest of the devices are connected and addresses set as shown in Figure 10-38. Note that this is just one possibility. Any node numbers could have been chosen. It is a good idea, however, to set the scanner to node, and to leave node 63 open so that new devices can be connected and then set to a new address.

Device	Node Address
Scanner	0
Drive	1
Photo Sensor	2
Limit Switch Through a DeviceLink	3
RediSTATION	4
KFD Module for Computer Link	62

Figure 10-38 Node addresses.

For our example we will utilize Rockwell Automation RSNetworx software (DeviceNet Manager software could also be used) and Rockwell products. Remember that any DeviceNet compatible software or hardware could be used.

Figure 10-39 shows the physical setup needed to set up our devices and network. Note the computer, KFD module, and photo sensor in this example.

The user would first need to change the node addresses of the devices in our application. Remember that new devices come with a default address of 63. The user must commission each device to the correct node number.

Next the user would construct the actual network. The user can then connect all of the devices together for the network. The KFD module is connected into the network also. RSNetworx is now able to communicate with all the devices and build the network on the screen. Next the user must build a scan list so that the scanner knows which devices it should be scanning. The devices must then be mapped to memory. The scanner can do this automatically or the user can do it manually.

Drive Example

A drive is an example of a device that uses multiple words in memory. For this example, we will use a Rockwell Automation 160 drive. A DeviceNet communications module can be attached to the front of the drive. The drive will be one node address in a DeviceNet system.

The address and baud rate are set with dip switches or configured through software. The front panel of the DeviceNet drive module has troubleshooting LEDs for communications, fault, and ready.

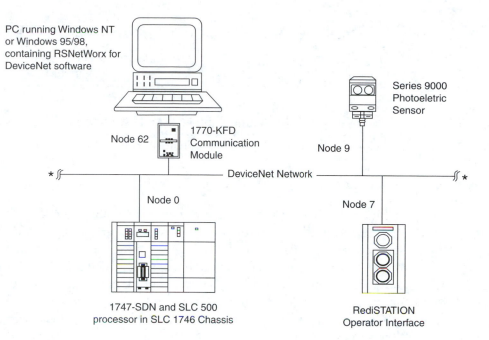

Figure 10-39 Computer, KFD communications module, and a series 9000 Rockwell Automation photo sensor. *(Courtesy Rockwell Automation Inc.)*

Byte	Bit 7	Bit 6	Bit 5	Bit 4	Bit 3	Bit 2	Bit 1	Bit 0
0		Net Reference	Net Control			Fault Reset	Run Reverse	Run Forward
1								
2		Speed Reference (RPM) Low Byte						
3		Speed Reference (RPM) High Byte						

Figure 10-40 Output data position in memory.

Figures 10-40 and 10-41 show the input and output words available to control and monitor the drive using DeviceNet. The user chooses from several choices of input and output selections for these tables. In this case, a reversing speed control drive format was chosen. The terms *output* and *input* are in relation to the scanner. So the output information would be used to send information to the drive such as a speed command (reference).

Byte	Bit 7	Bit 6	Bit 5	Bit 4	Bit 3	Bit 2	Bit 1	Bit 0
0	At Speed	Ref From Net	CTRL From Net	Ready	Running Reverse	Running Forward		Faulted
1								
2	Actual Speed (RPM) Low Byte							
3	Actual Speed (RPM) High Byte							

Figure 10-41   Input data position in memory.

Figure 10-41 shows the input information available from the drive. Remember that the information is in relation to the scanner so that input information for the scanner is output data from the drive. As you can see from Figure 10-41, bit 7 would be a 1 if the drive has achieved the commanded speed. Bit 2 would be a 1 if the drive is running forward. Bit 0 would be a 1 if the drive has faulted. Any of these bits can be used in ladder logic for logic or troubleshooting.

The drive outputs (input to scanner) the actual speed of the drive. That information is in bytes 2 and 3.

Revisit Figures 10-40 and 10-41. Note that there are 4 bytes of input information available and 4 bytes of output information available. These must be mapped to the DeviceNet scanner's memory. The user can choose where to map the drive's data in input and output memory or the scanner can automatically map the memory. Then the user would look at the starting memory location and determine where all of the drive parameters and information are in memory.

Once the scan list and memory mapping are complete and the scan list has been downloaded to the scanner, the DeviceNet system is ready to run. At this point, ladder logic in the SLC can control the devices.

Figure 10-42 shows an example portion of ladder logic used to control a drive. Note that in this case, the drive is mapped to discrete memory. Note also that the drive is a polled device. Rung 0 turns on the poll bit in the scanner so that the scanner polls all polled devices.

Remember that the scanner handles all communication with the network so that the CPU can worry about running the program (ladder logic). We can directly access the discrete information that we mapped to the scanner just like any other I/O. DeviceNet Manager enables us to configure the drive's parameters during setup if we wish.

The drive parameters can also be changed or monitored "on the fly." These can be accessed in a different manner, however, called explicit messaging. Explicit messaging utilizes M0 and M1 files. We would use copy (COP) instructions in the CPU to copy the M1 (input information from the scanner) files to integer files (N7) in the CPU. COP instructions would also be used to copy information (output information

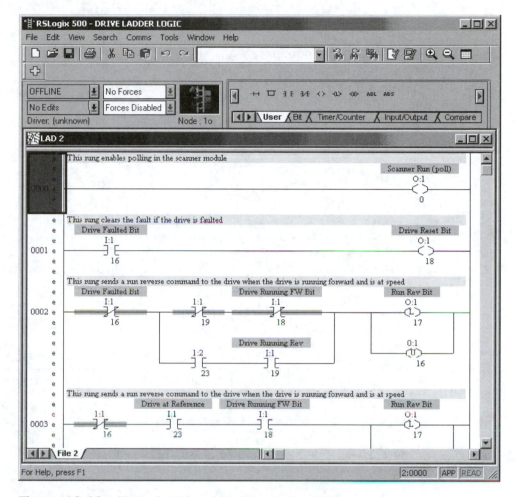

Figure 10-42 Note that the drive is mapped to discrete memory.

to the scanner—parameters in this case) from integer files (N7) to scanner memory. Scan time is optimized if we only copy M0 and M1 files when necessary. For example, if we want to change the acceleration parameter in the drive, we would copy the new value during one scan to M0 memory in the scanner and the scanner would write it to the drive.

RSLogix can also be used to examine the state of the devices. If a user wanted to see the states of DeviceNet inputs, the user would bring up the input file for slot 1. The scanner in this sample application was mounted in slot 1. The user can bring up the input or output files in the run mode and monitor DeviceNet I/O.

Figure 10-43 Top of scanner module showing status LEDs and numeric display. *(Courtesy Rockwell Automation Inc.)*

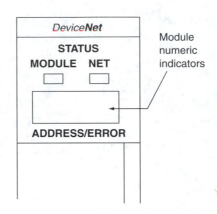

If the Module Indicator is:	Then:	Required Action:
Off	No Power to the Module	Apply Power
Green	Module Operating in Normal Mode	None
Flashing Green	Module Not Configured	Configure the Module
Flashing Red	Invalid Configuration	Check Configuration Setup
Red	Unrecoverable Fault in the Module	Replace the Module

Figure 10-44 Scanner module status LED indicators.

Troubleshooting

One of the greatest strengths of DeviceNet is the troubleshooting that is possible. There are two LEDs on the front of the scanner and a two-digit numeric display (Figure 10-43).

Figures 10-44 and 10-45 show the net and module status indicator conditions and troubleshooting help. Figure 10-46 shows some of the two-digit codes for troubleshooting the DeviceNet network. These two-digit codes are helpful in pinpointing the problem and correcting it. For example, if a node goes bad or a line gets cut, the scanner's readout will continually flash the error code and the nodes that are not communicating. Assume that the drop line to the photo eye was cut. The scanner readout would continually flash 72 and then 2. 72 means that a node has stopped

If the Net Indicator is:	Then:	Which Indicates:	Required Action
Off	The device has no power or the channel is disabled for communication due to a bus off condition, loss of network power, or has been intentionally disabled.	The channel is disabled for DeviceNet communication	Power-up the module, provide network power to the channel, and be sure that the channel is enabled in both the module configuration table and the module command word.
Green	Normal operation	All slave devices in the scan list are communicating normally with the module	None
Flashing Green	The two-digit numeric display for the channel indicates an error code that provides more information about the condition of the channel.	The channel is enabled but no communication is occurring	Configure the scan list table for the channel to add devices
Flashing Red	The two-digit numeric display on the scanner displays an error code that provides information about the cause	At least one of the slave devices has failed to communicate with the module	Examine the failed device and the scan list for accuracy
Red	The communications channel has failed. The two-digit numeric display for the scanner displays an error code that provides more information about the condition of the channel	The module may be defective	Reset the module. If failures continue, replace the module

Figure 10-45 Network status LED indicators.

Code	Description	Required Action
0-63	Under normal operation the display will show the network address of the scanner	None
70	Module failed the duplicate node address check	Change the module address to another available one.
72	Slave device stopped communicating—The node number of the device will flash alternately with the 72	Inspect the field devices and verify connections
75	No scan list is active in the module	Enter a scan list
78	Slave device in the scan list does not exist—The node number will alternately flash with the 78	Add the device to the network or delete the device from the scan list
80	The scanner is in idle mode	None
81	The scanner is in fault mode	None
92	No network power is detected on the communications port	Provide network power—Make sure that the DC power is present, clean and sufficient.

Figure 10-46   A partial list of the troubleshooting codes.

communicating and 2 is the node that is missing. If 3 was also missing it would flash 72-2-3. If there is a power problem the scanner will flash 92.

Devices also offer additional capability. For example, the Rockwell Automation photo sensor has a margin output bit that can be used in the user's logic. If the sensor is not receiving the amount of light it should be, it turns on the margin output. This could mean that the reflector for the sensor is dirty or misaligned. The user could use the margin bit as an input in the ladder logic to notify an operator or maintenance that this sensor has a margin problem. In this manner the sensor could be repaired or replaced before it failed.

DeviceNet Summary

DeviceNet is a simple, open networking solution that reduces the cost and time to wire and install automation. DeviceNet enables devices from any DeviceNet compatible vendors to be interchanged.

The troubleshooting it provides can also dramatically reduce downtime. The scanner module error codes can direct you to the malfunction and even the problem node. The user can also utilize ladder logic and the device's intelligence to pinpoint problems. An example would be using the light margin bit in the photo sensors in ladder logic to alert the operator when the sensor may need to be aligned, cleaned, or replaced.

QUESTIONS

1. Name and describe the three levels of communications.

2. What is daisy chaining?

3. What is DH+ and what is its purpose?

4. What is ControlNet used for?

5. What is DeviceNet used for?

6. Which of the following can a ControlLogix system be used for?
    a. Stand-alone controller
    b. Process controller
    c. Motion controller
    d. Communications gateway
    e. Only a, c, and d above
    f. All of the above

7. What is SERCOS?

8. How many nodes can a DeviceNet network have?

9. What is a scanner and what does it do?

10. What is a scanlist?

chapter 11

Safety and Lockout/Tagout

Safety should be the number-one concern in the workplace, because of the numerous dangers: machinery, electrical hazards, and so forth. Stay on guard of the dangers to protect yourself and others. In this chapter we examine safe practices and lockout/tagout procedures.

OBJECTIVES

Upon completion of this chapter, you will be able to:
1. Define an accident and why accidents happen
2. Describe how accidents can be prevented
3. Describe lockout/tagout and how it is used in industry
4. Develop a lockout/tagout procedure

SAFETY

Be mindful of your safety and the safety of others as you work.

What Is an Accident?

An accident is an unexpected action that results in injury to people, machines, or tools. Note that an accident is always *unexpected*. We never think accidents will happen to us, but they can happen to anyone. An accident can easily cause you to lose a limb, your sight, or even your life. Accidents cost enterprises huge amounts of money.

Most accidents are minor, such as minor cuts, but all are important. We should look for ways to prevent even minor accidents from reoccurring, because they can be worse than the first time. Every company has procedures for reporting even minor accidents, and all accidents should be reported. Companies often report accidents on Incident Report Forms.

CAUSES OF ACCIDENTS

Accidents can be prevented. Following are possible causes of accidents.

1. Carelessness
2. People who ignore safety rules or bypass safety equipment
3. The use of improper tooling, defective tools, or the improper use of tools
4. Unsafe working practices such as lifting heavy objects incorrectly
5. Horseplay (playing around on the job)

Common sources of accidents include the following:

1. Machines with moving or rotating parts
2. Electrical machinery
3. Equipment that uses high-pressure fluids
4. Chemicals
5. Sharp objects on machines or tools

Remember that every piece of equipment is dangerous!

ACCIDENT PREVENTION

Here are a few ways to prevent accidents.

1. *Design safety into the equipment.* This means that machinery is designed to prevent accidents. There are guards and interlocks on machines to prevent injury from moving parts and electrical shock. There are lockouts on electrical panels so that a worker can lock the power out to repair the equipment. Never remove guards or safety interlocks from machines while working on them.

2. *Use proper clothing, eye, and hearing protection.* You must have self-discipline. Safety glasses are required in most workplaces. If you are in a

noisy environment wear ear protection also. Never wear gloves, loose clothing, or jewelry around moving machinery.

3. *Follow warning signs.* Warning signs indicate high voltage and other dangers. A yellow/black line means Danger—Do Not Cross This Line.

4. *Follow safety procedures closely.* Know the company policies regarding safety in all areas.

SAFE USE OF LAB EQUIPMENT AND HAND TOOLS

It is important to follow safe procedures and learn good habits that will keep you safe on the job. Following is an important list of safety guidelines.

1. Wear proper safety equipment.
2. Wear proper eye protection.
3. Know how to use the equipment. Do not operate equipment you do not understand.
4. Do not hurry.
5. Do not fool around.
6. Keep the work area clean.
7. Keep the floor dry.
8. Always beware of electricity.
9. Use adequate light.
10. Know first aid.
11. Handle tools carefully.
12. Keep tools sharp. A dull tool requires more pressure and is more likely to cause injury.
13. Use the right tool.
14. Beware of fire or fumes. If you think you smell fire, stop immediately and investigate.
15. Use heavy extension cords. Thin extension cords can overheat, melting the insulation to expose the wires and cause a fire.

OVERVIEW OF LOCKOUT/TAGOUT

On October 30, 1989, the Lockout/Tagout Standard, 29 CFR 1910.147, went into effect. It was released by the Department of Labor. The standard is titled, "The Control of Hazardous Energy Sources (Lockout/Tagout)." The standard was intended to reduce the number of deaths and injuries related to servicing and maintaining machines and equipment. Deaths and tens of thousands of lost work days are attributable to maintenance and servicing activities each year.

The lockout/tagout standard covers the servicing and maintenance of machines and equipment in which the unexpected start-up or energization of the machines or equipment, or the release of stored energy, could cause injury to employees. The standard is intended to cover energy sources such as electrical, mechanical, hydraulic, chemical, nuclear, and thermal. The standard establishes only minimum guides for the control of such hazardous energy; Normal production operations, cords and plugs under exclusive control, and hot tap operations are not covered by the standard.

Hot tap operations are those involving transmission and distribution systems for substances such as gas, steam, water, or petroleum products. A hot tap is a procedure used in repair maintenance and in service activities that involve welding on a piece of equipment such as on pipelines, vessels, or tanks under pressure, to install connections or appurtenances. Hot tap procedures are commonly used to replace or add sections of pipeline without the interruption of service for air, gas, water, steam, and petrochemical distribution systems. The standard does not apply to hot taps when they are performed on pressurized pipelines, provided that the employer demonstrates that continuity of service is essential, that shutdown of the system is impractical, that documented procedures are followed, and that special equipment is used which will provide proven, effective protection for employees.

Employers are required to establish a program consisting of an energy control (lockout/tagout) procedure and employee training to ensure that before any employee performs any servicing or maintenance on a machine or equipment, where the unexpected energizing, start-up, or release of stored energy could occur and cause injury, the machine or equipment shall be isolated and rendered inoperative. The employer is also required to conduct annual inspection of the energy control procedure, to ensure that the procedures and the requirements of this standard are being followed.

The standard defines an *energy source* as any source of electrical, mechanical, hydraulic, pneumatic, chemical, thermal, or other energy. Machinery or equipment is considered to be energized if it is connected to an energy source or contains residual or stored energy. Stored energy can be found in pneumatic and hydraulic systems, springs, capacitors, and even gravity.

Servicing and/or maintenance includes activities such as constructing, installing, setting up, adjusting, inspecting, modifying, and maintaining and/or servicing machines or equipment. These activities include lubricating, cleaning, or unjamming machines or equipment, and making adjustments or tool changes, during which time the employee may be exposed to the unexpected energization or start-up of the equipment or release of hazardous energy.

Normal production operations are excluded from lockout/tagout restrictions. Normal production operation is the utilization of a machine or equipment to perform its intended production function. Any work performed to prepare a machine or equipment to perform its normal production operation is called setup.

If an employee is working on cord and plug–connected electrical equipment—for which exposure to unexpected energization or start-up of the equipment is controlled by the unplugging of the equipment from the energy source, and the plug is under the exclusive control of the employee performing the servicing or maintenance—this activity is also excluded from requirements of the standard.

Only authorized employees may lock out machines or equipment. An authorized employee is one who has been trained and has the authority to lock or tag out machines or equipment to perform the servicing or maintenance.

An energy isolating device is a mechanical device that physically prevents the transmission or release of energy. Energy isolating devices include the following: manually operated electrical circuit breakers; disconnect switches (Figure 11-1);

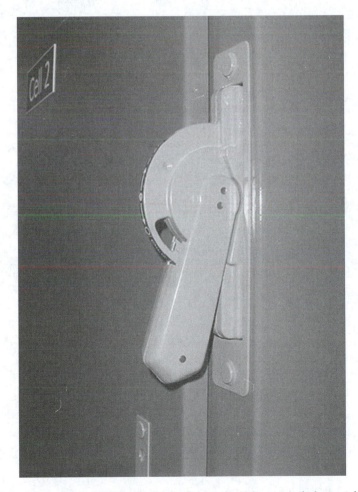

Figure 11-1 A typical electrical disconnect. In this case it is not locked out.

Figure 11-2 A typical pneumatic disconnect.

manually operated switches by which the conductors of a circuit can be disconnected from all ungrounded supply conductors and, in addition, no pole can be operated independently; line valves (Figure 11-2); and locks or similar devices used to block or isolate energy. Push buttons, selector switches, and other control circuit type devices are not energy isolating devices.

An energy isolating device is capable of being locked out if it has a hasp or other means of attachment to which, or through which, a lock can be affixed, or it has a built-in locking mechanism. Other energy isolating devices are capable of being locked out, if lockout can be achieved without the need to dismantle, rebuild, or replace the energy isolating device or permanently alter its energy control capability. Since January 2, 1990, industry has required that new machines or equipment with energy isolating devices be designed to accept a lockout device.

Lockout

Lockout is the placement of a lockout device on an energy isolating device, in accordance with an established procedure, to ensure that the device cannot be operated until the lockout device is removed.

A lockout device utilizes a positive means (such as a lock) to hold an energy isolating device in the safe position and prevent the energizing of a machine or equipment. A lock may be either key or combination type. If an energy isolating device is incapable of being locked out, then the employer's energy control program shall utilize a tagout system.

Notification of Employees Affected employees must be notified by the employer or authorized employee of the application and removal of lockout devices or tagout devices. Notification shall be given before the controls are applied, and after they are removed from the machine or equipment. Affected employees are defined as employees whose job requires them to operate or use a machine or equipment on which servicing or maintenance is being performed under lockout or tagout, or whose job requires them to work in an area in which such servicing or maintenance is being performed.

Tagout

Tagout is the placement of a tagout device on an energy isolating device, in accordance with an established procedure, to indicate that the energy isolating device and the equipment being controlled may not be operated until the tagout device is removed. Tagout shall be performed only by the authorized employees who are performing the servicing or maintenance.

A tagout device is a prominent warning device, such as a tag and a means of attachment, which can be securely fastened to an energy isolating device in accordance with an established procedure. This is to indicate that the energy isolating device and the equipment being controlled may not be operated until the tagout device is removed from each energy isolating device by the employee who applied the device. When the authorized employee who applied the lockout or tagout device is not available to remove it, that device may be removed under the direction of the employer, provided that specific procedures and training for such removal have been developed, documented, and incorporated into the energy control program.

Tagout devices, where used, must be affixed in such a manner as to clearly indicate that the operation or movement of energy isolating devices from the "safe" or "off" position is prohibited. Where tagout devices are used with energy isolating devices designed with the capability of being locked, the tag attachment must be fastened at the same point at which the lock would have been attached. Where a tag cannot be affixed directly to the energy isolating device, the tag must be located as close as safely possible to the device, in a position that will be immediately obvious to anyone attempting to operate the device.

TRAINING

Training must be provided by the employer to ensure that the purpose and function of the energy control program are understood by employees and that the knowledge and skills required for the safe application, usage, and removal of energy controls are attained by employees. Employees should be trained to do the following:

Recognize hazardous energy sources

Know the type and magnitude of the energy available in the workplace

Understand the methods and means for energy isolation and control

Understand the purpose and use of the lockout/tagout procedures

All other employees whose work operations are or may be in an area where lockout/tagout procedures may be used, shall be instructed about the procedure and about the prohibition against attempting to restart or reenergize machines or equipment which are locked or tagged out.

When tagout procedures are used, employees must be taught about the following limitations of tags.

Tags are really just warning devices and do not provide physical restraint on equipment.

When a tag is attached it is not to be removed without authorization of personnel responsible for it; and it is never to be bypassed, ignored, or otherwise defeated.

Tags must be legible. All authorized employees, affected employees, and others who work in the area must understand the tags.

Tags may create a false sense of security. Everyone must understand the purpose of them.

Retraining

Retraining shall be provided for all authorized and affected employees when there is a change in job assignments; a change in machines, equipment, or processes that present a new hazard; or a change in the energy control procedures.

Additional retraining shall also be conducted when a periodic inspection reveals, or when the employer has reason to believe, that there are deviations from or inadequacies in the employee's knowledge or use of the energy control procedures.

The retraining shall reestablish employee proficiency and introduce new or revised control methods and procedures, as necessary.

The employer shall certify that employee training has been accomplished and is being kept up to date. The certification shall contain each employee's name and dates of training.

REQUIREMENTS FOR LOCKOUT/TAGOUT DEVICES

Lockout and tagout devices must be singularly identified, must be the only device(s) used for controlling energy, and must not be used for other purposes. The devices must be durable, which means they must be capable of withstanding the environment to which they are exposed for the maximum period of time that exposure is expected. Tagout devices must be constructed and printed so that exposure to weather conditions or wet and damp locations will not cause the tag to deteriorate or the message on the tag to become illegible (Figure 11-3).

Tags must not deteriorate when used in corrosive environments such as areas where acid and alkali chemicals are handled and stored.

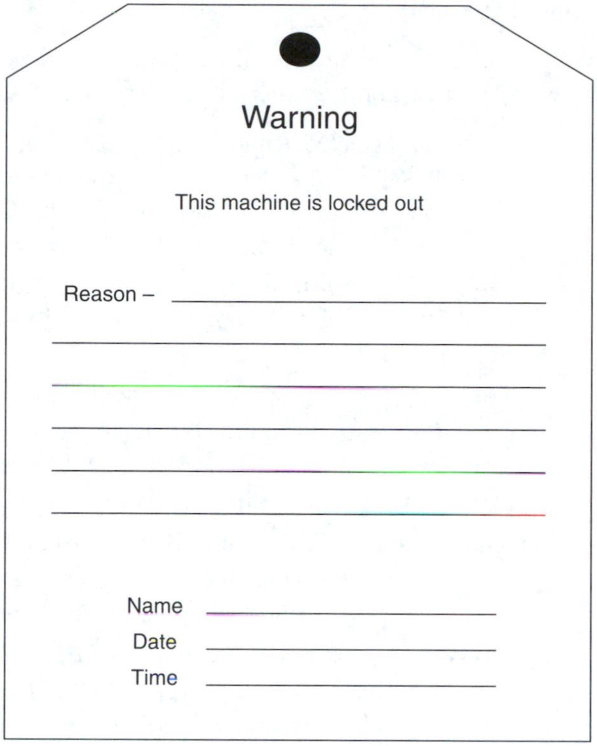

Warning

This machine is locked out

Reason – _____

_____

_____

_____

_____

_____

Name _____
Date _____
Time _____

Figure 11-3   A typical tagout tag.

Lockout and tagout devices must be standardized within the facility according to either color, shape, or size. Print and format must also be standardized for tagout devices.

Lockout devices must be substantial enough to prevent removal without the use of excessive force or unusual techniques, such as with the use of bolt cutters or other metal-cutting tools.

Tagout devices, including their means of attachment, shall be substantial enough to prevent inadvertent or accidental removal. Tagout devices must be attached with a nonreusable type of attachment. It must be attachable by hand, self-locking, and nonreleasable with a minimum unlocking strength of at least 50 pounds. It should have the general design and basic characteristics of being at least equivalent to a one-piece, all environment–tolerant nylon cable tie.

Lockout and tagout devices must identify the employee who applied them.

Tagout devices must clearly warn against hazardous conditions if the machine or equipment is energized, such as Do Not Start, Do Not Open, Do Not Close, Do Not Energize, or Do Not Operate.

APPLICATION OF CONTROL

The established procedures for the application of lockout or tagout shall cover the following elements and actions and shall be done in the following sequence.

1. Notify all affected employees that a lockout or tagout system is going to be used. They must also understand the reason for the lockout. Before an authorized or affected employee turns off a machine or equipment, the authorized employee must understand the types and magnitudes of the energy, the hazards of the energy to be controlled, and the method or means to control the energy for the machine or equipment being serviced or maintained.

2. The machine or equipment shall be turned off or shut down using the procedures established for the machine or equipment. An orderly shutdown must be utilized to avoid any additional or increased hazards to employees as a result of the equipment stoppage.

3. All energy isolating devices that are needed to control the energy to the machine or equipment shall be physically located and operated in such a manner as to isolate the machine or equipment from the energy sources.

4. Lockout or tagout devices shall be affixed to each energy isolating device by authorized employees. Lockout devices, where used, shall be affixed in a manner that will hold the energy isolating devices in a safe or off position.

5. Following the application of lockout or tagout devices to energy isolating devices, stored energy must be dissipated or restrained by methods such as repositioning, blocking, and bleeding down. If there is a possibility of reaccumulation of stored energy to a hazardous level, verification of isolation shall be continued until the servicing or maintenance is complete, or until the possibility of such accumulation of energy no longer exists.

6. Prior to working on machines or equipment that has been locked out or tagged out, the authorized employee shall verify that the machine or equipment has actually been isolated and de-energized. This is done by operating the push button or other normal operating controls to ensure that the equipment will not operate.

Caution: Be sure to return the operating controls to the neutral or off position after the test.

The machine is now locked or tagged out. Before lockout or tagout devices are removed and energy is restored to the machine or equipment, authorized employees take action to ensure the following:

The work area shall be inspected to ensure that nonessential items have been removed and ensure that machine or equipment components are operationally intact.

The work area shall be checked to ensure that all employees have been safely positioned or removed.

Before lockout or tagout devices are removed and before machines or equipment are energized, affected employees shall be notified that the lockout or tagout devices have been removed.

Each lockout or tagout device must be removed from each energy isolating device by the employee who applied the device. The only exception to this is when that person is unavailable to remove it. The device may then be removed under the direction of the employer, provided that specific procedures and training for such removal have been developed, documented, and incorporated into the employer's energy control program. The employer must demonstrate that the specific procedure includes at least the following elements.

The employer must verify that the authorized employee who applied the device is not at the facility.

All reasonable efforts must be made to contact the authorized employee to inform him or her that the lockout or tagout device has been removed.

The authorized employee must be made aware that the lockout/tagout device was removed before he or she resumes work at that facility.

TESTING OF MACHINES, EQUIPMENT, OR COMPONENTS

In certain situations, the lockout or tagout devices may be temporarily removed from the energy isolating device and the machine or equipment energized to test or position the machine, equipment, or component. In this case, the following sequence of actions must be taken.

1. Clear the machine or equipment of tools and materials.
2. Remove employees from the machine or equipment area.
3. Remove the lockout or tagout devices as specified in the standard.
4. Energize and proceed with testing or positioning.
5. De-energize all systems and reapply energy control measures in accordance with the standard to continue the servicing and/or maintenance.

Outside Personnel Working in the Plant

When outside servicing personnel (such as contractors) are to be engaged in activities covered by the lockout/tagout standard, the onsite employer and the outside employer must inform each other of the respective lockout or tagout procedures. The onsite employer must ensure that all employees understand and comply with the restrictions and prohibitions of the outside employer's energy control program.

GROUP LOCKOUT OR TAGOUT

When servicing and/or maintenance is performed by a group of people, they must use a procedure to protect them to the same degree as would a personal lockout or tagout procedure. The lockout/tagout standard specifies requirements for group procedures. Primary responsibility is vested in an authorized employee for a set number of employees. These employees work under the protection of a group lockout or tagout device (Figure 11-4). The group lockout device ensures that no individual can start up or energize the machine or equipment. All lockout or tagout devices must be removed to reenergize the machine or equipment. The authorized employee who is responsible for the group must ascertain the exposure status of individual group members with regard to the lockout or tagout of the machine or equipment. When more than one crew, craft, or department is involved, overall job-associated lockout or tagout control responsibility is assigned to an authorized employee. This employee is designated to coordinate affected workforces and ensure continuity of protection. Each authorized employee must affix a personal lockout or tagout device to the group lockout device, group lockbox, hasp (Figure 11-4), or comparable mechanism when beginning work, and shall remove those devices when stopping work on the machine or equipment being serviced or maintained.

Shift or Personnel Changes

Specific procedures must be utilized during shift or personnel changes to ensure the continuity of lockout or tagout protection, and therefore the orderly transfer of lockout or tagout device protection between shifts of employees, to minimize exposure to hazards from the unexpected energization or start-up of the machine or equipment, or the release of stored energy.

Figure 11-4 A hasp allows multiple personnel to lock out machines or equipment.

SAMPLE LOCKOUT PROCEDURE

Following is a sample lockout procedure. Tagout procedures may be used when the energy isolating devices are not lockable, provided the employer complies with the provisions of the standard which require additional training and more rigorous periodic inspections. When tagout is used and the energy isolating devices are lockable, the employer must provide full employee protection and additional training as well as more rigorous periodic inspections. When more complex systems are involved, additional comprehensive procedures may need to be developed, documented, and utilized.

Lockout Procedure for Machine 37

Note: This would normally name the machine when multiple procedures exist. If only one exists, it would normally be the company name.

Purpose

This procedure establishes the minimum requirements for the lockout of energy isolating devices when maintenance or servicing is done on machine 37. This procedure must be used to ensure that the machine is stopped, isolated from all potentially hazardous energy sources, and locked out before employees perform any servicing or maintenance during which time the unexpected energization or start-up of the machine or equipment or the release of stored energy could cause injury.

Employee Compliance

All employees, including authorized employees, are required to comply with the restrictions and limitations imposed on them during the use of this lockout procedure. All employees, upon observing a machine or piece of equipment locked out to perform servicing or maintenance, shall not attempt to start, energize, or use that machine or equipment.

A company may want to list disciplinary actions taken in the event of an employee violating the procedure.

Lockout Sequence

1. Notify all affected employees that servicing or maintenance is required on the machine and that the machine must be shut down and locked out to perform the servicing or maintenance.

   The procedure should list the names and/or job titles of affected employees and how to notify them.

2. The authorized employee must refer to the company procedure to identify the type and magnitude of the energy that the machine utilizes, must understand the hazards of the energy, and must know the methods to control the energy.

   The types and magnitudes of energy, their hazards, and the methods to control the energy should be detailed here.

3. If the machine or equipment is operating, shut it down by the normal stopping procedure (e.g., depress the stop button, open switch, close valve).

   The types and locations of machine or equipment operating controls should be detailed here.

4. Deactivate the energy isolating devices so that the machine or equipment is isolated from the energy sources.

   The types and locations of energy isolating devices should be detailed here.

5. Lock out the energy isolating devices with assigned individual locks.

6. Stored or residual energy (such as that in capacitors, springs, elevated machine members, rotating flywheels, hydraulic systems, and air, gas, steam, or water pressure) must be dissipated or restrained by methods such as grounding, repositioning, blocking, or bleeding down.

   The types of stored energy, as well as methods to dissipate or restrain the stored energy, should be detailed here.

7. Ensure that the equipment is disconnected from the energy sources by first checking that no personnel are exposed; then verify the isolation of the equipment by operating the push button or other normal operating controls or by testing to make certain the equipment will not operate. Caution: Return operating controls to neutral or off position after you verify the isolation of the equipment.

   The method of verifying the isolation of the equipment should be detailed here.

8. The machine or equipment is now locked out.

Returning the Machine or Equipment to Service

When the servicing or maintenance is complete and the machine or equipment is ready to return to normal operating condition, the following steps are taken.

1. Check the machine or equipment and the immediate area around the machine to ensure that nonessential items have been removed and that

the machine or equipment components are operationally intact. Check the work area to ensure that all employees have been safely positioned or removed from the area.

2. After all tools have been removed from the machine or equipment, and guards have been reinstalled and employees are in the clear, remove all lockout or tagout devices. Verify that the controls are in neutral and reenergize the machine or equipment. Note that the removal of some forms of blocking may require reenergization of the machine before safe removal. Notify affected employees that the servicing or maintenance is completed and the machine or equipment is ready for use.

SAMPLE LOCKOUT/TAGOUT CHECKLIST

NOTIFICATION

I have notified all affected employees that a lockout is required and the reason for the lockout.

Date _____ Time _____ Signature _____

SHUTDOWN

I understand the reason the equipment is to be shut down following normal procedures.

Date _____ Time _____ Signature _____

DISCONNECTION OF ENERGY SOURCES

I operated the switches, valves, and other energy isolating devices so that each energy source has been disconnected or isolated from the machinery or equipment. I have dissipated or restrained all stored energy such as springs, elevated machine members, capacitors, rotating flywheels, and pneumatic and hydraulic systems.

Date _____ Time _____ Signature _____

LOCKOUT

I have locked out the energy isolating devices using my assigned individual locks.

Date _____ Time _____ Signature _____

SAFETY CHECK

After ensuring that no personnel are exposed to hazards, I have operated the start button and other normal operation controls to ensure that all energy sources have been disconnected and that the equipment will not operate.

Date _____ Time _____ Signature _____

The Machine is Now Locked Out

QUESTIONS

1. What is an accident?

2. Explain three ways to prevent accidents.

3. Explain at least five things you can do to be safe in the lab.

4. List and explain the sources of energy that are typically found in an industrial environment.

5. Who is an affected employee?

6. Who is an authorized employee?

7. Define the term *lockout*.

8. Define the term *tagout*.

9. Describe the typical steps in a lockout/tagout procedure.

10. Write a lockout/tagout procedure for a cell that contains electrical and pneumatic energy.

chapter 12

Installation and Troubleshooting

Proper installation is crucial in automated systems. The safety of people and machines is at stake. Troubleshooting and maintenance of systems becomes more crucial as systems become more automatic, more complex, and more expensive. An enterprise cannot afford to have a system down for any length of time. The technician must be able to find and correct problems quickly.

OBJECTIVES

Upon completion of this chapter, you will be able to:
1. Describe safety considerations that are crucial in troubleshooting and maintaining systems
2. Explain such terms as *noise, snubbing, suppression,* and *single-point ground*
3. Explain correct installation techniques and considerations
4. Explain proper grounding techniques
5. Explain noise reduction techniques
6. Explain a typical troubleshooting process

INSTALLATION AND TROUBLESHOOTING

Installation, troubleshooting, and maintenance of an automated system is a crucial phase of any project. It is the point at which the hopes and fears of the engineers and technicians are realized. It can be a frustrating, exciting, and rewarding time. The installation, troubleshooting, maintenance, and operation of any automated system are highly dependent on the quality of the associated documentation. Documentation, unfortunately, is often an afterthought, although it should be developing as the system is developed. The system must be accurately and completely documented, to significantly reduce downtime. Fortunately, programming software for PLCs and other control devices has extensive documentation capabilities. Documentation should include the following:

Description of the overall system

Block diagram of the entire system

Program listing including cross referencing and clearly labeled I/O

Printout of the PLC or control device's memory showing I/O and variable usage

Complete wiring diagram

Description of peripheral devices and their manuals

Operator's manual including start-up and shutdown procedures

Notes concerning past maintenance

PLC INSTALLATION

Proper installation of a PLC is crucial. The PLC must be wired so that the system is safe for the workers. The system must also be wired so that the devices are protected from overcurrent situations. Proper fusing within the system is important. The PLC must also be protected from the application environment. Dust, coolant, chips, and other contaminants are usually found in the air. The proper choice of enclosures can protect the PLC. Figure 12-1 shows a block diagram of a typical installation.

Enclosures

PLCs are typically mounted in protective cabinets. The National Electrical Manufacturers Association (NEMA) has developed standards for enclosures (Figure 12-2). Enclosures are used to protect the control devices from the environment of the application. A cabinet type is chosen based on the severity of the environment in the application. Cabinets typically protect the PLC from airborne contamination. Metal cabinets can also help protect the PLC from electrical noise.

Heat is generated by devices. One must be sure that the PLC and other devices to be mounted in the cabinet can perform at the temperatures required. Remember that it will be even hotter in the cabinet than in the application, because of the heat

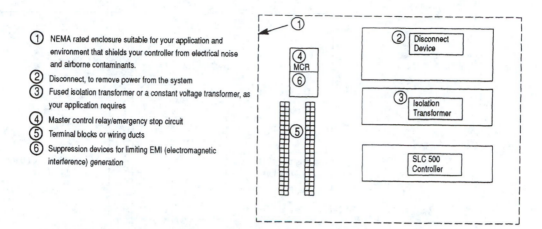

1. NEMA rated enclosure suitable for your application and environment that shields your controller from electrical noise and airborne contaminants.
2. Disconnect, to remove power from the system
3. Fused isolation transformer or a constant voltage transformer, as your application requires
4. Master control relay/emergency stop circuit
5. Terminal blocks or wiring ducts
6. Suppression devices for limiting EMI (electromagnetic interference) generation

Figure 12-1 Block diagram of a typical PLC control cabinet. *(Courtesy Rockwell Automation Inc.)*

Protection Against	Enclosure Type												
	1	2	3	3-r	3-s	4	4-x	5	6	6-p	1-1	1-2	1-3
Accidental contact with enclosed equipment	*	*	*	*	*	*	*	*	*	*	*	*	*
Falling dirt	*	*				*	*	*	*	*	*	*	*
Falling liquids, light splashing		*				*	*		*	*	*	*	*
Dust, lint, fibers, (noncombustible, nonignitable)					*	*	*	*	*			*	*
Windblown dust			*		*	*	*		*	*			
Hose down and splashing water						*	*		*	*			
Oil and coolant seepage												*	*
Oil or coolant spraying or splashing													*
Corrosive agents							*			*	*		
Occasional temporary submersion									*	*			
Occasional prolonged submersion										*			

Figure 12-2 Comparison of the features of NEMA cabinets versus enclosure type.

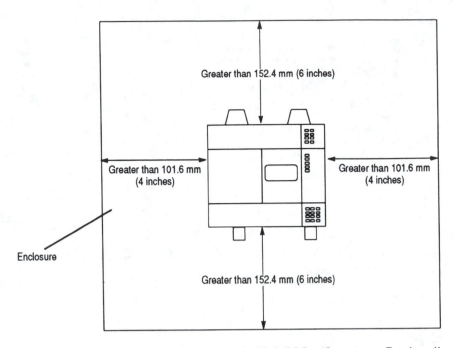

Figure 12-3   Proper mounting for an AB SLC-500. *(Courtesy Rockwell Automation Inc.)*

generated within the cabinet. In some applications, substantial heat may be generated by other devices in the system or cabinet. In this case, blower fans should be placed inside the enclosure to increase air circulation and reduce hot spots within the enclosure. These fans should filter the incoming air so that contaminants are not introduced to the cabinet and components.

The main consideration is adequate space around the PLC in the enclosure, to allow air to flow around the PLC. The manufacturer will provide installation requirements in the hardware manual for the PLC. Figure 12-3 shows an example for a AB SLC-500. Note that the dimensions shown from each side of the PLC to the cabinet are minimum distances. The actual distance between the PLC and the cabinet should be greater than those shown. Check the specifications for the PLC to determine temperature ranges. In most cases fans will be unnecessary. Proper clearances around devices will normally be sufficient for heat dissipation.

When drilling holes in the cabinet for mounting components, keep chips from falling into the PLC or other components. Metal chips or wire clippings could cause equipment to short circuit or could cause intermittent or permanent problems.

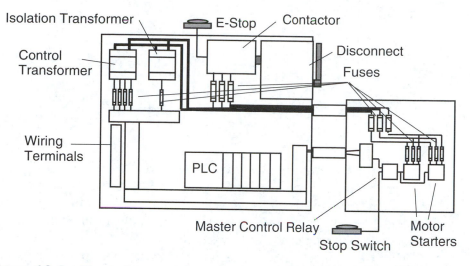

Isolation Transformer E-Stop Contactor

Control Transformer Disconnect Fuses

Wiring Terminals

PLC

Master Control Relay Stop Switch Motor Starters

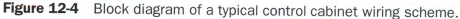

Figure 12-4 Block diagram of a typical control cabinet wiring scheme.

Wiring

Proper wiring of a system involves choosing the appropriate devices and fuses (Figure 12-4). Normally, three-phase power (typically 480 V) will be used in manufacturing. This will be the electrical supply for the control cabinet.

The three-phase power is connected to the cabinet via a mechanical disconnect. This disconnect is mechanically turned on or off by the use of a lever on the outside of the cabinet, and should be equipped with a lockout. This means that the technician should be able to put a lock on the lever to prevent anyone from accidentally applying power while it is being restored. This three-phase power must be fused. Normally, a fusible disconnect is used, which indicates that the mechanical disconnect has built-in fusing. The fusing is to ensure that too much current cannot be drawn. Figure 12-4 shows the fuses installed after the disconnect.

The three-phase power is then connected to a contactor. The contactor is used to turn all power off to the control logic in case of an emergency. The contactor is attached to hardwired emergency circuits in the system. If someone hits an emergency stop switch, then the contactor drops out and will not supply power. The hardwired safety should always be used in systems. This is called a master control relay.

Master Control Relay

A hardwired master control relay (MCR) is used for emergency controller shutdown (Figure 12-5). The MCR must be able to inhibit all machine motion by removing power to the machine I/O devices when the MCR relay is de-energized.

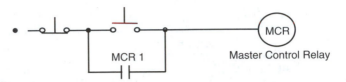

Figure 12-5 Example of a master control relay circuit.

If a DC power supply is used, the power should be interrupted on the load side rather than on the AC supply side, to provide quicker shutdown of power. The DC power supply should be powered directly from the fused secondary of the transformer. DC power from the power supply is then connected to the devices through a set of master control relay contacts.

Emergency stop switches can be placed at multiple locations. These should be chosen to provide full safety for anyone in the area. Switches may include limit-type switches for overtravel conditions, mushroom-type push-button switches, and other types. They are wired in series so that if any one of the switches is activated, the master control relay is de-energized. This removes power from all input and output circuits.

Never alter or bypass these circuits to defeat their function. Severe injury and/or damage can occur. These switches are designed to "fail safe": If they fail they should open the master control circuit and disconnect power. It is possible that a switch could short out and not offer further protection. Switches should be tested periodically to be sure they will still stop all machine motion if used.

The main power disconnect switch should be positioned in a convenient and easily accessible place for operators and maintenance personnel. The disconnect should be placed so that power can be turned off before the cabinet is opened.

The master control relay is not a substitute for a disconnect to the PLC. Its purpose is to quickly de-energize I/O devices. Figure 12-6 shows a cutoff system with a hardwired emergency switch connected to the master control relay. The figure also shows the wiring diagram. Note that the system provides for a mechanical disconnect for output module power and a hardwired stop switch for disconnecting the system power. The programmer should also provide for an orderly shutdown in the PLC control program.

The three-phase power must then be converted to single phase for the control logic. Power lines from the fusing are connected to transformers. In the case of Figure 12-7, there are two transformers: an isolation transformer and a control transformer. The isolation transformer is used to clean up the power supply for the PLC. Isolation transformers are normally used when there is high-frequency conducted noise in or around power distribution equipment. Isolation transformers are also used to step down the line voltage.

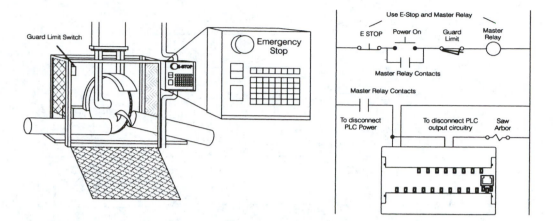

Figure 12-6 The use of a hardwired E-Stop and master control relay. *(Courtesy AutomationDirect Inc.)*

The control transformer is used to supply other control devices in the cabinet. The lines from the power supplies are then fused to protect the devices they will supply. These individual device circuits should be provided with their own fuses to match the current draw. DC power is usually required also. A small power supply is typically used to convert the AC to DC.

Motor starters are typically mounted in separate enclosures to protect the control logic from the noise these devices generate.

Within the cabinet, certain wiring conventions are typically used. Red wire is normally used for control wiring, black wire is used for three-phase power, blue wire is used for DC, and yellow wire is used to show that the voltage source is separately derived power (outside the cabinet).

Signal wiring, which is typically low voltage or low current, should be run separately from 120 V wiring. It could be affected by being too close to high-voltage wiring, so when possible, run the signal wires in separate conduit. Some conduit is internally divided by barriers to isolate signal wiring from higher voltage wiring.

Voltage is supplied to the PLC through wiring terminals. The user can often configure the PLC to accept different voltages (Figure 12-8). Here the PLC can be configured to accept either 220 or 110 V. In this case, the shorting bar must be installed if 110 V will be used.

Wiring Guidelines The following guidelines should be considered when wiring a system.

Always use the shortest possible cable.

Use a single length of cable between devices. Do not connect pieces of cable to make a longer cable. Avoid sharp bends in wiring.

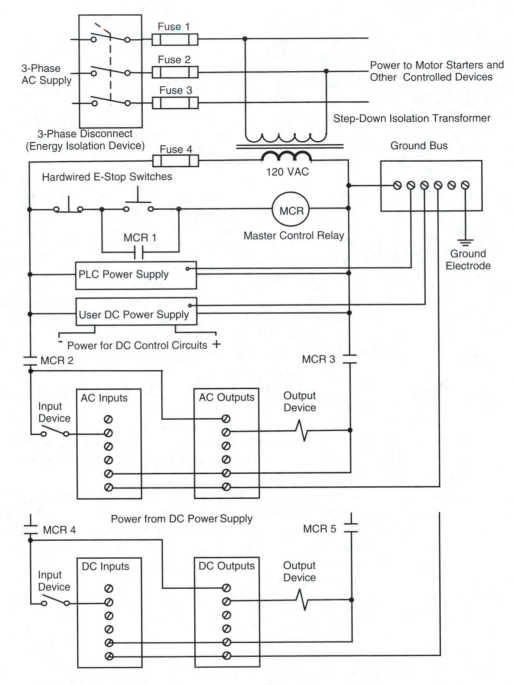

Figure 12-7 Control wiring diagram.

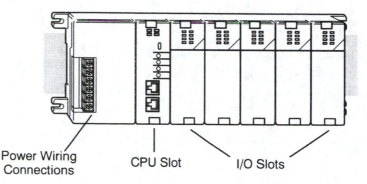

Power Wiring Connections   CPU Slot   I/O Slots

Figure 12-8 Diagram of PLC wiring.

Avoid placing system and field wiring close to high-energy wiring.

Physically separate field input wiring, output wiring, and other types of wiring. Separate DC and AC wiring when possible.

A good ground must exist for all components in the system (0.1 ohm or less).

If long return lines to the power supply are needed, do not use the same wire for input and output modules. Separate return lines will minimize the voltage drop on the return lines of the input connections.

Use cable trays for wiring.

Grounding

Neutral versus Ground   Grounding of electrical equipment is one of the least understood things about electrical systems. Beyond the use of grounding to ensure safety it must also ensure that the electrical devices do not interfere with each other in a cell or plant environment. The terms ground and neutral tend to cause confusion. They are not the same.

A ground represents an electrical path that is designed to carry current when an insulation breakdown occurs in a system. For example, a technician who drops a tool in an electrical cabinet may cause a breakdown if the tool touches a voltage source and the cabinet or other metal. It should be noted that some current will always flow through the ground path. This can be caused by capacitive coupling or inductive coupling between current conductors and the ground path.

Neutral represents a reference point within an electrical distribution system. Wires that are connected to neutral should normally be non-current carrying conductors. They should be sized to handle short term faults that may occur.

Neutral can be grounded, ground is not neutral.

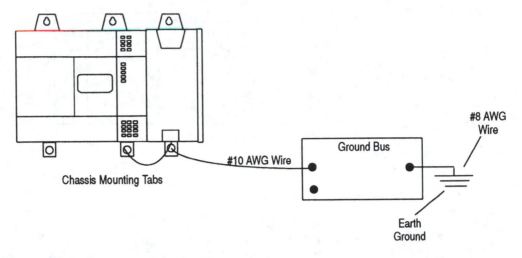

Figure 12-9   Grounding of an SLC-500 controller with a two-slot expansion chassis. *(Courtesy Rockwell Automation Inc.)*

Proper grounding is essential for safety and proper operation of a system. Grounding also helps limit the effects of noise due to electromagnetic interference (EMI). Check the appropriate electrical codes and ordinances to ensure compliance with minimum wire sizes, color coding, and general safety practices.

Connect the PLC and components to the subpanel ground bus (Figure 12-9). Ground connections should run from the PLC chassis and the power supply for each PLC expansion unit to the ground bus. The connection should exhibit very low resistance. Connect the subpanel ground bus to a single-point ground, such as a copper bus bar to a good earth-ground reference. There must be low impedance between each device and the single-point termination; a rule of thumb is less than 0.1 ohm DC resistance. This can be accomplished by removing the anodized finish and using copper lugs and star washers.

The PLC manufacturer will provide details in the hardware installation manual for their equipment. The National Electrical Code is an authoritative source for grounding requirements.

Grounding Guidelines   Figure 12-10 shows examples of ground connections. Grounding braid and green wires should be terminated at both ends with copper eye lugs to provide good continuity. Lugs should be crimped and soldered. Copper no. 10 or 12 bolts work well for fasteners that are used to provide an electrical connection to the single-point ground. This applies to device mounting bolts and braid termination bolts for subpanel and user-supplied single-point grounds. Tapped

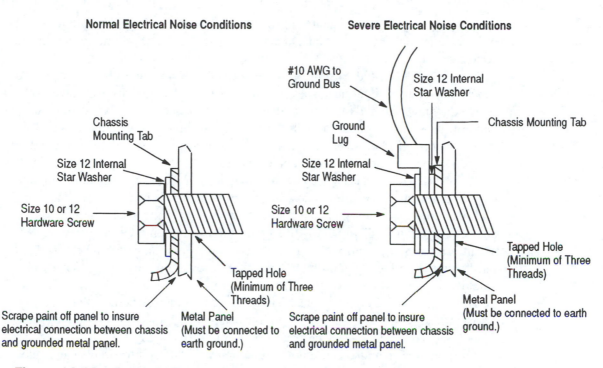

Normal Electrical Noise Conditions

Severe Electrical Noise Conditions

#10 AWG to Ground Bus

Size 12 Internal Star Washer

Chassis Mounting Tab

Ground Lug

Chassis Mounting Tab

Chassis Mounting Tab

Size 12 Internal Star Washer

Size 12 Internal Star Washer

Size 10 or 12 Hardware Screw

Size 10 or 12 Hardware Screw

Tapped Hole (Minimum of Three Threads)

Scrape paint off panel to insure electrical connection between chassis and grounded metal panel.

Metal Panel (Must be connected to earth ground.)

Tapped Hole (Minimum of Three Threads)

Scrape paint off panel to insure electrical connection between chassis and grounded metal panel.

Metal Panel (Must be connected to earth ground.)

Figure 12-10 Ground connections. *(Courtesy Rockwell Automation Inc.)*

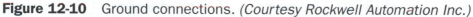

holes should be used rather than nuts and bolts. Note that a minimum number of threads are also required for a solid connection.

Paint, coatings, or corrosion must be removed from the areas of contact. Use external toothed lock washers (star washers). This practice should be used for all terminations: lug to subpanel, device to lug, device to subpanel, subpanel to conduit, and so on.

Check the appropriate electrical codes and ordinances to ensure compliance with minimum wire sizes, color coding, and general safety practices.

Handling Electrical Noise

Electrical noise is unwanted electrical interference that affects control equipment. The control devices in use today utilize microprocessors, which constantly fetch data and instructions from memory. Noise can cause the microprocessor to misinterpret an instruction or fetch bad data; and can cause minor problems or severe damage to equipment and people.

Noise is caused by a wide variety of manufacturing devices. Devices that switch high voltage and current are the primary sources of noise, including large motors and starters, welding equipment, and contactors that are used to turn devices on and off. Noise is not continuous; thus, it can be very difficult to find intermittent noise sources.

Noise can be created by power line disturbances, transmitted noise, or ground loops. Power line disturbances are generally caused by devices that have coils. When they are switched off they create a line disturbance. Power line disturbances can normally be overcome through the use of line filters. Surge suppressors such as MOVs or an RC network across the coil can limit the noise. Coil-type devices include relays, contactors, starters, clutches/brakes, and solenoids.

Transmitted noise is caused by devices that create radio frequency noise, in high current applications. Welding causes transmitted noise. When contacts that carry high current open, they generate transmitted noise. Application wiring carrying signals can often be disrupted by this type of noise. Imagine wiring carrying sensor information to a control device. In severe cases, false signals can be generated on the signal wiring. This problem can often be overcome by using twisted-pair shielded wiring and connecting the shield to ground.

Transmitted noise can also "leak" into control cabinets. The holes that are put into cabinets for switches and wiring allow transmitted noise to enter the cabinet. The effect can be reduced by properly grounding the cabinet.

Ground loops can also cause noise, and are often difficult to find because they produce intermittent noise. They generally occur when multiple grounds exist. The farther the grounds are apart, the more likely the problem. A potential problem can exist between the power supply earth and the remote earth, which can create unpredictable results, especially in communications.

Proper installation technique can avoid problems with noise. The two main ways to deal with noise are suppression and isolation.

Noise Suppression   Suppression attempts to deal with the device that is generating the noise. A very high-voltage spike is caused when the current to an inductive load is turned off.

Inductive devices include relays, solenoids, motor starters, and motors. Suppression is even more important if the inductive device is in series or parallel with a hard contact such as a push button or switch.

This high voltage can cause trouble for the device PLC. Lack of surge suppression can contribute to processor faults and intermittent problems. Noise can also corrupt RAM and may cause intermittent problems with I/O modules. Note that many of these problems are hard to troubleshoot because of their sporadic nature. Excessive noise also can significantly reduce the life of relay contacts. Some PLC modules include protection circuitry to protect against inductive spikes. A suppression network can be installed to limit the voltage spikes. Surge suppression circuits connect directly across the load device to help reduce the arcing of output contacts.

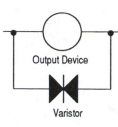
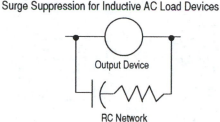
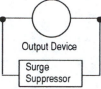

Surge Suppression for Inductive AC Load Devices

Output Device — Varistor

Output Device — RC Network

Output Device — Surge Suppressor

Surge Suppression for Inductive DC Load Devices

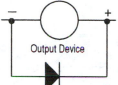

Output Device

Diode (A surge suppressor can also be used.)

Contact Protection Methods for Inductive AC and DC Output Devices

Figure 12-11   Surge suppression methods for AC and DC loads. *(Courtesy Rockwell Automation Inc.)*

Figure 12-11 shows how AC and DC loads can be protected against surges. Noise suppression is also called snubbing, which can be used to suppress the arcing of mechanical contacts caused by turning inductive loads off (Figure 12-12). Surge suppression should be used on all coils.

An RC or a varistor circuit can be used across an inductive load to suppress noise (1000 ohm, 0.2 microfarad). These components must be sized appropriately to meet the characteristic of the inductive output device that is being used. Check the installation manual for the PLC that you are using for proper noise suppression. A diode is sufficient for DC load devices. A 1N4004 can be used in most applications. Surge suppressors also can be used.

Noise Isolation   Besides suppression, the other way to deal with noise is isolation. The device or devices that cause trouble are physically separated from the control system. The enclosure also helps separate the control system from noise. In many cases field wiring must be placed in very noisy environments to allow sensors to monitor the process. This presents a problem especially when low voltages are used. Shielded twisted-pair wiring should be used for the control wiring in these cases. The shielding should only be grounded at one end. The shield should be grounded at the single-point ground.

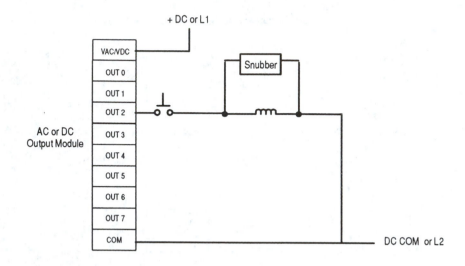

Figure 12-12   Example of snubbing. *(Courtesy Rockwell Automation Inc.)*

How to reduce the effects of noise:

Properly mount the PLC within a suitable enclosure.

Properly route all wiring.

Properly ground all equipment.

Install suppression to noise-generating devices.

INDUSTRIAL CONTROLLER MAINTENANCE

Industrial controllers are designed to be reliable devices. They are used in automated systems that are costly to operate. Downtime is costly in industry. The technician will be expected to keep the systems in operation and downtime to a bare minimum. Although industrial controllers have been designed to be low maintenance devices, certain tactics will help to reduce downtime.

It is important to keep the controllers clean. Industrial controllers are normally mounted in enclosures, which are typically air-cooled. A fan mounted in the wall of the enclosure circulates fresh air through the cabinet to cool the components. This enclosure can lead to the accumulation of dust, dirt, and other contaminants, which can cause short circuits or intermittent problems in electronic equipment. The fans for such enclosures must have adequate filters that are cleaned regularly. A preventive maintenance schedule will include a check of the enclosure to make sure the inside is free of contamination. This check should also include an inspection for loose wires or termination screws that could cause problems later. Vibration can loosen screws and cause intermittent or permanent problems. Modules should also be checked to make sure they are securely seated in the backplane, especially in high-vibration environments.

Many control devices have battery backup. Long-life lithium batteries are a good choice—they can have lifetimes of 2+ years; however, batteries will fail eventually. They will probably fail when least convenient. Their failure can cause unnecessary system downtime, which is often measured in hundreds or thousands of dollars. For this reason, regular battery replacement should be a part of the preventative maintenance schedule. Replacing the batteries once a year is a cheap investment to avoid costly downtime and potentially larger problems.

Companies must maintain an inventory of spare parts to minimize downtime. With the high cost of downtime, there is no reason to spend additional time repairing boards or other components. The technician must be able to find and correct the problem in a minimum amount of time, which means quick fault isolation and component replacement. It is wise to keep approximately one spare for each of the ten most used devices, including each type of input and output module, CPU, and other communication and special-purpose modules. Spare parts must also be maintained for sensors, drives, and other crucial devices. In many cases, modules may be returned to the manufacturer for repair. Having spare parts ensures that production can resume while the defective one is returned for repair. A reasonable selection of spare parts can drastically reduce downtime, firefighting, and frustration.

PLC Troubleshooting

The first consideration in troubleshooting and maintaining systems is safety. When you encounter a problem, remember that less than one-third of all system failures will be due to the PLC. Approximately 50 percent of the failures are due to input and output devices.

A few years ago, a technician was killed when he isolated the problem to a defective sensor. He bypassed the sensor and the system restarted with him in it. He was killed by the system he had fixed. You must always be aware of the possible outcomes of changes you make.

Troubleshooting is actually a straightforward process in automated systems. The first step is to think. This may seem rather basic, but many people jump to improper, premature conclusions and waste time finding problems. The first step is to examine the problem logically. Think the problem through using common sense first. This will point to the most logical cause. Troubleshooting is much like the game 20 Questions. Every question should help isolate the problem. In fact, every question should eliminate about half of the potential causes. Remember, a well-planned job is half done.

Think logically.

Ask yourself questions to isolate the problem.

Test your theory.

Next use the resources you have available to check your theory. Often the error-checking that is present on the PLC modules is sufficient. The LEDs on PLC

Output Condition	Output LED	Status in Ladder	Probable Problem
On	On	True ―●―	None
Off	Off	True ―●―	Bad fuse or bad output module
Off	Off	False ―○―	None
Off	On	True ―●―	Wiring to output device or bad output device

Figure 12-13 How to isolate a PLC problem by comparing the states of inputs/outputs, indicators, and the ladder status.

Figure 12-14 How to test an output, to help isolate the problem for the technician.

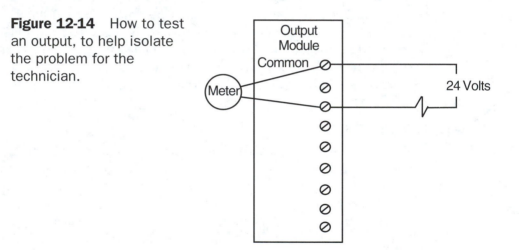

CPUs and modules can provide immediate feedback on what is happening. Many PLCs have LEDs to indicate blown fuses and other problems. Check these indicators first.

The usual problem is that an output is not turning on when it should. There are several possible causes. The output device could be defective. The PLC output that turns it on could be defective. One of the inputs that allow, or cause, the output to turn on could be defective. The sensor or the PLC input that it is attached to could be defective. The ladder logic could even be faulty. It is possible that a ladder can be written that performs perfectly the vast majority of the time but fails under certain conditions. Again the module I/O LEDs provide the best source of answers (see Figures 12-13 and 12-14). If the PLC module output LED is on for that output, the

Actual input condition	Actual module LED status	Ladder status		Probable problem
Off	Off	False ┤├	True ┤╱├	None
Off	On	True ┤■├	False ┤╱├	Short in the input device or wiring or a bad input module
On	Off	False ┤├	True ┤╱├	Wiring/power to I/O module or I/O module
On	On	False ┤├	True ┤╱├	I/O module
On	On	True ┤■├	False ┤╱├	None

Figure 12-15   Chart for troubleshooting inputs.

problem is probably not the inputs to the PLC. The device is defective, the wiring is defective, or the PLC output is defective.

The next step is to isolate the problem further. A multimeter is invaluable at this point. If the PLC output is off, a meter reading should show the full voltage with which the device is turned on. If the output is used to supply 115 V to a motor starter, the meter should show the full 115 volts between the output terminal and common on the PLC module (Figure 12-14).

If the PLC output is on, the meter should read 0 volts, because the output acts as a switch. If we measure the voltage across a switch, we should read 0 volts. If the switch is open, we should read the full voltage. If we read no voltage in either case, the wiring and power supply should be checked. If the wiring and power supply are good, the device is the problem. Depending on the device, there may be fuses or overload protection present.

Now pretend that the output LED is not turning on, so we must check the input side. If the input LED is on, we can assume that the sensor, or other input device, is operational (Figures 12-15 and 12-16). Next we must see if the PLC CPU really sees the input as true. At this point a monitor, such as a handheld programmer or a computer, is often used. The ladder is then monitored under operation. Note that many PLCs allow the outputs to be disabled for troubleshooting, which is a safe procedure. Check the ladder to see if the contact is closing. If it

Figure 12-16 How to isolate input problems.

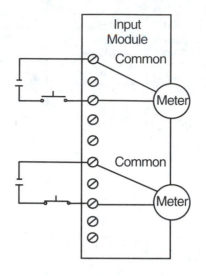

is seeing the input as false, the problem could be a defective PLC module input. Figures 12-17 and 12-18 show troubleshooting for input and output modules.

Potential Ladder Diagram Problems

Some PLC manufacturers allow output coils to be used more than once in ladders. This means that there can be multiple conditions that can control the same output coil. Sometimes technicians feel sure the output module is defective, because when they monitor the ladder, the output coil is on but the actual output LED is off. In this case, the technician inadvertently programmed the same output coil twice with different input logic. The rung being monitored was true, but one farther down in the ladder was false, so the PLC kept the output off.

The other potential problem with ladder diagramming is that the problem can be intermittent. Timing is crucial in ladder diagramming. Devices are often exchanging signals to signify that an action has occurred. For example, a robot finishes its cycle and sends a digital signal to the PLC to let it know. The programmer of the robot must be aware of the timing considerations. If the robot programmer turns it on for one step, the output may only be on for a few milliseconds. The PLC may be able to "catch" the signal every time, or it may occasionally miss it because of the length of the scan time of the ladder diagram.

This can be a tough problem to find, because it only happens occasionally. The better way to program is to handshake instead of rely on the PLC to see a periodic input. The programmer should have the robot output stay on until it is acknowledged by the PLC. The robot turns on the output and waits for an input from the PLC to ensure that the PLC saw the output from the robot.

Input LED State	Real-World State of Device	Condition	Cause	Action
Off	Off	Program operates as if the input is on.	Input is forced on in the program.	Check the forced I/O on the processor and remove forces, verify wiring. Try another input or replace the module.
			Input circuit is damaged.	Verify wiring. Try another input or replace the module.
	Off	Input device will not turn on.	The input device is damaged.	Verify device operation or replace if defective.
On	On	Input device will not turn off.	Device is damaged or shorted.	Verify device operation or replace if defective.
		Program operates as if the input device is off.	Input is forced off in program.	Check the forced I/O on the processor and remove forces.
			Damaged input circuit.	Verify the wiring. Try another input or replace the module.
	Off	Program operates as though the input is on and/or the input circuit will not turn off.	Damaged input circuit.	Verify the wiring. Try another input or replace the module.
			Input device is damaged or shorted.	Verify device operation or replace if defective.
			The leakage current of the input device exceeds the input circuit specification.	Use load resistor to bleed-off current.

Figure 12-17 Input troubleshooting.

Output LED State	Real-World State of Device	Condition	Cause	Action
Off	On	Output device will not turn off but the program indicates it is off.	Incorrect wiring.	Check the wiring. Disconnect the device and test.
			Output device is damaged or shorted.	Verify device, replace if necessary.
			Output circuit is defective.	Check the wiring. Try another output circuit, replace module if possible.
	Off	Program shows that the output circuit is on or the output circuit will not turn on.	Damaged output circuit.	Use the force function to turn the output on. If the output turns on, there is a programming problem. If not, there is an output circuit problem. Try a different output circuit and replace the module if necessary.
			Programming Problem.	Check for duplicate output addresses. If subroutines are being used, outputs are in their last state when not executing subroutines. Use the force function to force the output on. If the output does not turn on, the output circuit is damaged. Try a different output circuit and replace the module if necessary. If the output does force on, check for a programming problem.
			The output is forced off in the program.	Check the processor forced I/O or force LED and remove forces.
On	On	The program shows the output circuit off or the output circuit will not turn off.	Programming problem.	Check for duplicate output addresses. If subroutines are being used, outputs are in their last state when not executing subroutines. Use the force function to force the output off. If the output does not turn off, the output circuit is damaged. Try a different output circuit and replace the module if necessary. If the output does force off, check for a logic or programming problem.
			Damaged output circuit.	Use the force function to turn the output off. If the output turns off, there is a programming problem. If not, there is an output circuit problem. Try a different output circuit and replace the module if necessary.
			Output is forced on in the program.	Check the processor forced I/O or force LED and remove forces.
	Off	Output device will not turn on but the program indicates it is on.	Incorrect wiring or an open circuit.	Check the wiring and the common connections.
			Defective output circuit.	Try a different output circuit and replace the module if necessary.
			Low or no voltage across the load.	Measure the source voltage.
			Output device incompatibility.	Check the specifications—sink/source, etc.

Figure 12-18   Output troubleshooting *(Concept Courtesy of Rockwell Automation Inc.)*

SUMMARY

The installation of a control system must be carefully planned. People and devices are to be protected. Hardwired switching should be provided to drop all power to the system. Lockouts should be provided to ensure safety during maintenance. Proper fusing to ensure protection of individual devices is a must. The cabinet must meet the needs of the application environment. Control and power wiring should be separated to reduce noise. Proper grounding procedures must be followed to ensure safety.

Troubleshooting is done in a logical way: Think the problem through. Ask questions that will help isolate the potential problems. Above all, apply safe work habits while working on systems.

QUESTIONS

1. What is a NEMA enclosure?

2. Why should enclosures be used?

3. Describe how an enclosure is chosen.

4. What is a fusible disconnect?

5. What is a contactor?

6. What is the purpose of an isolation transformer?

7. What is the major cause of failure in systems?

8. Describe a logical process for troubleshooting.

9. Describe proper grounding techniques.

10. Draw a block diagram of a typical control cabinet.

11. Describe at least three precautions that should be taken to help reduce the problem of noise in a control system.

12. A technician has been asked to troubleshoot a system. The output device is not turning on for some reason. The output LED is working as it should. The technician turns the output on and places a meter over the PLC output, which reads 115 V. The device is not running. What is the most likely problem? How might it be fixed?

13. A technician has been asked to troubleshoot a system. The PLC does not seem to be receiving an input, because the output it controls is not turning on. The technician notices that the input LED is not turning on, but that the output indicator LED on the sensor seems to be working. A meter placed

across the input with the sensor on reads 24 V, but the input LED is off. What is the most likely problem?

14. A technician is asked to troubleshoot a system. An input seems to be defective. The technician notices that the input LED is never on. A meter placed across the PLC input reads 0 volt. The technician removes and tests the sensor. (The LED on the sensor comes on when the sensor is activated.) The sensor is fine. What is the most likely problem?

15. A technician is asked to troubleshoot a system. An output device is not working, but the technician notices that the output LED seems to be working. A meter placed over the PLC output with the output on reads 0 volt. Describe what the technician should do to find the problem.

16. What items should be included in system documentation?

chapter
IEC 61131-3
Programming
13

IEC 61131-3 is a standard for programming. It promises to revolutionize PLC and other controller programming.

OBJECTIVES

Upon completion of this chapter, you will be able to:
1. Describe the purpose of the IEC 61131-3 standard
2. List and explain each of the languages specified by IEC 61131-3
3. Explain how the languages can be integrated in programs
4. Explain the terms *function blocks, functions, and statements*
5. Explain how IEC 61131-3 will affect industrial automation

OVERVIEW OF IEC 61131-3

The International Standard IEC 61131 is a complete collection of standards on programmable controllers and their associated peripherals. It consists of the following parts: Part 1: General information, Part 2: Equipment requirements and tests, Part 3: Programming languages, Part 4: User guidelines, Part 5: Communications, Part 6 is reserved for future use, Part 7: Fuzzy control programming, and Part 8: Guidelines for the application and implementation of programming languages.

What is the '6' in IEC 1131?

You may be more familiar with the number IEC 1131. The International Electrotechnical Commission, IEC, is a world-wide standardization body. Nearly all countries have their own, national standards organizations. These organizations have agreed to accept the IEC approved and published standards. At local publication, the standard was often published under a local number. This local number often had no match to the number of the IEC published standard. To harmonize this, they searched for a worldwide numbering system. This is where the '6' came in.

The IEC 61131-3 standard has developed to meet a very natural need. Users have struggled for years with the problem of programming different brands of PLCs. Each brand has slightly different ladder logic. In some cases, different models from the same manufacturer often have different languages; thus users need multiple programming packages. It has also required users to learn the software and logic differences. Another change is that special-purpose controllers and languages emerged to fill the ladder logic gaps. Languages for more complex control and for special purposes such as motion control emerged, as did languages that attempted to simplify programming.

Ladder logic has some weaknesses: First, it is hard to reuse. Complex programs that have been developed are little use in developing new programs. Each application is essentially created from scratch. Ladder logic can be quite inconvenient and cumbersome to perform mathematical computations and comparisons. It is also difficult to segment ladder logic. Every line affects every other line, which means that it is difficult to control the execution of ladder diagrams, which are normally executed top to bottom. It would be advantageous to control which sections execute and in which order.

IEC 61131-3 emerged to meet these needs and establish a standard for programming. IEC 61131-3 was built using programming techniques that were already well established. The IEC standard specifies the following programming languages: ladder diagram, instruction list, function block diagram, structured text, and sequential function chart. The standard also allows the user to select any of the languages and mix their use in the program. The user can choose the best language for each part of the application. Three of the languages are graphics based and two are text based. The standard should ensure that the vast majority of software written for one PLC will run on PLCs from other manufacturers.

The first revision of IEC 61131-3 was published in 1993. Programs can be written using any of the IEC languages. A program is typically a collection of function blocks that are connected. Programs can communicate with other programs and can control I/O.

The IEC 61131-3 standard defines a program as "a logical assembly of all programming elements and constructs necessary for the intended signal processing required for the control of a machine or process by a programmable controller system."

Function Blocks

Function blocks are one of the keys in IEC 61131-3 programming. They allow a program to be broken into smaller, more manageable blocks. Function blocks can even be used to create new, more complex function blocks. They take a set of input data, perform actions or an algorithm on the data, and produce a new set of output data. Functions can hold data values between execution. You can think of a function block as a special-purpose integrated chip. We find special-purpose chips in many consumer products today. They take a set of inputs, process the data, and produce outputs. Think about the processors in automobiles and antilock braking systems. Like this example, a function block can be plugged in to programs and can perform a portion of the needed logic and control. Standard functions can be used off the shelf, or users can develop and use their own functions.

Function blocks can be used to solve control problems such as PID control. Temperature and servo controls are important in many industrial applications. The temperature and servo controls are typically only a portion of the control problem, however. Function blocks can be used to develop a PID or a fuzzy logic algorithm.

A function block defines the purpose of input and output data. These data can be shared with the rest of the control program. Only input and output data can be shared. A function block can also have an algorithm. These algorithms are run every time the block is executed. The algorithms process the current input data values and produce new output values.

Function blocks also have the ability to store data. Data can be used locally or may be used globally. Input or output data can be shared, but internal variables are not accessible to the rest of the program. This is an important feature in that it allows function blocks either to be modular and independent or to share their data.

The standard specifies some standard function blocks, for example, counters, timers (Figure 13-1), and clocks. Function blocks also can be developed by the user. Users can build new blocks using existing function blocks and other software logic.

Function blocks are crucial because they allow the user to develop very logical programs that are easy to understand and maintain.

Functions

IEC 61131-3 also specifies functions. Functions are different from function blocks. Functions are designed to perform common processing tasks such as trigonometric

Figure 13-1 A TON function block timer.

Figure 13-2   Example of a
limit function.

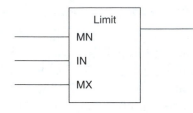

functions. They take a set of inputs and produce a result. Given the same input, the output will always be the same.

All standard trigonometric calculations are available as functions. All common arithmetic calculations such as add and subtract are also available as functions, as well as a variety of bit functions such as shifts and rotates, Boolean operators, and a set of selection type functions. Figure 13-2 shows an example of a limit function, which limits the value of an input data value between the values at minimum (MN) and maximum (MX) and sends out the result.

There are also comparison functions such as greater than (GT), greater than or equal to (GE), or equality (EQ). Character string function is also specified, as well as a wide variety of functions for working with the time and date.

STRUCTURED TEXT PROGRAMMING

Structured text (ST) is a high-level language that has some similarities to Pascal programming. The IEC standard defines structured text as a language in which statements can be used to assign values to variables. The use of structured text is wider than this, however.

Expressions

Structured text uses expressions to evaluate values that are derived from other constants and/or variables. Expressions can also be used to calculate values based on values of other variables or constants. When using expressions, the user must use a variable data type that will match the result of the expression.

Assignment Statements

Assignment statements are used to assign or change the value of a variable. An assignment statement in ST is similar to an assignment statement in any programming language, particularly Pascal.

An example of an assignment statement would be:

$$TEMP := Z$$

This would assign the value of whatever is in Z to TEMP. If the value of Z was equal to 78, the statement would put the value 78 into the variable called TEMP. (We could use a constant instead of Z.)

Operator	Description
(....)	Parentheses used to group for precedence
Function (....)	Used for function parameter list and evaluation
**	Exponentiation
-	Negation
NOT	Boolean complement
*	Multiplication
/	Division
MOD	Modulus
+	Addition
−	Subtraction
<,>, <=,> =	Comparison
=	Equality
<>	Inequality
AND,&	Boolean AND
XOR	Boolean exclusive OR
OR	Boolean OR

Figure 13-3   Structured text arithmetic operators.

Operators

Figure 13-3 shows the many arithmetic operators available. They are shown in their order of precedence, from the highest precedence to the lowest precedence.

Statements

Structured text language has a variety of statements that can be used to call functions, perform iteration (loops), or perform conditional evaluation.

Function blocks can be run using statements, for example:

Temp (PV := 74, SP := 83);

In this example a statement is used to call the Temp function (Figure 13-4). The Temp function requires two input values, PV and SP. Values are sent to the function by specifying them therein. In this case, 74 will be sent to the PV input of the function and 83 will be sent to the SP of the function. The function would

Figure 13-4   A Temp function.

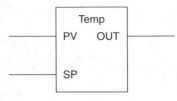

then calculate the output value. The output value is always available. It can be used in any assignment statement, for example:

Tval := Temp.Out;

This would assign the output of the Temp function to variable Tval.

Conditional Statements

Conditional statements are used to control which statements are to be executed. IF, THEN, ELSE, and CASE statements are allowed.

IF, THEN, ELSE Statements

The conditional statements IF, THEN, and ELSE evaluate a Boolean expression to determine whether to execute the logic they control. Consider the following example:

```
IF Tval = 87 THEN
  Var1 := 35;
  Var2 := 12;
ELSE
  Var1 := 54;
  Var2 := 17;
END_IF;
ELSIF can also be used.
IF Var1 < 83 THEN
  A:= 5;
ELSIF VAR1 = 83 THEN
  A:= 6;
ELSIF VAR1 > 83 THEN
  A:= 7;
END_IF;
```

CASE Statements

The CASE statement is also conditional. It is a useful statement when the user needs to execute a set of statements that are conditional on the value of an expression that returns an integer. In other words, a CASE statement evaluates an integer expression and executes the portion of the CASE code that matches the integer value.

```
CASE Var1 OF
1 : Var2 := 5;
```

```
2 : Var2 := 5; Pump1 := ON;
3,4 : Var2 := 5; Pump2 := ON;
5...7 : Var2 := 5; Alarm := ON;
END_CASE;
```

Loops

There are several types of loops available.

REPEAT . . . UNTIL Loop The REPEAT UNTIL loop is used to execute one or more statements while a Boolean expression is true. The Boolean expression is tested after execution of the statements. If it is true, the statements are executed again, for example:

```
Count := 1;
REPEAT
  Count := Count + 1;
  Pack := 5;
  Pump1 := OFF;
UNTIL Count = 5
END_REPEAT
```

FOR . . . DO Loop The FOR DO loop allows execution of a set of statements to be repeated based on the value of a loop variable, for example:

```
FOR I := 1 TO I < = 50 BY 1 DO
  Temp (PV := Var1, SP := Var2);
END_FOR;
```

WHILE . . . DO Loop The WHILE DO loop permits repeated execution of one or more statements while a Boolean expression remains true. The expression is tested before executing the statements. If the expression is false, the statements are not executed, for example:

```
WHILE Var1 < 95 DO
  Temp (PV := Var1, SP := Var2);
END_WHILE
```

RETURN and EXIT Statements

RETURN and EXIT statements can be used to end loops prematurely. The return statement can be used within functions and function block bodies. RETURN is used to return from the code. Consider the following example:

```
FUNCTION_BLOCK TEMP_TEST
VAR_INPUT
  PV, SP : REAL;
```

```
END_VAR
VAR_OUTPUT
  OUT : REAL;
END_VAR
IF PV > 100 THEN
  ALARM := TRUE; RETURN;
END_IF;
IF SV > 100 THEN
  ALARM := TRUE; RETURN;
END_IF;
END_FUNCTION_BLOCK;
```

If any IF is true, ALARM is set to TRUE and the RETURN statement is executed to end the execution of this function block.

EXIT Statement

The EXIT statement can be used to end loops before they would ordinarily end. When an EXIT statement is reached, the execution of the loop is ended and execution continues from the end of the loop. The following example shows a loop that increments through a single-dimensional array named TEMP. As the loop increments, the IF statement checks if the value of each element of the TEMP array is greater than 90. If it is, the loop is exited. Program execution would then proceed to the next statement following this loop.

```
FOR I:= 1 TO 10 DO
  IF TEMP[I] > 90 THEN
    EXIT;
  END_IF;
END_FOR;
```

FUNCTION BLOCK DIAGRAM PROGRAMMING

Function block diagram (FBD) programming is one of the graphical languages specified by the standard. FBDs can be used to show how programs, functions, and function blocks operate. An FBD looks like an electrical circuit diagram, where lines are used to show current flow to and between devices. There are typically inputs and outputs from each device. The diagram shows the overall system and the interrelationships of the components. This is similar to FBDs. Many people will find function block diagrams more friendly to program than language-based languages such as structured text.

FBD programming is used when the application involves the flow of signals between control blocks. Remember that we examined functions and function blocks earlier in the chapter. Figure 13-5 shows an example of a function block with in-

Figure 13-5 An example of a function block.

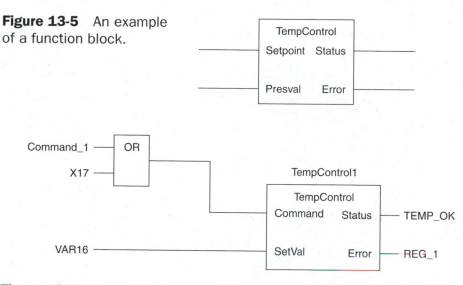

Figure 13-6 Use of Boolean operators in a simple FBD.

puts on the left and outputs on the right. The function block type name is shown inside the block (e.g., TempControl). Remember that the name shown in the block is the type name. The name shown above the block in a FBD will be the name of the function block instance. Again, the names of the inputs are shown on the left of the block and the output names are shown on the right.

Figure 13-6 utilizes Boolean functions. Remember that we can utilize standard functions such as Boolean, comparison, string, selection, time, mathematical, and numerical functions as well as user-created function blocks in FBDs.

Figure 13-7 shows an example of a function block diagram. This is a temperature control application, using two temperature control blocks. Note that the two blocks are of the same type. These blocks only needed to be created once. Note also that the name above each is different because each is a different use of the same function block type and the name identifies each particular instance. Note also that a block called TempMonitor has been used. It is providing the current temperature reading to the input called Presval in each of the TempControl blocks.

Variables or constants can be used as inputs to function blocks. Note also that the outputs from the function blocks are sent to variables. Outputs are used to supply values to variables and function block inputs (also variables).

The IEC 61131-3 standard also allows for values to be fed back to create feedback loops. Figure 13-8 shows an example of feedback. This allows values to be used as inputs to previous blocks. This means that the output value of Status from MachControl1 is used as an input value to the input (ComVal) of LoopCont1. What happens if LoopCont1 is evaluated before MachControl1?

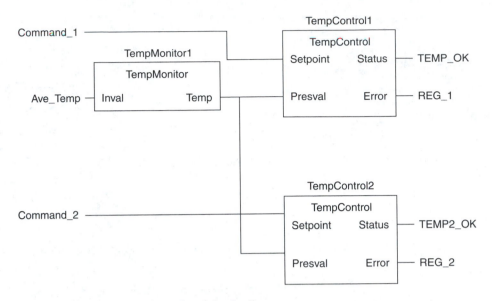

Figure 13-7   A small function block diagram.

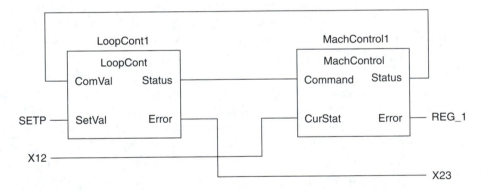

Figure 13-8   How a value can be used to create feedback.

Figure 13-9 shows a list of operators that are reserved for use with standard function blocks. The standard states that implementations may provide a facility so that the order in which functions are evaluated in a network can be defined. The standard does not define the method to be used. This means that different companies that sell FBD programming software can define their own method of determining how this would be evaluated. One method is a list to specify evaluation order.

Operator	Function Block Type	Use
CD, LD, PV	Down Counter CTD	Parameters for the CTD, to count down (CD), load (LD), and set the count preset (PV)
CU, R, PV	Up Counter CTU	Parameters for the CTU, to count up (CU), reset, (R), and load present value (PV)
CU, CD, R, LD, PV	Up/Down Counter	Same as for up and down counters
IN, PT	Pulse Timer TP	Parameters are IN to start timing and PT to set up the pulse time
IN, PT	On-Delay Timer TON	Parameters include IN to start timing and PT to set up the delay time
IN, PT	Off-Delay Timer TOF	Parameters include IN to start timing and PT to set up the delay time
CLK	R_Trig, Rising Edge Detector	Clock input to the rising edge detector function block
CLK	F-Trig, Falling Edge Detector	Clock input to the falling edge detector function block
S1, R	SR Bi-stable	Set and reset the SR bi-stable
S, R1	RS Bi-stable	Set and reset the RS bi-stable

Figure 13-9   A list of operators that are reserved for use with standard function blocks.

LADDER DIAGRAMMING

Ladder diagramming is also a graphical language that IEC 61131-3 defines. Ladder diagramming was a logical choice as a programming language for one of the standard languages as it is the most widely used. Ladder diagramming can also be used in combination with all of the other programming methods that IEC 61131-3 specifies. Figure 13-10 shows the contacts that are specified in IEC 61131-3. Figure 13-11 shows the coils that are specified in IEC 61131-3. Ladder logic can also be used with the other IEC 61131-3 languages. Figure 13-12 shows an example of ladder logic used with function blocks.

Figure 13-10 Contacts specified in IEC 61131-3.

| | | Normally Open Contact

| / | Normally Closed Contact

| P | Positive Transition Sensing Contact

| N | Negative Transition Sensing Contact

Figure 13-11 Coils specified in IEC 61131-3.

—( )— Coil

—(/)— Negated Coil

—(S)— Set Coil

—(R)— Reset Coil

—(M)— Retentive Memory Coil

—(SM)— Set Retentive Memory Coil

—(RM)— Reset Retentive Memory Coil

—(P)— Positive Transition Sensing Coil

—(N)— Negative Transition Sensing Coil

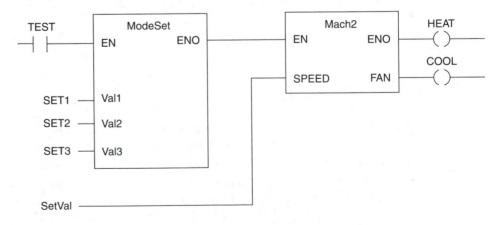

Figure 13-12 Use of ladder logic to combine function blocks.

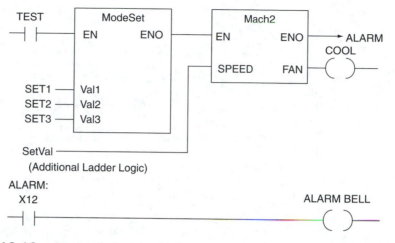

Figure 13-13 Jumps in ladder logic.

Jumps

The standard for ladder logic programming specifies jumps. A jump can be used to jump from one section of a ladder diagram to another, based on the condition of a rung of logic. This is accomplished by having the rung of logic end in a label identifier. The label identifier is a name which is then used to identify the start of the logic to which the user wishes to jump. Figure 13-13 shows an example of the use of a jump.

INSTRUCTION LIST PROGRAMMING

Instruction list (IL) programming is a low-level programming language, which means it is typically not very user-friendly. The higher the level of the language, the easier it is to use. Instruction list programming is much like assembly language programming. Figure 13-14 shows an example of IL programming.

IL programs can be used by experienced programmers to develop efficient, fast code. IL language is considered by many to be the base language for IEC-compliant PLCs. It is the language into which all of the other languages can be converted. IEC 61131-3 does not specify that any language is the base language, however. Figure 13-15 shows an example of arithmetic and Boolean instructions that can be used in IL programs. Figure 13-16 shows the comparison instructions that are available in IL programming.

Let us compare the IL program in Figure 13-14 to what it would look like in structured text.

```
IF Temp < 90 THEN
  CASES := Count / 6;
  Y12 := 0;
  Y23 := 0;
  Y5 := 1;
END_IF
ALARM : = 1;
```

Operator	Operand	Comments
LD	Temp	(* Load Temperature *)
LT	90	(* Test if Temperature < 90 *)
JMPCN	Temp_Hi	(* Jump to Temp_Hi if Temp is not < 90 *)
LD	Count	(* Load Count *)
DIV	6	(* Divide by 6 *)
ST	CASES	(* Store Result of Division to Cases variable *)
LD	0	(* Load 0 *)
ST	Y12	(* Turns Output Y12 Off *)
ST	Y23	(* Turns Output Y23 Off *)
LD	1	(* Loads 1 *)
ST	Y5	(* Turns on Output 5 *)
Temp_Hi: LD	1	(* Loads 1 *)
ST	ALARM	(* Stores a 1 in ALARM Variable *)

Figure 13-14   Instruction list program example.

Operator	Operand	Purpose
ADD	Any Type	Add
SUB	Any Type	Subtract
MUL	Any Type	Multiply
DIV	Any Type	Divide
LD	Any Type	Load
ST	Any Type	Store
S	Boolean	Set operand true
R	Boolean	Reset operand false
AND / &	Boolean	Boolean AND
OR	Boolean	Boolean OR
XOR	Boolean	Boolean exclusive OR

Figure 13-15   The arithmetic and Boolean instructions available in IL programming.

Operator	Operand	Purpose
GE	Any Type	Greater than or equal to
GT	Any Type	Greater than
EQ	Any Type	Equal
NE	Any Type	Not equal
LE	Any Type	Less than or equal to
LT	Any Type	Less than
CAL	Name	Call function block
JMP	Label	Jump to label
RET		Return from a function or function block
)		Execute last deferred operation

Figure 13-16 The comparison instructions available in IL programming.

Functions and function blocks can be called by using the CAL operator, for example:

CAL TEMP1(SETPT := 85, CYC := 5)

This would call and execute a function block called TEMP1. It would send the values of 85 to the SETPT input parameter and 5 to the CYC input parameter. These are the inputs that the TEMP1 function block requires. So as you can see, IL can be combined with the other types of programming languages that IEC 61131-3 specifies.

There is another way to load parameters and make a function block call. In the following example, the values are loaded and then stored to the input parameters for the function before the function is called. The LD function is used to load the value and then the ST is used to store the value into the parameter. The first ST stores 85 into the SETPT input parameter for the TEMP1 function block (TEMP1.SETPT). The same method is then used to load 5 into the CYC parameter. The function block is then called with the CAL operator.

```
LD 85.0
ST TEMP1.SETPT
LD 5
ST TEMP1.CYC
CAL TEMP1
```

Figure 13-17
Example of the
use of an OR.

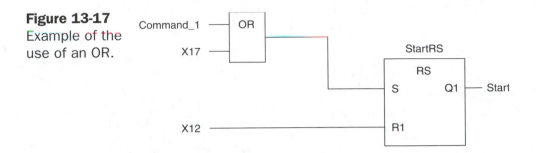

Figure 13-17 shows an example of a function block diagram for a start sequence. The equivalent logic is as follows:

```
LD Command_1
OR X17
ST StartRS.S
Load X12 Str\art.R1
LD StartRS.Q1
ST Start
```

SEQUENTIAL FUNCTION CHART PROGRAMMING

Sequential function chart (SFC) programming is a graphical programming method. SFCs are a useful method for describing sequential type processes. Figure 13-18 shows an example of a simple linear-type sequence. There are five steps in the sequence, and a condition must be fulfilled before moving from one step to the next. For example, to move from step 1 to step 2, S1 must be true. S1 in this case might be a start switch in the process. It could be anything that would evaluate to either a true (1) or false (0). There are conditions between each step in this example. Transitions can be defined by name.

Sequential function charts can also be used for processes that have portions of the applications whose steps are dependent on conditions. For example, imagine a bottling application (Figure 13-19). Two types of bottles come down a line at random.

A sensor mounted at the fill station identifies which bottle is present. The sensor has a tagname of Prod. If Prod is equal to 0, it should be filled with one product; and if it is equal to 1, it should be filled with a different product. Most of the processes (steps) in Figure 13-19 are the same. The fill processes are the only difference in this process. After the delay, the bottles are either filled in the Fill1 process or the Fill2 process. The processes following the fill processes are the same in this application. Sequential function charts handle these types of applications easily—it could have been much more complicated than this, for example, there could have been many alternative processes, or each path could have had multiple steps.

Figure 13-18 Example of a simple linear process.

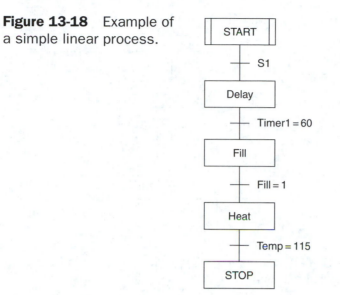

Figure 13-19 A simple process with alternate steps that are dependent on a condition.

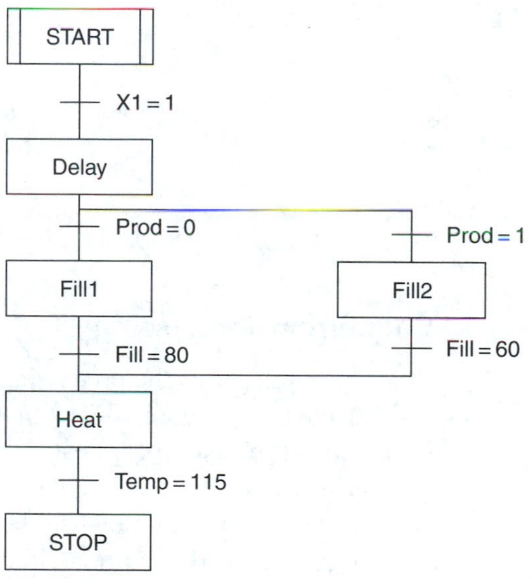

Branching

Branches can also be used to alter the sequence processing during operation (Figure 13-20). In this case, X17 is evaluated after the second step. If X17 is equal to 1, the sequence continues to the next step. If X17 is equal to 0, sequencing branches back to a position immediately following the start block.

Figure 13-20 An example of branching in a sequence.

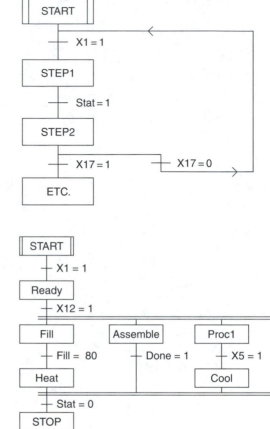

Figure 13-21 An example of concurrent processing.

Concurrent Processing

In many applications the processing is not linear, and several processes may occur at the same time (Figure 13-21). In this case, the three processes are all active at the same time. The first process has a Fill and a Heat step. The second process is an assembly process. The third contains two steps. Note that double lines are used to show where concurrent processes begin and end, and that there can be multiple steps in each process and conditions in each to control movement between steps. Concurrent processing is a powerful tool. As processors gain more power and speed, they have tremendous capability to control complex or even multiple processes.

Certain rules apply to how steps and transitions can be used. Transitions cannot be directly linked: There must be a step between any two transitions. If a transition leads to two or more steps, then all of the steps are executed independently and simultaneously. Two steps cannot be linked directly, either. Steps must be separated by a transition.

Figure 13-22 Use of the elapsed time flag for STEP1.

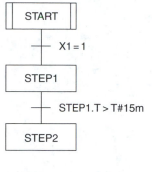

Figure 13-23 Use of the active flag to set Y21 when STEP1 is active.

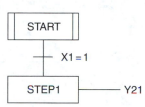

Step Variables

There are two variables associated with every step which the programmer can utilize. The first variable is set to a 1 while the step is active. This can be useful for monitoring and for logic. It is called the step active flag, named .X. To use it, the programmer uses the name of the step and adds the .X. There was a step named Ready in Figure 13-22. If the programmer wanted to use the active flag, he or she would simply use Ready.X. If the step is active, Ready.X would be equal to 1. If the step is inactive, Ready.X would equal 0. The active flag can be used in another way. Figure 13-23 shows how the active flag can be used directly. In this case, Y21 is set to a 1 when this step is active.

The second type of step variable is a time variable. Every step has a variable that contains the time that the variable has been active. The elapsed time variable can be used by giving the step name and adding a .T. Figure 13-22 uses the elapsed time variable to control the transition between Step1 and Step2. The logic essentially says if the elapsed time of Step1 is greater than 15 minutes, move to Step2 (Step1 > T#15m).

Ladder logic can be used as a transition condition between steps (Figure 13-24). In this example, when the rung is true, the program will move from the START step to STEP1.

Function blocks or FBDs can be used to control transitions between steps as long as their output is discrete (1 or 0). Figure 13-25 shows an example of a function block being used to control the transition from START to STEP1.

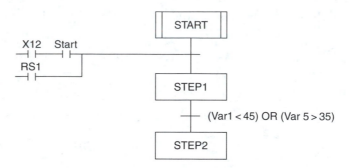

Figure 13-24 An example of ladder logic used as a transition condition.

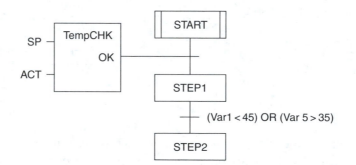

Figure 13-25 An example of a function block used as a transition condition between steps.

Ladder logic that ends in a transition connection can be used to control transitions between steps. Figure 13-26 shows a ladder diagram rung that ends in a transition connector named Alt1. Alt1 is also used as a transition condition in the sequential function chart.

Structured text expressions can be used as transition conditions. In Figure 13-27, an ST expression controls the transition between STEP1 and STEP2. The ST expression must result in a true or false. In this case, if Var1 is less than 45 or Var5 is greater than 35, the expression will result in a true (1) and the process will move from STEP1 to STEP2.

Transitions can also be defined by using IL programming. Figure 13-28 shows the use of an IL program to control a transition. In this case, the transition in the sequential function chart is called Cond1. Note that in the IL program the keyword TRANSITION is used to declare Cond1 as the name of the transition that is being defined. The conditions in the IL program are then evaluated when the program runs. If X12 or X15 is true, this IL program will result in a 1 and Cond1 will be true and cause the program to change from the Fill step to the Heat step.

Figure 13-26 An example of a ladder diagram rung that ends in a transition connector named Alt1.

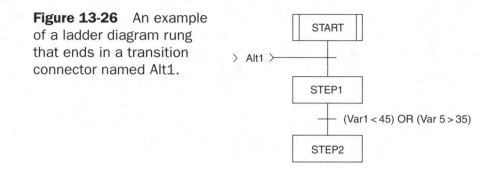

Somewhere else in the logic

Figure 13-27 Use of a structured text expression to control a transition.

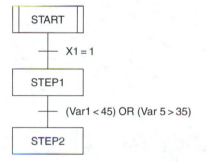

Figure 13-28 An example of the use of an IL program to control a transition.

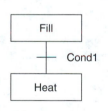

TRANSITION Cond1 :
  := X1 AND X15 OR X5;
END_TRANSITION

Instruction list programming can also be used to program transition conditions. Figure 13-29 shows an example. The IL program starts with the keyword TRANSITION followed by the name that the programmer assigns to the transition condition. In this case, the programmer chose Cond1 for the name; the logic would be that if X12 OR X18 is true, then Cond1 will be set to a 1, the transition condition between two steps will be met, and the program will move from one step to the next.

Figure 13-29   An example of instruction list programming to control a transition condition.

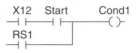

```
TRANSITION Cond1 :
    LD X12
    OR X18
END_TRANSITION
```

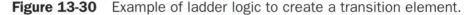

Figure 13-30   Example of ladder logic to create a transition element.

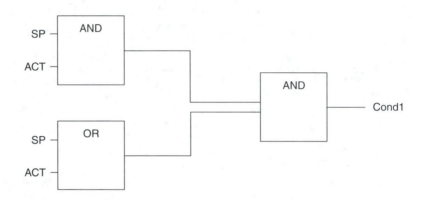

Figure 13-31   Example of an AND block ANDed with an OR block to define the transition logic.

Ladder logic can also be used to control transitions. The logic shown in Figure 13-30 is an example. Note that the transition name appears at the right of the controlling logic.

FBD language can also be used to define transitions. Figure 13-31 shows an example of an AND block ANDed with an OR block to define the transition logic.

Step Actions

Steps are used to control actions that occur during that step of the sequence. Steps can control multiple actions. Figure 13-32 shows the general format for an action. The action block is shown to the right of the step. The first part of the action block can contain a qualifier. The qualifier controls how the action is performed. The qualifier in this case is an N. An N means that the action will be executed while the associated step is active. Additional qualifiers are shown in Figure 13-33. The second part

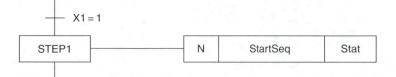

Figure 13-32 General format for an action.

Qualifier	Use
N	Not stored, executes while associated step is active
None	Default, not stored, executes while associated step is active
R	Resets a stored action
S	Sets an action active
L	Terminates after a given time period
D	Starts after a given time period
P	Pulse action that occurs only once when the step is activated and once when the step is deactivated
SD	Time delay and stored. The action is set active after a given period, even if the associated step has been deactivated before the time period elapsed
DS	Action is stored and time delayed. If the associated step is deactivated before the time period elapses, the action is not stored
SL	Time limited and stored. Action is started and executes for a given time period

Figure 13-33 Qualifiers that can be used with actions.

of an action block is the action to be performed. In this case the action is StartSeq. The third part of the action block is optional. The user may use a variable in the third part of the action block. The variable is called an indicator variable. The variable will indicate when the action has completed its execution. In this example, the variable is called Stat—when StartSeq has finished its execution Stat would be set to a 1.

Figure 13-34 shows an example of the use of an action. The action is associated with STEP1. The qualifier is N, so the action will be executed while STEP1 is active. There is no indicator variable. The action name is StartMotor. StartMotor is a

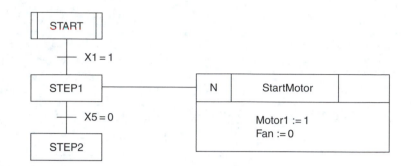

Figure 13-34   Example of the use of an action.

Figure 13-35   Example of the use of FBD language to define an action.

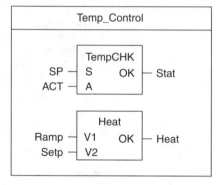

simple action that is used to turn Motor1 on and Fan off. This has been specified in the block under the StartMotor action name. There are only two outputs associated with this action, so the user programmed them with the action block. The action could have been defined on another page if it was more complex. Another valuable asset of action blocks is that once they are defined they can be used repeatedly with the qualifier and action name. So StartMotor could be used anywhere in our program now without redefining the actual I/O to be performed.

Actions can also be defined by using the FBD language. Figure 13-35 shows an example used to define an action. The FBD logic that the user creates is enclosed in a box with the name of the action that it defines at the top.

Ladder logic can be used to define what the action does. Figure 13-36 shows an example of the use of ladder logic for this purpose. The ladder logic is enclosed in a rectangle with the name of the action at the top.

Sequential function charts can also be used to describe the behavior of an action. Figure 13-37 shows how complex action behavior could be defined simply with

Figure 13-36 Example of the use of ladder logic to define an action.

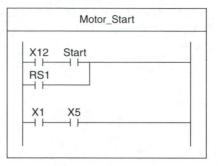

Figure 13-37 Example of how complex action behavior can be defined with SFC programming.

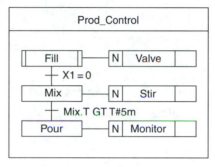

Figure 13-38 Structured text program used to define an action.

```
ACTION Stir :
IF Type = 1 THEN
    Speed1 = 75;
    Motor = ON;
ELSE
    SPEED1 = 25;
    Motor = ON;
    FAN = ON;
END_ACTION
```

SFC. In this case there are three basic steps in the SFC—Fill, Mix, and Pour. Also note the action associated with each step.

Figure 13-38 shows an example of the use of structured text to define the behavior of an action. Note that the keyword ACTION starts the structured text program. Then the name of the action that is being defined is shown. The name of the action is Stir. This action decides if Type is equal to 1 or not. If the Type is 1, then Speed1 is set to 75 and Motor is turned on. If Type is not equal to 1, then Speed1

Figure 13-39   Instruction
list program used to define
an action.

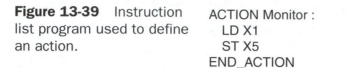

ACTION Monitor :
  LD X1
  ST X5
END_ACTION

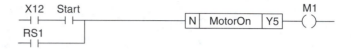

Figure 13-40   Example of the use of an action block in ladder logic.

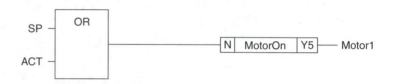

Figure 13-41   Use of an action in FBD language.

is set to 25, Motor is turned on, and Fan is turned on. The program is ended with
the keyword END_ACTION.

Figure 13-39 shows the use of instruction list programming to define an action's
behavior. The keyword ACTION begins the IL program, followed by the name of
the action. The IL program loads the state of X1 in this case and stores it to Y5. The
keyword END_ACTION ends the IL program.

Use of Action Blocks in Graphical Languages   Action blocks can be used in
ladder logic (Figure 13-40). When there is power flow into the action block, it is
active. The indicator variable (Y5) can be used to indicate when the action is
complete.

Figure 13-41 shows the use of an action in the FBD language. Note that the indicator variable (Y5) can be used elsewhere to indicate when the action is complete.

SUMMARY

This chapter has been a quick introduction to IEC 61131-3 programing. It is by no
means complete. A book could be written on each of the programming methods.
For those who want a more in-depth look at IEC 61131-3 programming, See R.W.
Lewis's, *Programming Industrial Control Systems Using IEC 61131-3.*

QUESTIONS

1. Explain why the IEC 61131-3 standard was developed.

2. Explain structured text programming.

3. Explain function block diagram programming.

4. Explain IEC 61131-3 ladder logic programming.

5. Explain instruction list programming.

6. Explain sequential function chart programming.

7. Explain how these languages can be combined in control programs. Examples might be helpful.

appendix

Control Logic Addressing and Project Organization

CONTROLLOGIX ADDRESSING

ControlLogix memory and addressing may be confusing at first for those who are already familiar with PLC addressing. The major difference is that there are no predefined data tables in the ControlLogix processor. There are, however, predetermined types of data. With ControlLogix you define tags instead of addresses. This is certainly the future of programming. Tags can be created before or after you develop the logic. Question marks (?) can be entered in place of the tag while programming and then the tag can be defined later. Once you are familiar with tag addressing you may like it more than traditional PLC memory addressing.

Tags

The naming of tags follows IEC 61131-3 rules. Tag names must begin with an alphabetic character (A_Z or a-z) or an underscore. They may be up to 40 characters long. Tag names are not case sensitive. They cannot have consecutive or trailing underscores.

Tag Types

There are three types of tags: base, alias, and consumed. A base tag is the most common. A base tag defines the memory location where a data element is stored. An alias tag references a memory location that has been defined by another tag. An alias tag can reference a base tag or another alias tag. In other words you can have more than one name for a specific tag. You can have a base tag and then other names to reference it. A consumed tag references data that comes from another controller.

The following information must be specified to define a tag:

Name	The tag name.
Description	This is optional. Descriptions can be up to 120 characters long. They are stored in the offline project file but are not downloaded to the controller.
Tag Type	User chooses base, alias, or consumed.
Data Type	User selects type from a list of predefined types or any user defined types. If the tag will be an array, you must specify the number of elements in up to three dimensions.
Scope	User selects the scope in which the tag is valid. The user can make the tag scope the whole controller or any of the existing program scopes. Note that a controller can have multiple programs.
Display Style	This defines the display type when the user is monitoring the tag in the programming software. The user chooses from the available types.
Produce This Tag	The user selects whether or not to make the tag available to other controllers. The user must also specify the number of other controllers that can consume the tag.

Data Types

ControlLogix has some predefined data types. There are two predefined types: basic and structure types. The basic types conform to the IEC61131-3 standard.

Basic Types (also called atomic data types)

BOOL	1-bit Boolean
SINT	1-byte integer
INT	2-byte integer
DINT	4-byte integer
REAL	4-byte floating point

Structure Types

AXIS	Control structure for an axis (controller-only tag)
CONTROL	Control structure for arrays
COUNTER	Control structure for counters
MOTION_INSTRUCTION	Control structure for motion instructions
PID	Control structure for a PID instruction
TIMER	Control structure for a timer
MESSAGE	Control structure for a message instruction (controller-only tag)
MOTION GROUP	Control structure for a motion group (controller-only tag)

Base Tags

All data in the controller is stored in a minimum of four bytes (32 bits). The types that can be used to define base tags are: BOOL, SINT, INT, DINT and REAL.

A BOOL (Boolean) base tag is stored in four bytes. A BASE tag's bit is stored in bit 0 of the 32 bits reserved for the tag. Bits 1–31 are not used.

A SINT (single integer) base tag consists of eight bits. Its value is stored in bits 0–7 (the low byte) of the 32 bits reserved for the tag. Bits 8–31 are not used.

An INT base tag consists of 16 bits and uses bits 0–15 (the lower two bytes) of the 32 bits reserved for the tag. Bits 16–31 are not used.

DINT (double integer) and REAL base tags use all 32 bits (4 bytes) of the memory reserved for them.

Structures

There are three types of structures: predefined, module defined, and user defined. Structures are used for groups of related data. Structures can contain multiple data types. In real life an address book is like a structure. There are many friends in an address book. For each friend there are several pieces and types of information. For each person there is a phone number, street address, email address, name, maybe even things like birthdays, and so on.

Some structures are predefined to make it easy for the programmer. Some of these were listed earlier.

Controller module-defined structures are created automatically when you configure I/O modules for the system. These structures contain information such as data, status, and fault information.

The user can define (create) structures that group different types of data into a single named entity, much like an address book groups like data. User-defined

User Defined Structure
Name: DATA

Member	Data Type
Inp_1	BOOL
Temp	SINT
Pressure	REAL

Memory Allocation for the Data

	Bits 24–31	Bits 36–23	Bits 5–15	Bits 0–7
Bit_0	Unused	Unused	Unused	Bit 0 used
Temp	Unused	Unused	Unused	First 8 bits
Pressure	Alsl 32 bit			

Figure A–1 Structure example.

structures contain one or more data definitions called members. The data type determines the amount of memory that is allocated for each. The data type for each member can be a basic type, a user-defined structure, a predefined structure, a single dimension array, a single-dimension array of a predefined structure, or a single dimension of a user-defined structure.

Creating a User-Defined Structure

To create a structure the user first enters a name and may enter a description (optional). The following parameters must be entered for each member:

Name	Name the member.
Data Type	The correct type is selected from the list.
Style	Select the desired style of the member from the list.
Description	Describe the member. This is optional.

Figure A-1 shows an example of a structure. This user created structure will hold a bit (BOOL), a single integer (SINT), and a real (REAL) number. The figure also shows how they are stored in memory.

Member Addressing

Members within a structure are addressed by using the tag name and a period, followed by the member name. For example, tag_name.member_name. If a structure is within a structure, the tagname of the highest level is followed by the substructure tag name, followed by the member name. For example: tag_name. structure_name.member_name.

Array-Temp	
Data Type SINT[5]	
	Temp[0]
	Temp[1]
	Temp[2]
	Temp[3]
	Temp[4]

Figure A–2 A one-dimension array to hold 5 temperature values.

Arrays

A user can utilize arrays to group sets of data, of the same type, in a contiguous block of controller memory. Note that arrays consist of one type of data, structures can hold multiple types. For example, an address book holds many types of data so it is a structure. A table of temperatures could be an array because it holds one type of data. Each tag within the array is one element of the array. The element can be a basic type or a structure type. Element numbering in arrays start with 0.

Figure A-2 shows an example of a one-dimension array. This array was created to hold 5 temperatures. Each element has an address. Temp[0] is the first address of the array and would hold the first temperature. Temp[4] is the 5th element of the array and would hold the 5th temperature. Note that the array was created with the name Temp. The array Temp was declared to be of type SINT (single integer) an has 5 elements. A particular element is addressed by using the array name followed by the number of the particular element in brackets. For example Temp[2]. A variable can also be used to identify the particular element. For example Temp[var1]. Whatever number is in var1 would specify the particular element of the Temp array. Math expressions can also be used in array addressing. For example Temp[count – 1]. This would specify the element that equals the value of count minus 1. If the present value of count is equal to 4, element 3 would be specified. Remember that this would be the 4th element because the first element is 0.

You can also specify the address for an element to the bit level. For example, Temp[1].2 would specify the third bit (bit 2) of Temp element 1 (the second element). You may also use variable addressing for bits. For example, Temp[1].count + 2.

If you are using variable addressing you must be sure that the address is within the array boundaries. If it is outside of the array, a major fault will occur.

Figure A-3 shows an example of a 2-dimensional array. The first column is used to store pressure values and the second column is used to hold temperature values. Note that both have to be the same type. Note that the array was named Machine_One and the data type for the array was specified to be DINT[5,2]. This

Array-Machine_One			
Data Type DINT[5,2]			
Pressure[0,0]			Temp[0,1]
Pressure[1,0]			Temp[1,1]
Pressure[2,0]			Temp[2,1]
Pressure[3,0]			Temp[3,1]
Pressure[4,0]			Temp[4,1]

Figure A–3 A two-dimension array with 10 rows and 2 columns.

means that the array was created to have 10 rows and 2 columns The array will hold double integers (DINT).

Three dimensional arrays can also be created.

CONTROLLOGIX PROJECT ORGANIZATION

To use a ControlLogix controller, you create a project file. The project file contains the programming and configuration information. Following is the information that is entered by the user when creating a project:

- The chassis size/type
- The slot number of the processor
- A description (optional)
- A file path
- A project name (this is also the file name)

    The file name is also assigned to the controller name.

    You may change the controller name if you wish.

    If you save the file under a different name, the controller name does not change.

    A file name can consist of up to 40 characters. It may be letters, numbers and underscores. The file name cannot have consecutive or trailing underscores.

There are three major components in a project: tasks, programs, and routines. Tasks are used to configure the controller's execution. Programs are used to group logic and data. Routines contain the executable code. A project may have multiple tasks. Only one task executes at a time. Other tasks may interrupt the controller and execute. When the interrupting task is done executing the original task is resumed. Only one task can operate at a time. Only one program within a task can operate at one time.

Tasks

Tasks schedule and prioritize programs or a group of programs that are assigned to that task. There are two types of tasks: periodic and continuous. The Logix5550 controller can support 32 tasks. There can only be up to 1 continuous task. If there is a continuous task there can only be 31 periodic tasks (total tasks = 32). Tasks are assigned priority numbers to determine which task has priority if multiple tasks are called. A continuous task always has the lowest priority. 1 is the highest priority and 15 is the lowest. A higher priority task interrupts a lower priority task.

Periodic tasks are triggered at a repetitive time period. The interruption can be set from between 1 ms to 2000 milliseconds. The default time is 10 milliseconds. Periodic tasks that have the same priority execute on a time slicing scheme at 1 millisecond intervals.

Programs

A task may have up to 32 programs assigned to it. Each program can have its own routines and tags. If a task is triggered, all of the programs associated with the task will execute in the order in which they are grouped. A program can be assigned to only one task in the controller.

Routines

A routine is a set of logic instructions that is written in a single programming language. Remember that IEC 61131-3 specifies different languages and Control-Logix can utilize some of them. The main program in a SLC 500 is similar to a routine. It consists of one language (ladder logic). Logic in the ladder logic (Jump to subroutines (JSRs)) can be used to call other subroutines (routines).

Glossary

Absolute pressure: The pressure of a gas or liquid measured in relation to a vacuum (zero pressure).

Acidity: A measure of the hydrogen ion content of a solution.

Accumulated value: The present count or time of timers and counters.

Accuracy: The deviation between the actual position and the theoretical position.

AC input module: A module that converts a real-world AC input signal to the logic level required by the PLC processor.

AC output module: A module that converts the processor logic level to an AC output signal to control a real-world device.

Action: Defines what is done to regulate the final control element to effect control of a controller action. Types include on-off, proportional, integral, and derivative.

Actuator: Output device such as an air valve or cylinder normally connected to an output module.

Address: A number used to specify a storage location in memory.

Alkalinity: A measure of the hydroxyl ion content of a solution.

Ambient temperature: The natural temperature in the environment such as a PLC in a cabinet near a steel furnace.

Analog: A signal with a smooth range of possible values. For example, a temperature that could vary between 60° and 300° would be analog in nature.

ANSI: American National Standards Institute.

ASCII: American Standard Code for Information Interchange. A coding system that represents letters and characters. Seven-bit ASCII can represent 128 different combinations, and 8-bit ASCII (extended ASCII) can represent 256 different combinations.

Asynchronous communications: A communication method that uses a series of bits including a start bit, data bits (7 or 8), a parity bit (odd, even, none, mark, or space), and stop bits (1, 1.5, or 2) to send data between devices. One character is transmitted at a time. RS232 is the most common.

Atmospheric pressure: The pressure exerted on a body by the air. It is equal to 14.7 pounds per square inch at sea level.

Backplane: A bus is a printed circuit board with sockets that accept various modules in the back of a PLC chassis.

Batch process: A process that processes a given amount of material in one operation to produce what is required.

Baud rate: The speed of serial communications, the number of bits per second transmitted. For example, RS232 is normally used with a baud rate of 9600 (about 9600 bits per second). It takes about 10 bits in serial to send an ASCII character so that a baud rate of 9600 transmits about 960 characters per second.

Bellows: A pressure-sensing element consisting of a metal cylinder that is closed at one end. The difference in pressure between the inside and outside of the cylinder causes the cylinder to expand or contract its length.

Beta ratio: The diameter of an orifice divided by the internal diameter of the pipe.

BEUG (BITBUS European Users Group): A nonprofit organization devoted to spreading the BITBUS technology and organizing a basic platform where people using BITBUS can share application experiences.

Binary: A base 2 number system using 1s and 0s to represent numbers.

Binary-coded decimal (BCD): A number system in which each decimal number is represented by four binary bits. For example, the decimal number 967 is represented by 1001 0110 0111 in BCD.

Bit: A binary digit; the smallest element of binary data; either a 0 or a 1.

BITBUS: Created by Intel in 1983 and promoted as a standard (IEEE-1118 1990) in 1990 by a special committee of the IEEE. It is one of the most widely used fieldbuses.

Boolean: A logic system that uses operators such as AND, OR, NOR, and NAND utilized by PLCs, although it is usually made invisible by the programming software for the ease of the programmer.

Bounce: An undesirable effect that is the erratic make and break of electrical contacts.

Branch: A parallel logic path in a ladder diagram.

Byte: Eight bits or two nibbles. (A nibble is 4 bits.)

Calibration: A procedure used to determine, correct, or check the absolute values corresponding to the graduations on a measuring instrument.

Cascade: A programming technique used to extend the range of timers and counters.

Celsius: The centigrade temperature scale on which the freezing point of water is 0° and the boiling point is 100°.

CENELEC: The European Committee for Electrotechnical Standardization develops standards that apply dimensional and operating characteristics of control components.

Central processing unit (CPU): The microprocessor portion of the PLC that handles the logic.

Closed loop: A system that has feedback and can automatically correct for errors.

CMOS (complementary metal-oxide semiconductor): The integrated circuits that consume very little power and have good noise immunity.

Cold junction: The point at which a pair of thermocouple wires is held at a fixed temperature; also called the *reference junction.*

Color mark sensor: A sensor designed to differentiate between two different colors on the basis of contrast between the two colors.

Compare instruction: PLC instruction used to test numerical values for equal, greater than, or less than relationships.

Complement: The inverse of a digital signal.

Contact: A symbol used in programming PLCs to represent inputs; can be normally open and normally closed; the conductors in electrical devices such as starters.

Contactor: A special-purpose relay used to control large electrical current.

CSA (Canadian Standards Organization): The organization that develops standards, tests products and provides certification for a wide variety of products.

CTD: Count down instruction.

CTU: Count up instruction.

Current sinking: An output device (typically an NPN transistor) that allows current flow from the load through the output to ground.

Current sourcing: An output device (typically a PNP transistor) that allows current flow from the output through the load and then to ground.

Cyclic redundancy check (CRC):   A calculated value based on the content of a communication frame. It is inserted in the frame to check data accuracy after receiving the frame across a network. BITBUS uses the standard SDLC CRC.

Dark-on: A photosensor's sensor output when no object is sensed.

Data highway: A communications network for devices such as PLCs. They are normally proprietary, which means that only like devices of the same brand can communicate over the highway. Allen Bradley calls its PLC communication network Data Highway.

Data table: A consecutive group of user references (data) of the same size that can be accessed with table read/write functions.

Debugging: The process of finding problems (bugs) in any system.

Derivative gain: The derivative in a PID system that acts based on the rate of change in the error. It has a damping effect on the proportional gain.

DeviceNet: An industrial bus for field-level devices; based on the controller area network (CAN) chip.

Diagnostics: The software routines that aid in identifying and finding problems and fault conditions in a system.

Digital output: An output that can have two states: on or off; also called *discrete output*.

Distributed processing: A concept that allows individual discrete devices to control their area and still communicate to the others via a network; its control takes the processing load off the "host" system.

Documentation: The descriptive paperwork that explains a system or program so that the technician can understand or change the system, install devices on it, troubleshoot it, and maintain it.

Downtime: The time a system is not available for production or operation because of breakdowns in systems.

EEPROM: Electrically erasable programmable read-only memory.

Energize: The instruction that causes a bit to be a 1. This turns an output on.

Examine-off: The (normally closed) contact used in ladder logic; is true (or closed) if the real-world input associated with it is off.

Examine-on: The (normally open) contact used in ladder logic programming; is true (or closed) if the real-world input associated with it is on.

Expansion rack: A rack added to a PLC system when the application requires more modules than the main rack can contain; sometimes used to permit an I/O to be remotely located from the main rack.

False: The disabled logic state (off).

Fault: A failure in a system that prevents its normal operation.

Firmware: The combination of software and hardware that is a series of instructions contained in read-only memory (ROM) used for the operating system functions.

Flowchart: An illustration used to make program design easier.

Force: The change in the state of actual I/O by changing the bit status in the PLC; normally used to troubleshoot a system.

Frame: A packet of bits to be transmitted across a network; contains a header, user data, and an end of frame; must contain all necessary information to enable the sender and receiver(s) of the communication to decode the user's data and to ensure that the data are correct.

Full duplex: Communications scheme in which data flows in both directions simultaneously.

Ground: Direct connection between equipment (chassis) and earth ground.

Half duplex: Communications scheme in which data can flow in both directions but in only one direction at a time.

Hard contacts: A physical switch connection.

Hard copy: A printed copy of computer information.

Hexadecimal: A numbering system that utilizes base 16.

Host computer: The computer to which devices communicate; may download or upload programs or be used to program the device.

HSC: High speed counter instruction.

Hysteresis: A dead band purposely introduced to eliminate false reads in a sensor. An encoder hysteresis is introduced in the electronics to prevent ambiguities if the system happens to dither on a transition.

IEC (International Electrotechnical Commission): An organization that develops and distributes recommended safety and performance standards.

IEEE: The Institute of Electrical and Electronic Engineers.

Image table: An area used to store the status of input and output bits.

Incremental: A description of an encoder that provides logic states of 0 and 1 for each successive cycle of resolution.

Instruction set: The instructions available to program the PLC.

Integral gain: The device in a PID system that corrects for small errors over time; eliminates offset and permanent error.

Intelligent I/O: The PLC modules that have a microprocessor built in, such as a module that controls closed-loop positioning.

Interfacing: The act of connecting a PLC to external devices.

I/O (input/output): A device used to speak about the number of inputs and outputs needed for a system or that a particular programmable logic controller can handle.

IP rating: The rating system established by the IEC that defines the protection offered by electrical enclosures; similar to the NEMA rating system.

Isolation: A process that segregates real-world inputs and outputs from the CPU to ensure its protection even if a major problem with real-world inputs or outputs (such as a short) occurs, normally provided by optical isolation.

K: The abbreviation for the number 1000; in computer language equal to 2^{10}, or 1024.

Keying: The technique to ensure that modules are not put in the wrong slots of a PLC.

Ladder diagram: The programmable controller language that uses contacts and coils to define a control sequence.

LAN: *See* Local area network.

Latch: An instruction used in ladder diagram programming to represent an element that retains its state during controlled toggle and power outage.

Leakage current: A small amount of current that flows through load-powered sensors.

LED (light emitting diode): A solid-state semiconductor that emits red, green, or yellow light or invisible infrared radiation.

Light-on sensor: A photosensor's output that is on when an object is sensed.

Linear output: The analog output.

Line driver: A differential output driver intended for use with a differential receiver; usually used when long lines and high frequency are required and noise may be a problem.

Line-powered sensor: A device powered from the power supply. These are normally three-wire sensors, although four-wire models also exist. The third wire is used for the output signal.

Load: A device through which current flows and produces a voltage drop.

Load-powered sensor: A sensor with two wires. A small leakage current flows through the sensor even when the output is off. The current is required to operate the sensor electronics.

Load resistor: A resistor connected in parallel with a high-impedance load to enable the output circuit to output enough current to ensure proper operation.

Local area network (LAN): A system of hardware and software designed to allow a group of intelligent devices to communicate within a fairly close proximity.

Lockout: The placement of a lockout device on an energy-isolating device in accordance with an established procedure to ensure that the energy-isolating device and the equipment being controlled cannot be operated until the lockout device is removed.

Lockout device: A device that utilizes a positive means such as a lock, either key or combination type, to hold an energy-isolating device in the safe position and prevent the energizing of a machine or equipment.

LSB: Least significant bit.

Machine language: A control program reduced to binary form.

MAP (manufacturing automation protocol): A "standard" developed to make industrial devices communicate more easily; based on a seven-layer model of communications.

Master: The device on a network that controls communications traffic.

Master control relay (MCR): A hardwired relay that can be de-energized by any hardwired series-connected switch and is used to de-energize all devices.

Memory map: A drawing showing the areas, sizes, and uses of memory in a particular PLC.

Microsecond: One-millionth (0.000001) of a second.

Milliamp: One-thousandth (0.001) of an amp.

Millisecond: One thousandth (0.001) of a second.

Mnemonic codes: A specific set of symbols designated to represent instructions in a control program; usually an acronym made by combining the initial letters or parts of words.

MSB: Most significant bit.

NEMA (National Electrical Manufacturers Association): An organization that develops standards that define a product, process, or procedure.

Network: A system connected to devices or computers for communication purposes.

Node: A point on the network that allows access.

Noise: The unwanted electrical interference in a programmable controller or network caused by motors, coils, high voltages, and welders that can disrupt communications and control.

Nonretentive coil: A coil that turns off upon removal of applied power to the CPU.

Nonretentive timer: A timer that loses the time if it loses the input enable signal.

Nonvolatile memory: The memory in a controller that does not require power to retain its contents.

NOR: The logic gate that results in zero unless both inputs are zero.

NOT: The logic gate that results in the complement of the input.

Octal: The number system based on the number 8, utilizing numbers 0 through 7.

Off-delay timer: A type that is on immediately when it receives its input enable and turns off after it reaches its preset time.

Offline programming: The programming occurs when the PLC is not attached to the actual device and can then be downloaded to the PLC.

On-delay timer: A timer that does not turn on until its time has reached the preset time value.

One-shot contact: A contact that is on for only one scan when activated.

Open loop: A system that has no feedback and no autocorrection.

Operating system: The fundamental software for a system that defines how it will store and transmit information.

Optical isolation: Technique used in I/O module design that provides logic separation from field levels.

OR: Logic gate that results in 1 unless both inputs are 0.

OSR: One shot rising instruction.

OTE: Output energize instruction.

OTL: Output latch instruction.

OTU: Output unlatch instruction.

Parallel communications: A method of communications data that transfers on several wires simultaneously.

Parity: A bit used to check for data integrity during a data communication.

Peer to peer: The communication that occurs between similar devices, such as two PLCs communicating.

PID (proportional, integral, derivative) control: A control algorithm used to closely control processes such as temperature, mixture, position, and velocity. Proportional portion takes care of the magnitude of the error; integral takes care of small errors over time; derivative compensates for the rate of error change.

PLC: Programmable logic controller.

PPR (pulses per revolution): The number of pulses an encoder produces in one revolution.

Programmable controller: A special-purpose computer programmed in ladder logic so that devices could easily interface with it.

Proportional gain: A device that considers the magnitude of error and attempts to correct a system.

Pulse modulated: Turning a light source on and off at a very high frequency. In sensors, the sending unit pulse modulates the light source. The receiver only responds to that frequency.

Quadrature: The situation in which two output channels are out of phase with each other by 90 degrees.

Rack: A PLC chassis in which modules are installed to meet the user's need.

Radio frequency (RF): A communications technology with a transmitter/receiver that can read or write to tags.

RAM (random access memory): The normally considered user memory.

Register: A storage area typically used to store bit states or values of items such as timers and counters.

Repeatability: The ability to repeat movements or readings; for a robot, how accurately it returns to a position time after time.

Resolution: A measure of how closely a device can measure or divide a quantity; for example, an encoder resolution is defined as counts per turn.

Retentive coil: A coil that will remain in its last state even though power was removed.

Retentive timer: A timer that retains the present count even if the input enable signal is lost.

Retroreflective: A photosensor that sends out a light that is reflected from a reflector back to the receiver when the receiver and emitter are in the same housing.

RF: *See* radio frequency.

ROM (read-only memory): The operating system memory that is nonvolatile and is not lost when the power is turned off.

RS232: A common serial communications standard that specifies the purpose of each of 25 pins.

RS422 and RS423: The standards for two types of serial communication. RS422 is a balanced serial mode. This means that the transmit and receive lines have their own common instead of sharing one like RS232. Balanced mode is more noise immune. This allows for higher data transmission rates and longer transmission distances. RS423 uses the unbalanced mode. Its speed and transmission distances are much greater than RS232 but less than RS422.

RS449: An electrical standard for RS422/RS423 that is more complete than the RS232 and specifies the connectors to be used.

RS485: An electrical standard similar to RS422 standard; its receivers have additional sensitivity that allows for longer distances and more communication drops.

RTO: Retentive timer instruction.

Rung: A group of contacts that control one or more outputs; horizontal lines on the diagram in a ladder diagram.

Scan time: The amount of time for a programmable controller to evaluate a ladder diagram once; typically in the low-millisecond range.

SDLC: The serial data link control, subset of the HDLC, used in many communication systems such as Ethernet, ISDN, and BITBUS; defines the structure of the frames and the values of a number of specific fields in these frames.

Sensitivity: A device's ability to discriminate between levels.

Sensor: Normally a digital device used to detect change.

Sequencer: An instruction type device used to program a sequential operation.

Serial communications: A system of data represented by a coding system such as ASCII that is one bit at a time.

Slave: The nodes of the network that can transmit information to the master only when they are polled (called) from it.

Speech modules: A device used by a PLC to output spoken messages to operators.

Tagout: A device placed on an energy isolating device, in accordance with an established procedure, to indicate that the energy isolating device and the equipment being controlled may not be operated until the tagout device is removed.

Tagout device: A prominent warning device, such as a tag and a means of attachment, that can be securely fastened to an energy isolating device in accordance with an established procedure to indicate that the energy isolating device and the equipment being controlled may not be operated until the tagout device is removed.

Thermocouple: A sensing transducer that changes a temperature to a current to be measured and converted to a binary equivalent that the PLC can understand.

Thumbwheel: A device used by an operator to enter a number between 0 and 9.

Timer: A device that changes its output state when a certain value is achieved.

TOF: Off-delay timer instruction.

TON: On-delay timer instruction.

TOP (technical and office protocol): A communication standard developed by Boeing that refers to the office and technical areas.

Transducer: A device that changes one form of energy to another.

Transitional contact: A contact that changes state for one scan when activated.

True: The enabling logic state generally associated with a 1 or a high state.

UL (Underwriters Laboratory): The organization that operates laboratories to investigate systems with respect to safety.

User memory: A device to store user information such as the user's program, timer/counter values, and input/output status.

Volatile memory: The memory that is lost when power is lost.

Watchdog timer: A timer that can be set to shut the system down if the time is exceeded.

Word: Length of data in bits (16 or 32) that a microprocessor can handle.

XIC: Examine if closed instruction. Also known as a normally open instruction.

XIO: Examine if open instruction. Also known as a normally closed instruction.

Index